Bandwagon Effects in High-Technology Industries

Bandwagon Effects in High-Technology Industries

Jeffrey H. Rohlfs

The MIT Press
Cambridge, Massachusetts
London, England

First MIT Press paperback edition, 2003
©2001 Massachusetts Institute of Technology

This book was set in Sabon by Best-set Typesetter Ltd., Hong Kong.
Printed and bound in the United States of America.

Library of Congress Cataloging-in-Publication Data

Rohlfs, Jeffrey H.
  Bandwagon effects in high-technology industries / Jeffrey H. Rohlfs.
    p. cm.
  Includes bibliographical references and index.
  ISBN 0-262-18217-3 (hc. : alk. paper), 0-262-68138-2 (pb)
    1. High technology industries—United States—Case studies. I. Title.
HC110.H53 R64   2001
338.4'762'000973—dc21

                                                              2001030659

10 9 8 7 6 5 4 3 2

For Joan, the love of my life

Contents

Acknowledgments

Many persons contributed to the creation of this book, and I would like to thank them for their efforts. Chuck Jackson suggested that I undertake this venture and cajoled me into doing so. The book has been substantially improved as a result of helpful comments from John Haring, Jackson, Chip Shooshan, Hal Varian, and three anonymous referees. I am also grateful for the support and encouragement that I received from all my colleagues at Strategic Policy Research. In particular, I would like to thank David Fintzen for his research support and Adrienne Vendig, who typed numerous revisions of the text. I am, of course, solely responsible for any remaining errors.

Foreword

I first met Jeff Rohlfs back in 1973 when I visited Bell Labs. During this visit he told me about "network externalities." This was a new term to me—and to everyone, I suppose, since Jeff had just invented it. He told me how AT&T had spent millions of dollars on Picturephone, and explained to me how it had flopped. He showed me his model of network effects, and I remember being impressed by its elegance. Little did I realize just how powerful and important this idea was to become!

Jeff's paper on network effects was published in 1974. The rest of the world was slow to recognize its significance. Figure 1 shows the citations to Jeff's paper from 1975 to 2000. As with many papers, it had a few citations early on, then a drop off. But unlike most papers, citations to Jeff's paper picked up again as people began to recognize the importance of network effects in high-technology industries. In fact, the citations to Jeff's paper look a bit like the dynamics associated with networks: a slow period, followed by a burst of rapid growth.

I conjecture that the long time that it took to recognize the importance of network effects was due to the nature of the example Jeff chose to motivate the investigation (Picturephone) and the nature of technology innovation in the 1960s and 1970s. Picturephone was a loser—it never achieved critical mass and market success. No one seems to cares why a loser lost—they only care why a winner wins.

Furthermore, from roughly 1950 to 1980, there were no really prominent example of network effects that caught the public imagination. True, there was the spread of the television networks, but these didn't really exhibit network externalities in the Rohlfs sense of the word. The

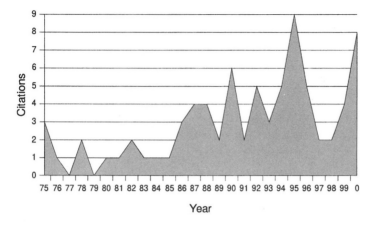

Figure 1
Citations to "A Theory of Interdependent Demand for a Communications Service."

fact that one family bought a television had little direct effect on the value that another family would place on a TV.

The combination of these effects meant that Rohlfs's analysis of network dynamics in 1970s didn't really resonate with potential readers. Things were quite different in the 1980s and 1990s when we saw several technologies that exhibited classic network externalities: ATM machines, fax machines, VCRs and prerecorded videos, and e-mail to name just a few. People began to notice there was something interesting going on!

This wasn't really "new." These industries exhibited the same dynamics as telegraph, telephone and wireless technologies had exhibited a century or so earlier. But they were new in our lifetimes, and that's what mattered.

It's great to see Jeff's new book network externalities and positive feedback in high-tech markets. He has pulled together the theory and the examples necessary to understand how these markets work and provided valuable insight for future economists and entrepreneurs.

Let the band(wagon) play on!

Hal R. Varian
University of California, Berkeley

I

Introduction

The literal meaning of *bandwagon* is an ornately decorated wagon that carries musicians in a parade. This type of bandwagon is from a gentler era and rarely seen any more. Nevertheless, just about everyone today knows the figurative meanings of *bandwagon*. In U.S. presidential primaries, the bandwagon is, according to many political commentators, what the winner of the last primary has. This candidate risks losing the bandwagon unless he or she wins the next primary. Some commentators appear unable to describe an election campaign without using the word *bandwagon*. The word is never defined but seems to mean what sports commentators call "momentum"—that is, a general tendency of success to breed further success.

Bandwagons are also used to characterize "irrational exuberance" of investors in the stock market.[1] According to this view, investors observe that others have recently been highly successful in the market. They then follow their example, regardless of market fundamentals. Bandwagon effects in this context are a type of herd behavior.

Both these concepts bear some similarity to what we (and other economists) mean by "bandwagon effects," but they are not precisely the same. Since we are using language somewhat differently from others, our first order of business is to define our terms precisely. Our definition of a **bandwagon effect**[2] is as follows: a benefit that a person enjoys as a result of others' doing the same thing that he or she does. In particular, a consumer may enjoy bandwagon benefits as others consume the same product or service that he or she does. The consumer then enjoys a "rational exuberance" as the user set expands.

1
The High-Technology Bandwagon

Young musicians are unlikely to ride on a literal bandwagon, but they nevertheless learn about bandwagon effects at an early age. If the rest of the band has reached a particular place in the score, that is the place to be. Even if the others have miscounted, their sheer number makes them right. There is no good alternative to getting on the bandwagon.

Consumers of high-technology products learn this same lesson. For example, not too many years ago, two technical standards existed for videocassettes in the United States: Beta and VHS. Beta was widely regarded to have better picture quality, but VHS cassettes could run longer and be used to record longer television programs. For a while, video-rental stores carried cassettes of both types. But for bandwagon effects, both standards might have coexisted indefinitely. Consumers who strongly preferred Beta's picture quality would have chosen Beta, while those who recorded long television programs would have opted for VHS. In reality, the selection of Beta cassettes in rental stores shrank over time, ultimately down to zero. Eventually, *all* consumers—even those who strongly preferred Beta's picture quality and never recorded long television programs—had no choice but to get on the VHS bandwagon. The bandwagon effect is apparent here. If a consumer plays along with the band, he or she has a good selection available at the video-rental store. If the consumer plays his or her own tune, there is little or no selection.

Henry Ford, the father of mass production, once stated that customers could get Model Ts in any color they wanted, so long as it was black. Ford's goal was to drive down the costs of production so that cars would be available to "the other 90 percent" of the population. That cost-cutting required uniformity of design; so customers had no choice.

Modern technology has ameliorated this problem. Today's consumers can buy low-cost automobiles (and other manufactured goods) and still have a variety of options. Bandwagon effects, however, create new pressures for uniformity in high-technology industries. Today's consumers can get VCRs of any technical standard they choose, so long as it is VHS.

Much the same phenomenon has occurred in personal computer (PC)[1] operating systems. In our experience, users of Apple computers almost invariably insist that the Macintosh operating system is/was superior to Microsoft Windows. Nevertheless, Windows became the industry standard, and many more applications programs were written for Windows than for Macintosh. PC users who want access to this broad range of applications programs can choose any operating system they want, so long as it is Microsoft Windows.

Those who resent the lack of choice in videocassette technical standards have no specific person to blame. But computer users all across the globe know whom to blame (though perhaps unfairly) for the lack of choice in PC operating systems—namely, Bill Gates, the chairman and former chief executive officer of Microsoft Corporation, the once (and perhaps future) richest man in the world.

The history of Microsoft illustrates how bandwagon effects can lead to market concentration and market power. A successful proprietor of a bandwagon technology generally has the ability to abuse market power. The U.S. Department of Justice, in its antitrust case, alleged that Microsoft did, indeed, abuse its market power.

Bandwagon effects, notwithstanding their pressure toward uniformity and their potential for abuse of market power, can be viewed in a positive light. They enable consumers to benefit if they can somehow contrive to do the same thing. Suppliers in bandwagon markets are band conductors who try to get consumers to play in concert to achieve that goal.

Bandwagons have dynamics that differ from those of conventional products and services. They are quite difficult to get started and often end up in a ditch before they can get under way. Once enough consumers have gotten on a bandwagon, however, it may be unstoppable.

Picturephone service, which was introduced by the Bell System in the early 1970s, shows how easily a bandwagon can end up in a ditch. The service was offered at $86.50 per month—equivalent to over $175 per month in current dollars. The service, by its nature, could be used for communicating only with other subscribers. At the beginning, there were inevitably very few subscribers—primarily large Bell System suppliers who were interested in maintaining good relations with Bell. Virtually no one thought it was worth $86.50 per month to communicate via video with this small set of subscribers. The service therefore flopped and has become, along with the Edsel, a classic example of marketing failure.

The largest and most successful bandwagon, apart from telephone service, has been the Internet. It has, indeed, achieved unstoppable momentum. The Internet makes available to most computer users a huge range of information on just about any subject. It has become indispensable to universities and other research institutions. In some recent years, Internet stocks have been among the hottest on Wall Street. Perhaps most important, the Internet serves as a vast resource to facilitate free speech and free expression across the globe.

In its early development, the Internet faced the same start-up problem as Picturephone. The precursor to the Internet then provided limited value, since it could be used to communicate only with a small set of other users. The Internet evolved from a specialized telecommunications system funded by the Defense Advanced Research Projects Agency (DARPA) and used primarily by the Department of Defense (DoD) and its contractors. Key policymakers in the federal government had the insight that a larger, more general telecommunications system would be a valuable national resource. With relatively modest expenditures by federal government standards, they initiated one of the greatest economic success stories of modern times.

Of course, some bandwagon products grow rapidly with no money from the public till. In particular, fax machines grew from a relatively few specialized applications to ubiquitous usage over a period of about ten years. Telephone service also grew on its own, albeit much more slowly, when it was first introduced over 100 years ago.

Not surprisingly, firms in high-technology industries clearly understand the importance of bandwagon effects. When a new service is first introduced, competitors often wage a fierce battle. Each tries to have its own technology become the industry standard. The contenders all know that the lion's share of the profits will go to the bandwagon technology.

A more conciliatory approach to standard setting is also possible. For example, several major producers of compact discs (CDs) and CD players successfully agreed to a single technical standard. Such agreements avoid the economic waste associated with producers' developing a losing standard and consumers' being stuck with products that embody it. A supplier with a truly superior technology may, however, prefer to go for broke and battle it out in the market. Sony did precisely that, to its own regret, by introducing the Beta videocassette recorder (VCR) without getting industry consensus on a technical standard.

Such battles take quite a different form when governments become involved in setting technical standards. Each market participant then competes to persuade public policymakers that its technology is superior. There has been an active debate among economists and policy analysts on the advantages and disadvantages of having governments set technical standards.

Public policymakers sometimes fully determine a technical standard. For example, the Federal Communications Commission (FCC) fully determined the technical standards for analog television transmission. Alternatively, public policymakers may choose to set some aspects of the technical standard, while leaving other important aspects to be determined by the market. The FCC followed this latter course with respect to digital television.

Bandwagon effects pervade high-technology industries. They raise a host of interesting issues for economic analysis and public policy. Economic analysis of bandwagon effects provides valuable insights into what is going on and what policymakers should do about it.

2
A Bandwagon Tour

In this book, we take readers on a wide-ranging tour on the high-technology bandwagon. We encounter many interesting passengers on the trip:

The major Japanese electronics firms occupy several seats on the bandwagon. These passengers brought you the fax and VCR and have played major roles with respect to CDs and television. They are often referred to collectively as "Japan Inc.," because of the close cooperation among Japanese firms and the Japanese government. Nevertheless, we will see one instance (Beta versus VHS) in which Japanese cooperation broke down completely.

Since our bandwagon travels across time as well as space, we see *Ma Bell* and her entourage. The Department of Justice (DOJ) alleged that Ma, notwithstanding her staid image, frequently "reached out to crush someone." Ma was even feistier in her younger days. Her ride ended abruptly after Judge Harold Greene wrote a scathing rejection of AT&T's petition to dismiss DOJ's antitrust case. Then, DOJ and AT&T threw Ma off the bandwagon.

Some European firms, most notably the Dutch firm *Philips*, ride the bandwagon. Philips distinguished itself by its excellent management of the bandwagon for CDs and CD players. That effort remains, in our view, the best model from actual practice of how to start up a bandwagon product.

IBM, the ancient (by high-technology standards) titan of the computer industry, is also on board. IBM was almost left behind by the PC bandwagon and had to fight to get a seat. In recent years, a bunch of clones who look just like IBM have been crowding its space.

We get a chance to observe *Bill Gates*, the supreme virtuoso in the management of bandwagon effects. Gates has become the real-life personification of the revenge of the nerds. Twenty years ago, nerds were regarded as persons unlikely to achieve real success. Notwithstanding their possible (narrowly focused) brilliance, they were expected to be ruled and exploited by those having greater presence and social skills. Gates showed that a person perceived (albeit inaccurately in his case) to be a nerd can nevertheless amass enormous wealth and wield great economic power.

Finally, Uncle Sam is on the bandwagon. He has intervened (some would say "meddled") in all the bandwagon markets that we see on the tour. With respect to the Internet, his intervention (initially in the guise of DARPA and later as the National Science Foundation (NSF)) had spectacular success. It created from whole cloth the largest, most successful, and most profitable bandwagon since the telephone.

The high-technology bandwagon is a tour like no other. Readers will get to see some of the world's greatest technological thinkers grapple with the exceedingly difficult problems posed by bandwagon markets. Those thinkers have had widely varying degrees of success. Sometimes they ate the bear; sometimes the bear ate them.

2.1   A Guide to the Tour

Our tour begins by first exploring how bandwagons work. We focus on the problem of getting the bandwagon rolling for newly introduced products and services.

We distinguish between two general types of bandwagon effects:

• **Network externalities.** These apply to products and services that use telecommunications networks. As the set of users expands, each user benefits from being able to communicate with more persons (who have become users of the product or service).

• **Complementary bandwagon effects.** These apply to products whose value derives, at least in part, from use of competitively supplied complementary products. For example, as more consumers purchase a hardware product, software vendors have greater incentives to produce software for that product. As the vendors respond to those incentives, purchasers of the hardware benefit from greater availability of software.

Part II (chapters 3–5) develops the theory of bandwagon demand and supply. These chapters are equation-free; 100 percent of the intellectual nutrients are in the form of complex verbal ideas. Some mathematical results are given in the mathematical appendix, but they may be skipped by readers who are not interested in the mathematical elaboration.

The demand theory in chapter 3 is drawn largely from Rohlfs (1974), with some extensions that are useful for the empirical analysis in part III. A key concept in the demand theory is **critical mass**. Bandwagon products and services that do not reach a critical mass can have only limited success and may fail altogether. Those that do reach a critical mass often grow thereafter at a very rapid rate. Chapter 3 also discusses **Metcalfe's Law**, which states that the value of a network increases as the square of the number of users.

Chapter 4 analyzes the impact of bandwagon effects on the supply side of the market. Rohlfs (1974) analyzed bandwagon supply only for the case of a monopoly.[1] Starting in the mid-1980s, a number of papers analyzed bandwagon supply for the more interesting and important case of competition.

An important consideration in the supply analysis is whether a consumer enjoys bandwagon benefits with respect to (a) all other consumers; or (b) only the customers of his or her own supplier. We have coined the term **interlinking** to refer to case a. The term **interconnection** is often used to refer to interlinking of telecommunications networks. We use the term "interlinking" more broadly to encompass complementary bandwagon effects, as well. Our treatment of interlinking (or its absence) as a critical generic aspect of bandwagon supply is, so far as we know, a new approach. The degree of interlinking has key importance in all our case studies of high-technology industries.

Interlinking can enormously increase the value of a bandwagon product or service to consumers. With respect to network externalities, interlinking is achieved by interconnection of the networks of all suppliers. With respect to complementary bandwagon effects, interlinking is achieved through **compatibility**, which allows the same complementary products (e.g., software) to be used in conjunction with the base products (e.g., hardware) of all suppliers.

The whole nature of competitive rivalry depends on whether the products or services of suppliers are interlinked. Bandwagon markets without interlinking have a tendency to gravitate toward a dominant supplier. Bandwagon markets *with* interlinking have no such tendency.

Technical standards play an important role in bandwagon markets. An agreed-upon technical standard interlinks the products of all suppliers. Technical standards can be set through industry agreement or through government intervention. The alternative is for multiple suppliers to promote their own proprietary standards. Each then tries to become the dominant supplier in the noninterlinked bandwagon market.

Chapter 5 summarizes the results of bandwagon theory. It provides a cheat sheet for readers who wish to skip, or at least to postpone reading, the theory in chapters 3 and 4.

Part III (chapters 6–13) discusses case studies of bandwagon products and services. The case studies illustrate the application of bandwagon theory in a variety of real-world contexts. These chapters may be read in any order, depending on the reader's interests. The chapters appear roughly in order of increasing complexity of bandwagon effects. Chapters 6–8 discuss products and services that are subject to network externalities. Chapters 9–12 discuss products that are subject to complementary bandwagon effects. Chapter 13 discusses the Internet—the most complex bandwagon service of all. The Internet is subject to both network externalities and complementary bandwagon effects.

Chapter 6 describes the development of the fax. This case study illustrates how good a product must be to succeed in a bandwagon market. Earlier versions of fax machines worked well and could meet important business needs. It was only in the 1980s, however, that technological progress had improved the product sufficiently to allow it to reach a critical mass.

Chapter 7 reviews the early rollout of telephone service. This case study illustrates the cost to bandwagon suppliers of being too greedy for short-run profits. The Bell-affiliated companies charged high prices during the period of Bell's patent monopoly. They would have been better off charging lower prices to generate more bandwagon benefits and increase their competitive advantage as the dominant suppliers in bandwagon markets in which their services were not interlinked with those of their competitors. If they had done so, they would probably have had an unassailable first-mover advantage when the Bell patents expired. As it was, the Bell companies were unnecessarily vulnerable to competition when the patents expired and paid a high price for their earlier greed.

Chapter 8 recounts the introduction of Picturephone service in the early 1970s. The introduction was a fiasco that illustrates the consequences of introducing a bandwagon service with no advance consideration of the start-up problem.

Chapters 9 and 10 deal with players of recorded programming. The big producers of complementary products for these machines are the major record companies (for CDs) and Hollywood studios (for videocassettes). There is no bandwagon for the playing machines unless the producers of the complementary products are on board. The complementary producers have acted in a variety of ways. Record companies played an important supporting role in the introduction of CD players, but their lack of support doomed digital audiotape (DAT) players to failure. With regard to VCRs, Hollywood had to be dragged, kicking and screaming, into the bandwagon that was rolling down the road to riches.

Chapter 9 discusses the introduction of the CD player by Philips and Sony. That introduction is a model of how to introduce a new product in a market that involves complementary bandwagon effects. Chapter 10 describes the introduction of the VCR. The highlight was the standards war between Sony (Beta) and Matsushita/JVC (VHS). That history illustrates what happens when suppliers with proprietary standards duke it out in the marketplace. Chapters 9 and 10 also recount the market failures of several other players of recorded programming—namely, DAT players, digital compact cassette players, minidisc players, and video disc players. These failures illustrate how difficult it is to successfully introduce new products in bandwagon markets.

Chapter 11 recounts the history of the personal computer industry. That history illustrates the tendency of bandwagon markets without interlinking to gravitate toward a dominant supplier: in this case, Intel for microprocessors and Microsoft for operating systems. Microsoft's success indicates how profitable such markets can be—*if the supplier is not too greedy for short-run profits.* The history also illustrates the enduring effects of misjudgments by suppliers in bandwagon markets without interlinking. The whole current structure of the personal computer industry has been largely determined by misjudgments that IBM and Apple made during the late 1970s and early 1980s.

Chapter 12 deals with the history of television. It recounts the original introduction of television, the introduction of color television, and recent attempts to introduce high-definition television (HDTV). Governments have been deeply involved with all these activities. The case study illustrates the benefits and costs of government intervention in bandwagon markets. It also provides some guidance on how governments should go about setting technical standards.

Chapter 13 describes the evolution of the Internet. That evolution had three distinct stages: (1) the development of packet switching as a cost-effective means of data communications; (2) the proliferation of a large number of commercial and noncommercial packet-switched networks that were not interlinked; and (3) the interlinking of those networks to form the Internet. The extraordinarily rapid growth of the Internet since 1986 shows how important and beneficial interlinking can be.

Part IV (chapters 14 and 15) states our conclusions. It summarizes the lessons learned on our tour on the high-technology bandwagon.

II

Bandwagons: How They Work

The real world was in color even when all film was black and white. Similarly, bandwagon effects existed in the real world long before economists got around to coining the term. Nevertheless, the importance of bandwagon effects has increased dramatically in recent years as a result of a number of high-technology innovations. Not surprisingly, therefore, most of the economic work on bandwagon effects has been done relatively recently.

Nevertheless, bandwagon effects were first analyzed half a century ago—by Harvey Leibenstein in 1950. In Leibenstein's analysis, bandwagon effects are purely psychological—a quirk in the individual's preferences. That is, a consumer may feel better doing the same as others do. Leibenstein contrasted bandwagon effects to "snob" effects, whereby a consumer feels better doing as others do not. These concepts are illustrated in the following stories:

(Story A): Betty and Veronica buy new dresses for a high-school event, each hoping to catch Archie's eye. They are dismayed to find that they have bought the same dress. Archie, who is generally clueless, never notices. Nevertheless, Betty and Veronica are very upset.

(Story B): One day when Betty and Veronica were pre-teens, they were delighted to discover that they had worn the same dress to school. As a result, they had a feeling of camaraderie. Archie, who was even more clueless at that age, did not notice. Back then, however, Betty and Veronica did not care what Archie thought.

Story A illustrates Leibenstein's concept of snob effects, while Story B illustrates his concept of bandwagon effects. Since Archie did not notice anything, both these effects occurred entirely within Betty and Veronica's heads.

In contrast, bandwagon effects in high-technology industries often have a basis that goes beyond what is in the consumer's head. In particular,

• Consumers of a product or service that uses a telecommunications network may benefit from being able to communicate with more persons as the set of users expands. These effects are known as network externalities for reasons discussed below.

• Consumers of a product (e.g., hardware) may benefit from greater availability of competitively supplied complementary products (e.g., software) as the set of users of the product expands. We denote these effects as complementary bandwagon effects.

The fax is an example of a product that is subject to network externalities. A fax machine is worth more to each consumer if there are 10 million machines in use than if there are only 100,000. As the user set expands, each consumer can benefit by sending faxes to more people. Other examples of services that are subject to network externalities are the telephone and e-mail. Users of all these services benefit from being able to communicate with more persons as the user set expands.

In formal economics terms, these benefits are characterized as **external demand-side scale economies**. The elements of this characterization can be parsed as follows:

• **Demand-side scale economies** are conditions that impart benefits to each consumer as the user set expands. They are analogous to **supply-side scale economies**, which impart benefits to suppliers (through reductions in unit costs) as output expands.

• When a new user subscribes to a service[1] with network externalities, other users benefit. The benefits to these other users are *external* to the new user. For this reason, bandwagon benefits in networks are known as "network externalities."

Even where bandwagon effects are absent, consumers benefit from internal supply-side scale economies as output increases. For example, the unit cost of producing a particular model of automobile is generally lower if 10 million are produced than if only 100,000 are produced.

These economies are **internal supply-side scale economies,** because they accrue to the firm that expands production and not to other firms. The savings in unit costs from internal supply-side scale economies are likely to be passed on, at least in part, to consumers.

In our two examples of fax machines and automobiles, the gain to each consumer from expansion of supplier output could be the same.[2] As more fax machines are deployed, the consumer might be willing to pay $500 more for a machine (but does not have to). As output of the automobile model expands, the consumer may be able to purchase the automobile for $500 less (though he or she derives the same benefit from the automobile). It is also possible that the consumer benefits from *both* network externalities and internal supply-side scale economies as output expands. In the case of the fax, unit production costs and prices might be $500 lower when 10 million machines are sold than when 100,000 are sold. In that case, the total consumer gain would be $1,000. The machine is worth $500 more to the consumer, but he or she pays $500 less.

Although network externalities and internal supply-side scale economies both benefit consumers as output expands, the two effects are easily distinguished. The consumers' benefits from network externalities derive from observable effects on the demand side of the market, for example, the sending of more faxes by each user. The consumers' benefits from internal supply-side scale economies derive from observable effects on the supply side of the market, for example, cost savings through automation and centralization. Bandwagon theory, as described in this book, is useful for modeling network externalities. Internal supply-side scale economies can, however, be modeled without recourse to bandwagon theory.

Complementary bandwagon effects involve complex interactions between supply and demand. The nature of those effects depends on whether the same supplier or different (unaffiliated) suppliers produce the complementary products.

One possibility is that a fully integrated supplier provides the hardware and all the complementary software that the user needs and does not write himself or herself. This is a form of **vertical integration,** because it spans (vertical) stages of the production process. Such integration is common for special-purpose equipment, for example, some telecommunications switches.

Under vertical integration, complementary bandwagon effects are simply internal supply-side scale economies. As output expands, the supplier can spread the cost of writing software over more units of production. Consequently, writing more and better software is likely to be profitable. Users then benefit from greater availability of software. Since users benefit (indirectly) from the expansion of the user set, one can view this phenomenon as a bandwagon effect. Actually, it is no different from other kinds of internal supply-side scale economies that benefit users as output expands. Consequently, where supply is fully (vertically) integrated, one does not need bandwagon theory to model complementary bandwagon effects (notwithstanding their name).

Bandwagon theory is, however, useful for modeling these effects where supply of hardware and software is not vertically integrated. In that case, the bandwagon effects are *external* economies of scale. The economic consequences of such economies differ considerably from those of *internal* supply-side scale economies, which apply to output of a single firm.

Examples of complementary bandwagon effects where supply is *not* fully integrated are the following:

• Owners of CD players and VCRs benefit as other consumers buy products using the same technical standard, because a wider range of prerecorded CDs and videocassettes will become available.

• Owners of PCs benefit as others buy compatible systems, because a wider range of applications software will become available.

• Owners of digital television sets benefit as others buy such sets because a wider range of digital television programs will become available.

• Internet users benefit as the Internet grows and a wider range of information becomes available on-line.

These external bandwagon effects sometimes give rise to a **chicken-and-egg problem**. There may be no incentive for any firm to supply the complementary product (the "egg") until there is a sizable user set for the base product (the "chicken"). But there may also be no incentive for any firm to produce the base product or for any consumers to purchase it until the complementary product is available. The chicken-and-egg problem and its solution had critical importance for the introduction of CD players and CDs. They had similar importance with respect to the introduction of television, color television, and HDTV.

3

Bandwagon Demand

Supply in bandwagon markets is like a game of chess played on the board of high technology, according to a set of complex rules. Bandwagon demand theory is the set of rules that determine whether the bandwagon will roll. Getting the bandwagon rolling is essential for success. It adds a whole new dimension to strategic planning.

By comparison, supply in non-bandwagon markets can be likened to a game of checkers (draughts). Substantial skill (not to mention a good product) may be required to win, but there is much less scope for strategic maneuvering.

Many of the rules of bandwagon demand are stated in terms of equilibrium analysis. An **equilibrium** is an economic state that has no tendency to change. It contrasts with **disequilibrium**, which is an economic state that *does* tend to change. In particular, a disequilibrium usually tends to gravitate toward an equilibrium.

Equilibrium theory does not posit that demand is always in equilibrium. On the contrary, the equilibrium may recently have changed, but demand has not yet had time to adjust. For example, an individual whose income has recently increased may, in equilibrium, demand a more expensive car. Nevertheless, this individual may wait until his or her current (less expensive) car is ready to be traded in before moving to the new equilibrium. In this case the individual's demand has a tendency to increase toward equilibrium in the future. More generally, if the actual level of purchases exceeds equilibrium demand, it tends to decline over time. If the actual level of purchases is less than equilibrium demand, it tends to increase over time.

Bandwagon models always posit a tendency for users to derive greater benefit from the bandwagon service as the user set expands. The **pure bandwagon model** posits that as the user set expands, the service becomes more valuable to some persons and does not become less valuable to anyone.

Readers will immediately perceive the weakness of the latter part of this assumption, as it applies to the most important bandwagon service, namely, telephone service. Telemarketers have become a scourge of modern life. Since modern technology has lowered telecommunications costs, telemarketers can often operate profitably, even if they make only one sale in one hundred attempts. They can and do disregard the bother and inconvenience that they cause the other ninety-nine persons, since they are not required to pay that cost. The other ninety-nine persons may well feel that they would be better off if telemarketers unsubscribed to telephone service.

Much the same phenomenon occurs with respect to other bandwagon services. Junk faxes appear on the office fax machine every morning. E-mail provides the means for low-cost, pervasive proliferation of junk mail, which is usually bothersome and sometimes offensive. E-mail has also recently provided the means for spreading computer viruses.

For these reasons, real-world services and products generally do not conform precisely to the pure bandwagon assumptions, described above. Nevertheless, the pure bandwagon model is often a reasonable approximation. It provides useful insights into demand for services and products that are subject to substantial (although not pure) bandwagon effects.

3.1   Equilibrium User Sets

For some services, a reasonable bandwagon model could specify that each user's demand depends on the number of other users. In general, however, demand in a bandwagon model also depends on who those users are. In this regard, a famous economist once remarked in discussing universal-service policy for telephone service, "A marginal telephone subscriber [i.e., one who would unsubscribe if the price were slightly higher] isn't anyone I would want to talk to." The remark was obviously intended to be jokingly elitist, but it (like many jokes) contains a kernel of truth. The economist, like many other persons of his intellectual and socioeconomic status, really does not have much occasion to talk to marginal telephone subscribers. To be sure, Thomas Jefferson got it right when he said, "All men are created equal." It does not follow, however, that one derives equal benefit from talking on the telephone to any of them. More generally, all bandwagon effects are not created equal.

In terms of bandwagon theory, a consumer's demand depends on the number of users with whom that consumer has some **community of interest**. For example, communities of interest include

• for a telecommunications service, those persons with whom the consumer wants to communicate;

• for a computer operating system, those persons whose needs for applications software resemble the consumer's; and

• for a machine that plays prerecorded programming, those persons whose tastes resemble the consumer's.

Because communities of interest are often important, the basic theoretical concept in the bandwagon model is not the number of users, but the user set—that is, the set of consumers who have for some reason (perhaps animal spirits) chosen to consume the bandwagon service. A user set is an **equilibrium user set** if and only if

• no consumer who has chosen to consume the service would be better off not consuming it—given the other users of the service; and

• no consumer who has chosen *not* to consume the service would be better off consuming it—given the users of the service.[1]

Under these conditions, the demand of each user and nonuser has no tendency to change.

3.1.1 Interlinking

All the users considered in this equilibrium analysis are presumed to be interlinked. If customers of multiple suppliers are, in reality, not interlinked, the demand facing each supplier must be analyzed separately. Customers of other suppliers are then simply considered to be nonusers that do not provide any bandwagon benefits.

Interlinking expands the relevant user set. After interlinking, each user enjoys bandwagon benefits from the combined user sets of all suppliers. These increased bandwagon benefits may substantially increase demand. In particular, suppose that the noninterlinked market is originally in equilibrium. The new equilibrium resulting from interlinking would include all the original users, but it could also include many other users, as well. This is precisely the story of the Internet, as we shall see in chapter 13.

3.1.2 Multiple Equilibria

A key result of bandwagon demand theory is that there are generally multiple equilibria, which may differ substantially. This point is illustrated in the following simple example:

Suppose that each consumer has five principal contacts. He or she demands the bandwagon service if and only if all five of those contacts consume that service. In this model:
- The null set (no users) is an equilibrium user set.
- The entire population is also an equilibrium user set.

  Suppose that society is partitioned into two groups, and no member of either group has a principal contact in the other group. In that case,
  - all members of first group and no members of the second group is an equilibrium user set; and
  - all members of the second group and no members of the first group is also an equilibrium user set.

In the real world, communities of interest are not this precise. An individual generally belongs to many partially overlapping communities of interest. Some small groups may have strong communities of interest. The individual may additionally have weaker communities of interest with larger groups. In addition, it is often reasonable to model the individual as having some community of interest with the population as a whole. Multiple equilibria are possible—indeed likely—in this more complex framework, as well as in simpler models.

If perfect cooperation were possible among all members of society, the best (maximum) equilibrium user set could always be attained. In general, if all members of that user set could agree to consume the bandwagon service, they would thereby all benefit. More generally, through cooperation persons may be able to act as a group, rather than as individuals. Bandwagon benefits that are external to individuals may be internal to the group. In formal economics terms, this type of group activity can **internalize the externality**.

There are, of course, limits to the degree of cooperation that a diverse group can realistically achieve. For any large group, perfect cooperation is not possible; nor is anything remotely resembling perfect cooperation. Indeed, one can reasonably assume that cooperation is limited to the following:

• An organization may be able to make decisions, taking into account bandwagon benefits within the organization.

• Small groups (in most cases, probably two persons or two organizations) can jointly make decisions to consume a bandwagon service.

Ronald Coase, in the work for which he was awarded the Nobel Prize, used the term **transactions costs** to include all barriers to achieving cooperation to internalize externalities. In general, such transactions costs grow very rapidly as the size of the potentially cooperating group increases.

In any event, suppose that the **initial user set** consists of all individual entities and small groups (mainly pairs) of entities that that can justify purchasing the service, even if no others purchase it. This set may possibly be the null set. For example, the bandwagon service may have little utility within an organization, and the bandwagon benefits for small user sets do not justify the (high) price. In that case, the initial user set is an equilibrium user set, and there is no tendency for demand to grow.

For many services, however, the initial user set is not the null set. In that case, it is probably not an equilibrium user set and demand will expand until an equilibrium user set is reached. We refer to the resulting equilibrium as the **demand-based equilibrium user set**. This equilibrium derives solely from demand adjustments—assuming that suppliers simply offer the service at some price.[2] It depends on price and on the initial user set. It does not (in this model) depend additionally on the dynamics of demand adjustment. (In section 3.4, we consider more complex models in which the dynamics do, indeed, affect the equilibria for products involving complementary bandwagon effects.)

In this chapter on bandwagon demand, we treat the initial user set as given. In reality, the initial user set depends on the culmination of supplier strategies, which may be quite elaborate. In particular, the initial user set depends on

• the quality of the product;
• the promotion of the product, prior to its being offered;
• the marketing campaign; and
• the available supply of complementary products.

Supplier strategies that affect the initial user set are the focus of chapter 4 and all the case studies.

The demand-based equilibrium user set may, unfortunately, be far from optimal. There may exist a much larger equilibrium user set wherein all consumers are better off. The original subscribers would all be better off with a larger equilibrium user set because of bandwagon benefits. Moreover, if new subscribers make voluntary decisions to subscribe, they are presumably better off as well. The ideal in this regard is the **maximum equilibrium user set**.[3]

To the extent that the maximum equilibrium user set is larger than the demand-based equilibrium user set, ordinary demand adjustments do not provide a path to the optimum. Later in this book, we examine various ways that one might get there through supply-side activities or government intervention.

3.2   Demand as a Function of Price

The discussion of equilibrium user sets above is based on the assumption that the bandwagon service is offered at some fixed price. Let us now consider how demand varies as price varies.

In bandwagon models, a general tendency exists for demand to be negatively related to price. In particular, starting from any given equilibrium user set, equilibrium demand declines as price rises; it rises as price declines.

Nevertheless, the level of demand depends on the starting point as well as price. Consider the following two cases:

A. Price is high, but the starting point is a large user set; and

B. Price is low, but the starting point is a small user set.

It is quite possible that demand in case A exceeds demand in case B.

In particular, suppose that the five-contact model described above in section 3.1.2 holds at both the high and low prices. That is, at either price a consumer demands the service if and only if all five of his or her principal contacts are users. Suppose that in case A, the initial user set is the entire population. That starting point is an equilibrium user set; so demand does not decline. Suppose that in case B, the initial user set is the null set. That starting point is also an equilibrium user set; so demand does not grow. Thus, demand at the higher price is the entire population, while demand at the lower price is the null set. In this example, the starting point—not the price—is completely determinative.

Having made the case that it is generally unrealistic to assume that demand depends only on the number of subscribers, we now ask readers to bear with us while we analyze precisely that model. In particular, suppose that the maximum price that an individual would be willing to pay for the service (his or her **reservation price**) depends only on the number of subscribers. Under these assumptions we can develop a bandwagon analogue to the familiar **demand curve.**

Figure 3.1 depicts such a demand curve. The equilibrium quantity demanded (q) is modeled to depend on the price (p). For any price p_o, the demand curve indicates the equilibrium level of demand q_o.

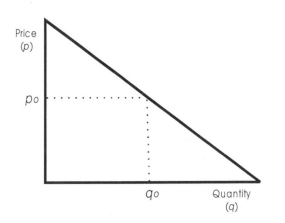

Figure 3.1
Demand curve.

Figure 3.1 can alternatively be viewed as an **inverse demand curve**, in which p is modeled as a function of q. For each value of q_o, the inverse demand curve indicates the price p_o for which that level of demand is an equilibrium.

The relation between price and equilibrium quantity is more complex in bandwagon markets. The simplest shape for the inverse demand curve in a bandwagon market is depicted in figure 3.2.[4] The quantity variable in the figure (q) indicates the equilibrium number of users. The first users to join in equilibrium are those who value the service the most, *for any given q*. Then additional users who value the service progressively less (for any given q) join. The price variable indicates the price at which the user set with q subscribers is an equilibrium user set. For any given q, p in figure 3.2 (as in any inverse demand curve) is the reservation price of the **marginal user**, that is, a user who would not consume the service if the price were slightly higher.

Because additional users value the service progressively less, ordinary (nonbandwagon) inverse demand curves are necessarily downward sloping. The reservation price of the marginal user declines as q increases.

For bandwagon services, however, there is an additional consideration. As more users join, bandwagon benefits increase the value of the service to each user. For services in the start-up phase, this bandwagon effect usually dominates the normal tendency toward a downward-sloping

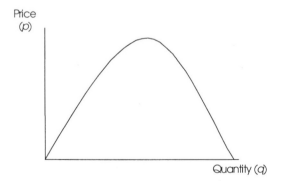

Figure 3.2
Equilibrium demand versus price: Simplest shape.

inverse demand curve. That is, the reservation price of the marginal user *increases* as additional users join. Thus, we have the anomalous result that the inverse demand curve in the left part of figure 3.2 is upward sloping!

The downward-sloping part of figure 3.2 has properties similar to those of ordinary (nonbandwagon) inverse demand curves. For any given price, actual (disequilibrium) demand tends to gravitate toward the inverse demand curve, which indicates the equilibrium at that price. That is, each of the equilibria is a **stable equilibrium.**

In contrast, each point on the upward-sloping part of figure 3.2 is an **unstable equilibria.** Demand has no tendency to gravitate toward that part of the inverse demand curve. On the contrary, if demand is to the left of the upward-sloping curve, it tends to contract toward zero, which is a stable equilibrium. If demand gets past the upward-sloping part of the curve, it tends to expand until it reaches the downward-sloping part.[5] Thus, for any price, the upward-sloping part of the inverse demand curve can be considered the critical mass at that price. In this example, the service cannot be successful unless critical mass is somehow achieved. If critical mass is achieved, the service can take off, and a positive level of demand can be sustained.

Once critical mass is achieved, demand becomes subject to what is known as **positive feedback.** Virtually everyone is familiar with a common example of positive feedback, namely, a speaker's talking too loudly into a microphone. The speaker's voice first gets amplified. Then, the amplified sound is picked up by the microphone and amplified again. Then the further amplified sound is picked up and amplified still again; and so forth. The result is a deafening roar, which ends when the speaker is frightened into utter silence. More generally, positive feedback is a process in which increases in an activity lead to further increases in that activity, which lead to still further increases, and so forth.

Bandwagon effects lead to positive feedback of a much pleasanter sort. The feedback starts when enough users join the bandwagon to exceed critical mass. The initial user set then provides sufficient bandwagon benefits to induce additional users to join. When the additional users join, more bandwagon benefits are generated, inducing still more users to join.

In the model illustrated in figure 3.2, this positive feedback continues until the maximum equilibrium user set is achieved.

Figure 3.2 is the simplest possible bandwagon inverse demand function. The economics become more complicated when we take into account communities of interest among individuals. In that case, a tight community of interest might have its own critical mass. Its achieving critical mass may or may not suffice to allow other groups that have some community of interest with the original group to achieve critical mass.

In the simplest model (figure 3.2), the service is either a market success or failure, depending on whether critical mass is achieved. In more complex models, gradations of market success may be realized, depending on the number and sizes of community-of-interest groups that achieve critical mass.[6] Even in more complex models, however, demand growth to the maximum equilibrium user set *may* be sustained when the user set expands beyond a certain point—the same as in figure 3.2.

In several of the case studies, we observe that rapid demand growth was sustained after the user set reached a certain level. We find it natural in such situations to say that demand achieved a critical mass. Nevertheless, readers should note several important differences between any real-world situation and the model depicted in figure 3.2:

• Critical mass in the real world is not a unique user set. Many alternative user sets of different sizes involving different users may suffice to propel demand to the maximum equilibrium user set (which *is* unique). Thus, it is more accurate to say that *a* critical mass—not *the* critical mass—was achieved.

• Failure to achieve a critical mass does not imply complete failure, as in figure 3.2. Indeed, the product may still be a commercial success.

• Even though the final user set is very large, one can never be sure in practice that it is the maximum equilibrium user set. It is always possible that some actual nonusers are really members of the maximum equilibrium user set. It may be that their communities of interest never attained their individual critical masses.

3.3   Metcalfe's Law

A principle often ascribed to network services is Metcalfe's Law, namely, the value of a network goes up as the square of the number of users. The law is named for Bob Metcalfe, the inventor of Ethernet and the founder of 3Com.[7]

The assumption underlying Metcalfe's Law is that the value that any user A derives from a communications link with any other user B is the same for all users A and B. For a user set of n users, each user enjoys the value of n links.[8] The sum of the values derived by all n users is therefore the value of n^2 links.

In reality, the values that users derive from links are likely to differ considerably. Some users will derive much more value from links than will other users. Moreover, any given user will derive very different values from links with different users.

In general, one would expect that the first users would be those who derive the most value from links. Then, users who derive progressively less value from links would follow. Under these circumstances, the value of a network increases *much less than proportionately* to the square of the number of users. Indeed, the total value of a bandwagon service may go up less than proportionately to the number of users—let alone the square of the number of users. Such an outcome could occur, for example, if a service in equilibrium has a low price, but some enthusiastic users value it very highly. Because the price is low, we know that the value of the service to marginal users must also be low. That value, in turn, may be low because marginal users do not use the service very much. Under these circumstances, it is likely that existing users would derive only small bandwagon benefits as marginal subscribers join. The sum of these two low values (benefits to marginal subscribers and bandwagon benefits to existing subscribers) may be far less than the average value of the service to enthusiastic users (for communicating with one another). This point is developed more rigorously and in more detail in the mathematical appendix.

The fundamental insight underlying Metcalfe's Law—that bandwagon effects raise the value of a service to each user—is certainly correct, indeed, the point of this whole book. Nevertheless, the precise statement of the law is wrong as a matter of economic theory. In practice, it is likely to substantially overstate the value of large networks.

An important possible exception is internal networks, such as a local area network (LAN) within an organization. It is, for example, quite plausible that a LAN is four times as valuable for an organization that has twice as many connected computers. This is, perhaps, the application that Metcalfe had in mind.

Internal networks are bandwagon products in a sense. Nevertheless, the managers of the organization can internalize the network externality by simply taking bandwagon effects into account in making their decision whether to set up the network. The theory developed in this book applies to external bandwagon effects that cannot be internalized so easily. It is neither necessary nor appropriate to use that theory to analyze decisions involving (purely) internal networks.

3.4 Dynamics of Complementary Bandwagon Effects

The bandwagon benefits from network externalities generally accrue concurrently with consumption of the bandwagon service. In contrast, part of the benefits from complementary bandwagon effects usually accrue after some lag. In particular, the base product (e.g., a CD player) is often durable. It provides some benefits right away, but purchasers may anticipate much greater benefits in the future. For example, early CD purchasers anticipated (correctly) that a greater variety of the complementary products, CDs, would become available in the future as the set of users of CD players expanded.

Under these circumstances, the decision whether to purchase the base product is complex. The potential purchaser must balance the expected future bandwagon benefits against the up-front cost of the purchase. The decision may depend not only on the demand equilibrium, but also on how quickly that equilibrium is likely to be reached.

A further consideration is that the future benefits are uncertain. In markets with complementary bandwagon effects, expectations about such benefits tend to be self-fulfilling. That is, if everyone expects the user set to grow rapidly, purchase of the base product will seem more attractive; and the user set may, indeed, grow rapidly. Pessimistic expectations may also be self-fulfilling and doom a product that is subject to complementary bandwagon effects.[9]

These dynamic factors interact with the equilibria. In particular, the equilibrium may depend, in part, on the speed with which demand adjusts to that equilibrium. For example, more rapid adjustment to equilibrium makes the purchase of the (durable) base product more attractive and may lead to a larger equilibrium user set. It may also cause a smaller initial user set to constitute a critical mass.

Dynamic factors are generally subject to some control by suppliers. For example, a supplier may choose to offer an exceptionally high-quality product. That product may inspire consumers to believe that the user set will grow rapidly, and that belief may be self-fulfilling. More generally, the management of dynamic factors can be an important part of a supplier's strategy for solving the start-up problem for a product involving complementary bandwagon effects.

4

Bandwagon Supply

The theory of bandwagon supply defines the rules of the road for bandwagons. Those rules become quite complex when several bandwagons are trying to head down the same road. Sometimes the rules lead all of them to proceed in an orderly fashion. Sometimes, the rules amount to a game of bumper cars wherein each bandwagon tries to force all the others into a ditch.

The rules obviously depend on the number of bandwagons and the differences among them. One possibility is that many similar bandwagons are on the road—**pure competition.** In that case, bandwagon supply theory reduces to the usual (nonbandwagon) model used to analyze such competition.

In reality, however, relatively few firms are usually at the forefront of technology. Sometimes only a single bandwagon is on the road—**monopoly.** More usually, several bandwagons are on the road—**oligopoly.** In practice, the rivalry among high-technology oligopolists tends to be intense, but some firms may have a substantial competitive advantage over the others, for example, because of better technology or a bigger bandwagon.

4.1 Monopoly versus Competition

It is possible that the bandwagon supplier is a monopolist. In a high-technology industry, monopoly can derive from a proprietary technology. For example, Alexander Graham Bell's original monopoly over telephone service was based on his patents. Alternatively, monopoly may derive from public policies. For most of the twentieth century, the Bell

System was granted monopoly franchises over much of the United States and was subjected to regulation.

In many bandwagon industries, a single supplier amasses a large market share. Indeed, bandwagon markets often have a tendency to gravitate toward a single supplier. The supplier in such cases is sometimes called a de facto monopolist. Here, however, we use the term "monopoly" to refer to markets in which a single firm faces no actual or potential competition in supplying the bandwagon service.

Monopoly in this sense is uncommon today in industries that supply bandwagon services. Even the local telephone industry has been subjected to competition in recent years. Indeed, apart from Picturephone, varying degrees of competition are now prevalent in all the examples of bandwagon services and products discussed in this book.

4.2   Interlinking

Where bandwagon services are competitively supplied, a key issue is interlinking. If bandwagon services are interlinked (in the bandwagon sense), the bandwagon effects apply to total industry output by all suppliers. If they are not interlinked, bandwagon effects are limited to the output of a single supplier.

In some markets (e.g., digital fax machines and CD players), suppliers voluntarily interlink their services. In other markets (e.g., local and long-distance telephone service), the government mandates interlinking. In still other bandwagon markets (e.g., the Internet), the government has facilitated, but not mandated, interlinking. Nevertheless, in many bandwagon markets suppliers are not interlinked or are only partially interlinked. For example, Apple computers are only partially interlinked with "IBM-compatible" computers—that is, those that are based on Intel microprocessors and run Microsoft Windows.

Interlinking can be implemented by various means. In telecommunications, it involves physical linking of wires and radio facilities (interconnection). As a result of interconnection, electronic or optical signals can be sent from subscribers of one carrier to subscribers of another. Government policies often require incumbent telecommunications carriers to interconnect with new entrants at regulated prices.

The term "interconnection" is also used to refer to interlinking of data communications systems, including e-mail. The issue is whether a subscriber of one network can communicate with (e.g., send e-mail to or receive e-mail from) subscribers of other networks. All types of interconnection require cooperation between the interconnecting networks.

Interlinking of computer systems means compatibility. The ideal is that an applications program written for one system works equally well on all other systems. Rarely is that goal ever fully achieved, but it may be easier or harder to transport programs from one system to another.[1] For players of recorded programming (e.g., CD players and VCRs), interlinking refers to the ability of players of different manufacturers to play the same recorded programming.

Interlinking always bestows direct benefits on consumers, who thereby enjoy bandwagon benefits with respect to a larger population. These benefits are almost always quite large. Indeed, if there are *n* equal suppliers, interlinking increases the total value of the network by a factor of *n* under the assumptions underlying Metcalfe's Law. The benefits can be very large even if those assumptions are substantially relaxed. (See the mathematical appendix.)

Nevertheless, interlinking also involves costs, which depend on the type of interlinking involved. In some cases, interlinking is not cost-effective. Indeed, it may not even be feasible at reasonable cost.

Apart from the direct consumer benefits, interlinking profoundly affects the nature of competitive rivalry among suppliers. In bandwagon markets with interlinking, competitive rivalry is not much different than in nonbandwagon markets. Bandwagon markets without interlinking tend to generate a winner-take-all contest among suppliers.

4.3 Solving the Start-Up Problem

The nature of the start-up problem depends on industry structure and interlinking arrangements. We consider three possibilities:

• The supplier is a monopolist.

• Multiple rivals operate in the market and interlink with one another. Bandwagon effects therefore apply to total industry output.

• Multiple rivals operate but they do not interlink with one another. Bandwagon effects for each subscriber are therefore limited to subscribers of the same supplier.

4.3.1 Monopoly

The simplest start-up strategy for the monopolist is as follows:

1. Offer the service at a fixed price.

2. The initial user set then depends on that price.

3. Because of bandwagon effects, demand grows to the demand-based equilibrium user set, which depends on the price.

4. The monopolist can then choose the price that leads to the most profitable demand-based equilibrium.

This strategy is not fundamentally different than the usual problem of monopoly profit maximization without bandwagon effects. In this case, bandwagon effects are simply part of the reason that demand is what it is. Whatever the reason, the usual economic model of monopoly profit maximization applies.

Where bandwagon effects are present, more complex start-up strategies may be more profitable. In particular, it may be profitable for the monopolist to sacrifice profits in the short run. He or she may lower prices in the hope that demand will reach a critical mass and become subject to positive feedback. He or she may also hope to be able to raise prices profitably in the future, after demand has grown and consumers are enjoying bandwagon benefits.[2]

This point is a recurring theme in both our theoretical and empirical analysis. It is especially relevant for our analysis of PCs and early telephone service. A firm in a bandwagon market should not be greedy for short-run profits during the start-up phase. Its goal should be to increase sales to solve the start-up problem. This strategy can be very profitable for a monopolist and may be essential for survival in an oligopolistic bandwagon market.

It is quite likely that consumers benefit as a result of a monopolist's solving the start-up problem. Consumers benefit from the lower promotional prices in the short run. In the long run, they benefit from bandwagon effects, though the monopolist can be expected to expropriate some of the benefits by raising prices.

An alternative approach to solving the start-up problem is to have **multipart tariffs** that include a fixed monthly charge and usage charges. This approach was discussed briefly in Rohlfs (1974, 34–35) and analyzed in much greater depth by Oren and Smith in 1982. It has the advantage that the amount paid by each subscriber grows automatically over time as he or she uses the service more and derives more benefit therefrom. With a low fixed charge and high usage charges, the following occurs:

• While the user set is small, the usage of most subscribers is low. The amount paid by each subscriber is therefore small; it includes only the small fixed charge and the charges for little usage. Since users need pay only a small amount, they may choose to subscribe, even though the value that they derive from the service is also small.

• As the user set grows, the usage of most subscribers grows. With the high usage charges, the supplier can then hope to recoup initial losses.

This approach seems like quite a good way to solve the start-up problem. It has the advantage that the amount paid *by each user* rises automatically as he/she uses the service more (and presumably derives more value from it). This approach may be more effective than the alternative of periodic increases in the fixed monthly charge, which apply to all subscribers, regardless of their usage. The alternative may cause some users to unsubscribe if their usage (and the value they derive from the service) has not increased as rapidly as the price.

In nonbandwagon markets, multipart tariffs may be far more efficacious than a single fixed price, even if the latter is chosen optimally.[3] The advantage of additional pricing variables may be even greater during the start-up phase of a bandwagon service. All the pricing variables can then be optimized to solve the start-up problem, while minimizing initial losses.

4.3.2 Competition with Interlinking
The combination of competition and interlinking provides substantial benefits for consumers. Competition limits the extraction of profits by a

monopolistic supplier, while interlinking allows consumers to benefit from bandwagon effects that apply to total industry output—not just the output of a single supplier.

Unfortunately, interlinking is generally costly.[4] Interlinking of networks usually requires additional transmission facilities. The cost is, however, usually moderate. Making incompatible products compatible can be a much more a costly activity. Furthermore, compatible products may be less suitable for meeting specialized needs of diverse consumers. To decide public policies regarding interlinking, one must weigh the large benefits of interlinking against these possibly substantial costs.

In general, interlinking makes the start-up problem much easier to solve. With interlinking, consumers enjoy bandwagon benefits with respect to the entire customer base—not just the customers of a single supplier. Thus, initial demand is likely to be substantially greater, and it is easier to reach a critical mass.

On the other hand, interlinking also reduces the incentives of suppliers to solve the start-up problem. Indeed, if it were not possible to gain an enduring competitive advantage, no supplier would have any incentive to incur short-run losses to promote the service. In this case, the market equilibrium is likely to be the demand-based equilibrium user set. The maximum equilibrium user set may be a much nicer place, but there is no way to get there.

In reality, suppliers who incur short-run losses to promote a service are likely to derive a substantial **first-mover advantage.** They will be the recognized supplier and can establish enduring relationships with customers. They also have a head start in moving down the learning curve to reduce costs and improve service quality. These competitive advantages often allow firms to earn large profits.[5] The profits deriving from a first-mover advantage are, however, lower than the profits that a monopolist could earn in the same market. Competitive suppliers therefore have less incentive than a monopolist would to promote a bandwagon service. Nevertheless, the benefits of the first-mover advantage may suffice to induce a supplier to promote the service.[6]

The above results are analogous to some famous results of the economist Joseph Schumpeter. Schumpeter observed that in order to undertake risky ventures, a firm needs the prospect of some degree of **market power**—that is, the ability to earn a greater return on investment than a competitive firm could expect to earn. If the firm had no way to acquire market power, it would lose if the venture failed and earn only a competitive return if the venture succeeded. Since the firm could probably earn a competitive return by investing in safer ventures, the odds of the risky venture are, "Heads I lose; tails I break even." To avoid this unfavorable gamble, the firm would choose to avoid risks and pursue only safe ventures. But firms in high-technology industries must take calculated risks for technology to advance rapidly and for social welfare to be maximized in the long run. Schumpeter's inescapable conclusion is that firms must have some degree of market power if social welfare is to be maximized in the long run.[7]

Schumpeter further reasoned that market power is likely not to be permanent. Technological progress and the successful bearing of new risks by other firms can be relied upon to erode the original firm's market power. Schumpeter named this process "creative destruction."[8]

We find, analogously, that suppliers must have the prospect of market power to induce them to incur short-run losses to develop a bandwagon service. Where the maximum equilibrium user set is much larger than the demand-based equilibrium user set, this market power is necessary to generate the bandwagon benefits that maximize social welfare. Given that the firm interlinks with its rivals, we can also reason, as Schumpeter did, that the market power is likely not to be permanent. The value of first-mover advantages tends to dissipate over time, and technological progress will eventually destroy the very basis of any first-mover advantage.

This outcome is not, however, guaranteed. It may be that the first-mover advantage does not suffice to induce firms to solve the start-up problem. In that case, no value is created, and the process of creative destruction never gets under way.

From a theoretical perspective, any number of products may conceivably have been successful, but no firm had the incentive to solve the start-up problem. In practice, identifying such products is exceedingly difficult. To be sure, we can identify many bandwagon products that were not developed and/or marketed. What we cannot easily ascertain is whether the products would have been duds, even apart from the start-up problem.

4.3.3   Competition without Interlinking

As discussed in section 4.3.2, the start-up problem is more difficult to solve where there are multiple suppliers whose services are not interlinked. Each consumer then enjoys bandwagon benefits only with respect to the customers of his or her own supplier. Initial demand is therefore reduced, and critical mass is harder to achieve.

At the same time, suppliers have greater incentives to promote their services, even at the cost of suffering losses during the start-up period. Each supplier has a strong incentive to amass more subscribers than other suppliers amass, so that his or her customers enjoy greater bandwagon benefits. He or she hopes thereby to be able to attract other suppliers' customers who wish to enjoy the greater bandwagon benefits. This leads to an unstable process in which success breeds further success. Ultimately, one supplier may have a virtual monopoly.

This instability is analogous to that deriving from internal supply-side scale economies in standard economic models. Under standard assumptions, competition among firms with internal scale economies is unstable, leading ultimately to a single survivor that has a monopoly with lower unit costs than any competitor or potential competitor. Bandwagon effects without interlinking have this same tendency toward monopoly.

In markets without interlinking, bandwagon effects always augment the first-mover advantage, often substantially. Nevertheless, the emergence of a single supplier is not inevitable. In the analogous case of internal supply-side scale economies, the outcome of a single supplier may be averted through product differentiation. That is, each supplier can provide products specially designed to meet the needs of a subset of consumers. Multiple suppliers can then survive, each catering to its own niche in the market. Product differentiation of this sort is not necessarily desirable. The lost scale economies may outweigh the benefits of product differentiation. Product differentiation may, however, be the only practical way that consumers can reap the benefits of competition, as compared to a monopoly supplier of an undifferentiated product. The key issue is whether the benefits of product differentiation *plus* the benefits of competition outweigh the lost scale economies.

Communities of interest play a precisely analogous role in bandwagon models. They allow the possibility that consumers with a strong community of interest choose one supplier, while other community-of-interest groups choose another supplier. Apple, for example, carved out such a niche in the educational community. Likewise, early telephone competitors had serving areas that were not completely overlapping and thereby catered to geographic communities of interest.

This industry structure is not economically efficient, since each consumer does not enjoy bandwagon benefits from customers of other suppliers. The alternative may, however, be monopoly supply. The issue then is whether the benefits of competition outweigh the loss of bandwagon benefits.

Regulation is another alternative. If a nonbandwagon industry (e.g., suppliers of water) is regulated, consumers may be able to enjoy the full benefits of internal supply-side scale economies, while the excesses of monopoly are mitigated. Similarly, regulation in bandwagon markets may allow consumers to enjoy full bandwagon benefits, while the excesses of monopoly are mitigated. In both cases, the inherent costs and inefficiencies of regulation must be weighed against the expected benefits deriving from regulation.

In any event, since the rewards of being the victor in a bandwagon market without interlinking can be enormous, firms often compete fiercely in such markets. Indeed, each of several firms may choose to incur initial short-run losses to promote its particular product. Each firm may do so, knowing full well that most of the firms will be unable to recoup their losses. The potential rewards may be so great that the gamble is good, even with only a moderate chance of success.

This sort of competition, while fierce, bears little resemblance to the competition posited in standard economic models. One cannot, therefore, presume that it yields the benefits usually associated with competition. Rather, we need to examine the benefits and drawbacks to consumers for this particular kind of competition.

Consumers may potentially be harmed by being stuck with an orphaned product (e.g., a Beta VCR) that loses the bandwagon race. To be sure, they should have been aware of that risk when they bought the product. Furthermore, the supplier may have offered the consumer a special deal in order to induce him or her to bear the risk. Nevertheless, consumers' being stuck with an orphaned product is a form of economic waste.

Another type of economic waste is the duplication of development efforts by competing suppliers. Quite possibly, the development efforts of the losers of the bandwagon race will turn out to be largely wasted effort.

Consumers directly benefit from this form of competition via the special deals that they receive while competing suppliers are promoting their products (each hoping to win the bandwagon race). These consumer benefits may be considerable.

Unfortunately, there is no free lunch. Suppliers do not offer these special deals out of altruism. They do so because they have some expectation of earning **monopoly profits** (i.e., profits over and above what a competitive firm could expect to earn) in the future. If suppliers act rationally, the expected value of the monopoly profits to each supplier is no less than the losses that the supplier expends in promoting the product. It follows that consumers will, in an expected-value sense, pay for all the costs that all the suppliers expend. Moreover, they must also bear the costs of the inefficiencies. These include

• the costs of consumers' being stuck with orphaned products,

• the wasteful duplication of producers' development costs,

• the loss of the benefits of competition in the inevitable future monopoly, and

• the loss of intersupplier bandwagon benefits during the start-up period, until the winner in the bandwagon race emerges.

Put another way, consumers may be enjoying a foolish prosperity while suppliers offer special deals to promote their products. Ultimately, those consumer gains may have to be paid back with usurious interest.

The preceding discussion demonstrates that competition without interlinking involves substantial economic waste. Nevertheless, it may under some circumstances be a better industry structure than the alternatives. Possible countervailing harms associated with interlinking are as follows:

- *Increased costs.* Interlinking may be very costly.

- *Reduced incentives to innovate.* A supplier with a new technology may gain a valuable competitive advantage by declining to interlink. Without the prospect of such advantage, firms might have insufficient incentives to develop technological innovations. For this reason, the right to refuse to interlink may be analogous to patent rights. Such rights reduce consumer benefits in the short term but may increase them in the long term.

- *Reduced incentives to solve the start-up problem.* With interlinking, it may be that no supplier has a sufficient incentive to incur the initial losses necessary to solve the start-up problem.

These factors, if applicable, must be weighed against the aforementioned economic waste of bandwagon markets without interlinking.

We conclude this section by discussing two further defects of competition without interlinking. These defects must also be considered in evaluating the efficacy of that industry structure.

4.3.3.1 The Best Product Does Not Necessarily Win the Bandwagon Race On the contrary, if an inferior product for any reason gets an early edge in number of customers, it may well win the race.[9] Suppose, for example, that firm A introduces a successful bandwagon product. Sometime later, firm B introduces a better product. Firm B may be unsuccessful, even if everyone knows that its product is better. Consumers may be reluctant to give up the bandwagon benefits that they currently enjoy from A's product.[10] These considerations were especially important with respect to digital compact cassettes, minidiscs, and video disc players, as discussed in chapters 9 and 10.

Another possibility is as follows: Suppose that firm A and firm B enter the market at the same time. Suppose further that firm A is well known and has a good product; firm B is lesser known but has a better product. In a nonbandwagon market, A would initially have greater sales. Firm B would gain market share over time as more and more people learned about the quality of its product. It would eventually prevail. In a bandwagon market, however, B may be unable to overcome A's initial lead in the bandwagon race.

Consider a third example: Suppose that firm A and firm B have equally good reputations and enter the market at the same time. Firm B makes some serious marketing misjudgments, losing the advantage to firm A, but it (otherwise) has the better product. In a nonbandwagon market, firm B would often get a second chance (perhaps under new management). In a bandwagon market, however, misjudgments can have much more enduring consequences. By the time firm B recovers from its misjudgments, firm A may have an insurmountable lead in the bandwagon race. In a bandwagon market, it can be, "One strike and you're out!" For example, the short playing time of Sony's initial Beta videocassettes is often cited as a fatal misjudgment, even though later Beta videocassettes had longer playing times.

As previously discussed, expectations also play a critical role in competition involving complementary bandwagon effects. The extreme example is as follows: Suppose that everyone knows that firm B's product is superior but expects that Firm A will win the bandwagon race. In that case, everyone may choose to purchase A's product, notwithstanding its inferiority.

Liebowitz and Margolis challenge the practical relevance of this model. They ask why everyone would expect firm A to win the bandwagon race under these circumstances. That is a good question. In reality, it seems likely that most people would expect Firm B to win the bandwagon race if it is widely known to have the better product.

Expectations can, however, be determinative under less extreme circumstances. Suppose, for example, that firm A has a good product but not the best. Suppose further that it has considerably greater financial resources than the other firms and is (say, because of animal spirits) committed to win the bandwagon race, by winning a price war, if necessary. As a result, everyone may expect A to win the bandwagon race and choose A's product. Firm A may therefore win the bandwagon race without the price war.[11] This type of effect probably contributed to the initial success of the IBM PC.

The above example highlights two interesting characteristics of competition in markets with complementary bandwagon effects:

• Small firms may have a marketing disadvantage because they lack credibility. This disadvantage is over and above their inability to enjoy technological economies of scale. Financially weak firms may also lack credibility, in addition to the other problems caused by a weak financial condition. These are two further ways in which rich suppliers get richer and poor suppliers get poorer in bandwagon markets.

• The most rational strategy for a financially strong firm may be to signal an irrational commitment to win the bandwagon race at all costs. This is analogous to a well-known result of oligopoly theory; namely, the most rational strategy for an oligopolist may be to signal an irrational commitment to punish price cutters—regardless of the ruinous cost that it may incur by doing so.

4.3.3.2 The Resulting Monopoly May Be Quite Enduring Even if new technology allows other producers to offer better products at lower prices, they may be unable to prevail, because customers of the monopolist enjoy large bandwagon benefits. Where there are bandwagon effects without interlinking, the Schumpeterian process of creative destruction bogs down.

Of course, no monopoly lasts forever. Nevertheless, bandwagon effects may substantially lengthen the duration of the monopoly—so long as the monopolist avoids serious misjudgments. Note, however, that this qualification is not trivial. As we shall see in part III, avoiding serious misjudgments is far from easy in high-technology markets.

4.4 Incentives of Suppliers to Interlink

An incumbent supplier in a bandwagon market often has little incentive to interlink with new entrants. By refusing to interlink, the incumbent may retain an insurmountable competitive advantage in the market. Entrants, even if they have a superior product and superior service, may be unable to match the bandwagon benefits that the incumbent (with its larger user set) offers its customers. Thus, entrants may go out of business or remain small indefinitely.

It is possible, however, that two or more firms each amass a large user set. Such an outcome can be sustainable if the user set of each supplier has a substantial community of interest within itself. Because of that community of interest, the customers of each supplier may find the services of other suppliers unattractive.

Under these circumstances, interlinking involves the following trade-offs for the suppliers:

• As a result of interlinking, each supplier's service becomes more valuable because of increased bandwagon benefits to customers. Demand therefore increases, perhaps substantially.

• Each supplier faces more intense competition, because all suppliers can provide full bandwagon benefits to all customers.

These trade-offs depend critically on the likely nature of competition after interlinking. If the suppliers can agree to "live and let live" (a strategy often dubbed "implicit collusion" by proponents of antitrust enforcement), they can all be better off by interlinking. Interlinking is especially likely to be profitable if the suppliers are not well positioned to compete in each other's markets—for example, because each specializes in offering complementary products (e.g., specialized software) that are especially valuable to its own customers but not to the customers of the other supplier.[12] If competition takes the form of frequent price wars, however, the suppliers are almost certainly better off maintaining unlinked services.

Suppliers sometimes agree to interlink prior to beginning operations—for example, by agreeing to a single technical standard—as discussed below in section 4.6. Such an agreement increases demand, because consumers will be able to enjoy greater bandwagon benefits. It also avoids a costly competitive battle to establish the industry standard and the large economic waste associated therewith. The downside (from the perspective of suppliers) is that competition to win customers will be more intense. This trade-off could go either way; for example:

• The proprietor of a clearly superior technology may be reluctant to enter into an agreement, since it stands to win outright in the competitive battle. Theoretically, it could achieve the same profits by negotiating favorable contracts with competitors, but designing airtight contracts is exceedingly difficult—especially where technology is rapidly changing.

• Absent such an agreement, consumers will be reluctant to purchase the product of any supplier, because they fear being stuck with a product that embodies a losing technology. As a result, a supplier may have to incur prohibitive losses in order to solve the start-up problem.

• An agreement is most advantageous where multiple suppliers have technologies that are viable, even if the technologies are not equally meritorious. By reaching an agreement, the suppliers may all have the prospect of earning substantial transitory profits during an initial period of rapid growth. During that period, the main problem may be to grow rapidly enough to meet increases in demand. Farther down the road, suppliers face the prospect of a shakeout after growth has attenuated, and they start to compete more vigorously with one another. But having put a lot of money in the bank, they may be willing to take their chances in the shakeout.

As might be expected from this discussion, the willingness of suppliers in the real world to interlink is a mixed bag. Sometimes they do; sometimes they do not. The choice depends largely on the considerations identified in this section.

4.5   Supply Coordination with Complementary Bandwagon Products

Coordinating supply is always problematic for complementary bandwagon products. Where the chicken-and-egg problem exists (as described at the beginning of part II), coordination is absolutely essential. Even where there is no chicken-and-egg problem, coordinating supply is generally constructive. At a minimum, base-product suppliers can profit by ensuring that their product designs work well with the product designs of the complementary products.

Coordination may go further, and a base-product supplier may offer inducements to complementary-product suppliers. Such inducements internalize the external benefits that accrue to base-product suppliers from the supply of complementary products. Complementary-product suppliers cannot be expected to take such external benefits into account in their supply decisions. Consequently, their supply is likely to be too little and/or too late, from the perspective of the base-product suppliers. Inducements can encourage sufficient and timely supply of complementary products.

Such inducements can also become a form of competitive rivalry. For example, IBM offered inducements to software suppliers to promote its original PCs.[13] Microsoft has continued this practice in recent years.[14]

Vertical integration is another way to internalize the externality. As previously discussed, it converts external complementary bandwagon effects into internal supply-side economies of scale.

Even apart from internalizing the externality, vertical integration may yield significant internal supply-side economies of scale, for example, from centralized administration. It can also facilitate transactions where the output and/or its quality cannot be precisely defined.

On the downside, vertical integration also has some serious disadvantages, including the following:

• Under vertical integration, production of the downstream (or upstream) output is governed by internal incentives within the firm. Unfortunately, internal incentives to improve efficiency are generally duller than the incentives afforded by competitive markets. As a result, quality of output may decline, and costs may rise.

• In practice, vertical integration often has the effect of reducing the variety of output. Competitive markets generally do far better than any single firm in meeting diverse customer needs.[15]

For these reasons (among others), the production of base products (e.g., hardware) and complementary products (e.g., software) are often not vertically integrated or are integrated to only a limited extent.

4.6   Technical Standards

Agreements on technical standards interlink the products and services of all suppliers. For services that use telecommunications networks, interlinking is achieved through agreements on transmission protocols. For example, protocols have been agreed upon for both television and Internet transmission. For complementary bandwagon effects, interlinking is achieved through agreements on compatibility standards. Such standards have been agreed upon for CD players and VCRs (now that Beta has left the field). Also, IBM-compatible PCs are all interlinked and can use the same applications software. On the Internet, technical standards have been agreed upon for the standard applications of Telnet, file-transfer protocol (FTP), and e-mail. More recently, in order to facilitate Internet use, software standards have been developed to interlink a broad range of computers, including IBM compatibles, Apple computers, and those that run variants of the Unix operating system. These standards include HTML for input and output and Java for computer programs.

Competition in bandwagon industries often revolves around technical standards. Each supplier may have its own proprietary technology and seeks to have that technology become the industry standard. Without government intervention, competition might take the form described in section 4.3.3.

To avoid the economic waste associated with that competition, government setting of technical standards is often proposed, but government setting of standards involves a whole set of problems of its own. The most obvious problem is that public policymakers may be clueless about which is the best technology. The technological choice inherently involves uncertainties on the forefront of technological knowledge. Public policymakers do not generally have the high level of technical expertise required to evaluate such uncertainties. The problem is compounded, because the most knowledgeable persons (viz., those whose jobs are to develop the competing technologies) usually have incentives to deceive the policymakers—in particular, to exaggerate the strengths of their own technology and the weaknesses of the opposing technology. Because public policymakers lack sufficient knowledge, they may choose the wrong technology and get an important new industry off on the wrong foot.

One can argue that public policymakers may nevertheless be able to muddle through. Notwithstanding their lack of knowledge, they may do better than an inefficient competitive process. In particular, they may be able to discard the technologies that are markedly inferior. An arbitrary choice among the remaining technologies, which may be approximately equally meritorious, may suffice.

Another potential problem with governmental choice of technology is that the process may be corrupted. In many countries, the likely winner would be the technology whose proprietors offered the largest bribes to key governmental officials. Alternatively, the "race" may be won by the firm that offered substantial participation to close relatives of high governmental officials. Such a process is almost surely destructive—however otherwise persuasive the theoretical case for government intervention.

In many other countries, bribery would not be an especially serious problem. Nevertheless, the prospect of governmental selection would almost certainly spawn a contest to exert political influence on the process. Such a contest is inherently wasteful. It may also lead to the selection of an inferior technology—even if (expert) subordinates of the influenced public officials know that another technology is better.

Good public policy thus boils down to selecting the lesser of two evils: namely,

• the economic inefficiency that is certain to result if proprietors of competing technologies battle in the market; or

• the economic inefficiency that is certain to result if governmental officials choose the winning technology.

Chapter 12 sheds some light on this trade-off, as it has arisen in one particular industry, namely, television.

4.7 Proprietor Services versus Customer Equipment

A key distinction in bandwagon theory is between proprietor services and customer equipment.[16] Customer equipment may be the bandwagon product itself. Alternatively, customers may have to own or lease equipment and operate it on their premises in order to consume a bandwagon service. In either case, the benefits from obtaining the customer equipment grow as the user set expands—the bandwagon effect. Examples of customer equipment are telephones, VCRs, and PCs.

In contrast, service suppliers operate equipment on their own premises in order to provide proprietor services to customers. A service supplier may enjoy internal supply-side scale economies and be able to provide greater value to its customers by operating over a broad geographic region. Nevertheless, the supply of proprietor services does not generate (external) bandwagon effects. Examples of suppliers of proprietor services are Western Union (telegraph), movie theaters, and computer-service bureaus.

Although the supply of proprietor services does not generate bandwagon effects, the suppliers may enjoy bandwagon benefits in their role as customers. For example, the availability of movies (in a particular format) may depend on the number of movie theaters (that show movies in that particular format). Thus, proprietor services may not eliminate bandwagon effects but rather shift them farther upstream in the production process.

Customer equipment often offers greater benefits to customers than the analogous proprietor services could. In particular, customers enjoy the convenience of being able to use the equipment on their own premises.

Proprietor services are a low-cost alternative. The same facilities can be used to provide services to many customers. Moreover, the supplier may have special expertise in operating the equipment. The VCR may approach the limit on how complicated customer equipment can be to operate for home use. In contrast, a proprietor service (e.g., telegraph) may require substantial skill to provide.

In many cases, proprietor services are offered initially. Then, only after technological progress has driven down costs and/or improved quality is customer equipment supplied commercially. At that time, suppliers must deal with the start-up problem. The examples of proprietor services and customer equipment listed above were introduced in that sequence.

4.8 Mature Services

This book focuses on bandwagon effects as they apply to new products and services and suppliers thereof. Bandwagon effects also apply to mature services. There, the start-up problem has already been solved. Nevertheless, the resulting market equilibrium is generally suboptimal. In particular, there may be individuals such that

• the benefit *to the individual* of consuming the bandwagon service does not justify incurring the (incremental) cost of serving him or her, but

• the benefit *to society*, including bandwagon benefits that would be enjoyed by other users, does justify incurring the cost.

Under these circumstances, economic efficiency would be improved if the individual consumed the service; but he or she will choose not to do so.

More generally, mature bandwagon services involve external economies, the same as start-up services. Such externalities can, at least in principle, justify government intervention. In this case, the goal of the government policy would be to lower the price of the bandwagon service to stimulate its consumption and generate bandwagon benefits.[17] This argument is the economic rationale for public policies to promote universal telephone service.

Issues to be considered in implementing such a policy include the following:

• *To what extent can users internalize the externality, in the absence of corrective pricing?* Users may be able on their own to work out an arrangement that leads to efficient expansion of the user set. We have already discussed the possibility that small groups of users (mainly pairs) may jointly decide to subscribe to the bandwagon service. Market forces also sometimes internalize externalities. For example, a business may subscribe to telephone service as an accommodation to its customers. It presumably passes the cost on to those customers. As a result, the beneficiaries are the payers, and the benefits are therefore not external. To the extent that users can internalize the externality by such means, corrective pricing is unnecessary.

• *Who will pay for lunch?* It is all very well to say that the price of a bandwagon service should be reduced below cost, but there is no free lunch. Someone will have to pony up the money to cover the resulting deficit. In general, raising money to cover the deficit—either through taxes or increased prices for nonbandwagon services—has drawbacks. These drawbacks must be balanced against the benefits from the corrective pricing.

The relevant economics literature for addressing these issues is not that of bandwagon effects, as discussed in this and the previous chapter. Rather it is the literature on externalities and economically efficient pricing; see, for example, Pigou (1912, 1920), Coase, Ramsey, Boiteaux, and Baumol and Bradford. Rohlfs (1978) addresses these issues as they apply to pricing telephone services. Such analysis is beyond the scope of this book.

4.9 Predatory Pricing

Under antitrust law, firms with substantial market power are prohibited from **predatory pricing**—that is, the offering of low prices with the intent of eliminating competition. Even if present, however, anticompetitive intent is generally difficult to prove directly. Furthermore, firms that lower prices always do so in the full knowledge (and probably pleasurable anticipation) that the price reduction will make life more difficult for their competitors. Yet, antitrust laws obviously should not be construed to prohibit all price decreases.

A common judicial solution to this conundrum is to prohibit firms with substantial market power from pricing below the relevant measure of cost. The reasoning is that below-cost pricing, properly defined, cannot be profit maximizing. If a firm with substantial market power does, indeed, price below relevant cost, anticompetitive intent can be presumed.

As might be expected, there has been considerable controversy about the appropriate measure of relevant cost.[18] Whatever the cost measure, however, one cannot infer anticompetitive intent from below-cost pricing during the start-up period for bandwagon products. We previously observed that firms may maximize long-run profits by pricing below cost (however defined) for an extended period of time. Such pricing can maximize long-run profits even if there is no competition at all. If there *is* competition, such pricing can maximize profits even if there is no prospect of eliminating the competition. Of course, below-cost pricing *may* reflect anticompetitive intent—even during the start-up period of a bandwagon product. But one would need additional evidence, other than below-cost pricing itself, to demonstrate such intent.

A further consideration is that in bandwagon markets without interlinking, the goal of *all* competitors is to drive their rivals out of the market, or at least to marginalize them. "Predator" is the wrong metaphor in this case. The lion is not eating the zebras. Rather, the lions are killing each other off. One can argue that lesser beasts do not belong on this particular savannah. Nevertheless, in the high-tech world, the most ferocious denizen of all can turn out to be a start-up software house in Seattle.

In a bandwagon market without interlinking, an equilibrium in which several firms survive and have sizable market shares may not be possible. It is hard to define "predatory pricing" in this case so as not to include normal competitive behavior. More generally, antitrust enforcement is problematic in bandwagon markets without interlinking. The de facto monopoly resulting from the winner-take-all struggle may be better for consumers, because of bandwagon benefits, than a government-contrived market structure with several sizable suppliers that are not interlinked.

Nevertheless, bandwagon markets without interlinking do tend to bestow substantial market power on the winner of the competitive struggle. It may be good public policy to avert this outcome by facilitating interlinking (as with the Internet) or mandating it (as in telecommunications). Where such policies are not efficacious, there may be no constructive way to prevent the bandwagon market from being dominated by a single firm for some period of time.

Given this outcome, antitrust enforcement to prevent extension of monopoly can be especially important. It can serve the valuable function of preventing the winner in a bandwagon market from unfairly and inefficiently extending its market power into other (bandwagon or nonbandwagon) markets.

5

Summary of Results of Bandwagon Theory

We are aware that some readers are impatient to get to the analysis of real-world bandwagon markets and will have skipped chapters 3 and 4. For those readers, we now offer a "cheat sheet," that is, a brief summary of the theoretical results. The cheat sheet will suffice to let you understand part III. We hope, however, that you will return to the theoretical chapters after seeing how useful the theory is for understanding the real-world markets.

5.1 The Cheat Sheet

Bandwagon effects[1] increase the benefits that consumers derive from a product or service as the user set expands. In the formal terms of economic theory, bandwagon effects are **external demand-side scale economies**. Where they apply to networks, they are often called **network externalities**. **Complementary bandwagon effects** obtain where the benefits of a product (e.g., hardware) depend at least partially on the supply of complementary products (e.g., software) produced by independent vendors.

A property sometimes ascribed to network services is **Metcalfe's Law**, which states that the value of a network increases proportionately to the square of the number of users. The fundamental insight underlying this law—that bandwagon effects increase the value of a network to each user—is certainly correct. Nevertheless, the quantitative statement of Metcalfe's Law is incorrect as a matter of economic theory and likely to substantially overstate the value of large networks—except possibly for internal networks within organizations.

Bandwagon markets usually have multiple equilibria. The key user sets for our analysis are as follows:

- the **initial user set;**
- the **demand-based equilibrium user set,** to which demand converges starting from the initial user set; and
- the **maximum** (largest possible) **equilibrium user set.**

Consumers are generally better off at the maximum equilibrium user set than at any other equilibrium. Unfortunately, demand adjustments lead only to the demand-based equilibrium user set, which may be a far smaller and less satisfactory equilibrium. Concerted efforts by suppliers and/or government intervention may be required to solve the start-up problem and get to a larger, better equilibrium. Solving the start-up problem is often a question of reaching a **critical mass.** After a critical mass is achieved, demand for the product is subject to **positive feedback.** Then, growth in demand generates bandwagon effects, which lead to further increases in demand; and so forth. As a result, demand may grow extremely rapidly.

In the early stages of a bandwagon product, suppliers should not be greedy for short-term profits. On the contrary, their best strategy is usually to maximize growth of sales, subject to reasonable financial constraints. The suppliers can thereby enjoy the prospect of large profits in the future, after demand reaches a critical mass and becomes subject to positive feedback.

A key concept in bandwagon markets is **interlinking.** With interlinking, each consumer enjoys bandwagon benefits with respect to *all* consumers—not just those of his or her own supplier. Interlinking is sometimes achieved if the physical networks of various suppliers are interconnected. It is sometimes achieved if the products of various suppliers are compatible, for example, if the hardware produced by different suppliers can use the same software.

Interlinking almost always has substantial benefits. It increases the value of the product or service to each user. It therefore increases demand. It eases the start-up problem, because this expansion of demand makes it easier to reach a critical mass.

Interlinking does, however, involve costs, which vary, depending on the particular circumstances. The costs of interlinking are lowest before a new product is manufactured. Manufacturers can interlink their products at relatively little cost by adopting a single **technical standard** that achieves **compatibility** for their products. Once incompatible hardware is produced, however, interlinking may not be economically feasible. Interlinking (**interconnection**) of physical networks is an intermediate case. The costs are significant but not especially large with modern technology.

Bandwagon markets without interlinking have a tendency to gravitate toward a single supplier. In such markets, firms often engage in fierce competitive battles to determine which will become the dominant supplier. Bandwagon markets *with* interlinking have no such tendency to gravitate toward a single supplier.

Notwithstanding the benefits of interlinking, a supplier may have an incentive *not* to interlink its product with those of other suppliers. Interlinking allows all suppliers to provide full bandwagon benefits to, and compete aggressively for, all customers. This prospect is especially unattractive to a supplier who would otherwise have a good chance of being the dominant supplier in the bandwagon market without interlinking. Even in this case, however, the benefits of interlinking to the supplier (e.g., expanding demand and making it easier to achieve a critical mass) sometimes outweigh such considerations.

Bandwagon services usually involve customer equipment that resides on the customer's premises. Proprietor services are low-cost alternatives that often predate bandwagon services and perform similar functions. Service suppliers provide such services on their own premises. Proprietor services are subject to internal supply-side scale economies, but they are not subject to external bandwagon effects.

In bandwagon markets, low prices do not necessarily constitute **predatory pricing**, even if the prices are below the relevant measure of cost. Low prices increase bandwagon benefits and can increase the supplier's long-run profits, apart from any anticompetitive consequences. Of course, the pricing may be driven by predatory intent, but other evidence, in addition to below-cost pricing, would be required to demonstrate that intent.

III
Case Studies

Bandwagon markets are not for the faint of heart. Innovators always face the difficulties of working with new technology, which always develops unexpected problems. In bandwagon markets, they must additionally convert a vehicle with no passengers into a bandwagon. All the while, they face great uncertainty regarding market demand and future technological developments.

More often than not, the whole effort ends in failure. Where the suppliers succeed, however, the endeavor can have exquisite beauty. The beauty is all the greater because society benefits, often substantially, from their efforts.

It is now time to observe in action the innovators who dared try to meet this challenge. Let the bandwagon tour begin.

6

Fax

The facsimile ("fax") machine seems to be a bandwagon product that grew rapidly and effortlessly to maturity. The start-up problem was obviously solved. Indeed, viewing the rapid growth of the fax in the mid- to late 1980s, one might ask, "What start-up problem?" One might even be tempted to infer that if you build a truly better mousetrap, the world will beat a path to your door, and you need not be concerned about the start-up problem.

In reality, the fax grew from original invention to ubiquitous deployment over a period of about 150 years![1] The original fax machine was built in 1843, and commercial fax service was offered between Paris and Lyons in 1865. With the technology of that period, a raised image was sensed by a stylus and communicated by telegraph.

This variant of the fax was a proprietor service (as described in section 4.7). The service was not especially successful and did not make the transition to customer equipment that embodied bandwagon effects.

The service's lack of success is easy to understand. To utilize it, a customer had to go to the telegraph office. Once there, he or she could alternatively use the old technology at lower cost to send verbal messages. The fax technology at that time additionally afforded an awkward way to transmit low-quality pictures. The cost was presumably rather large, because transmission required substantial labor input and lengthy use of the telegraph line. The user had the further option of sending much better pictures by mail. Thus, the market niche for the fax consisted of occasions for which words alone would not do, a low-quality picture would suffice, time was of the essence, and cost was no object. Not surprisingly, this niche turned out to be quite small.

A key technological development for the fax was the invention of photoelectric cells in the 1870s. This invention enabled the development of wirephoto technology, which was first deployed in 1902. Subsequently, wirephoto technology was widely utilized by newspapers across the globe.

The rapid adoption of wirephoto by the newspaper industry is readily understandable. Time is always of the essence in the newspaper business. A photograph of today's news is far more valuable if it arrives today than if it arrives tomorrow or the day after. Wirephoto was always the least-cost way, and often the only way, to get photos of today's news today.

An additional consideration is that a wirephoto transmitted to a single newspaper could be viewed by tens of thousands of readers. Such a transmission could have substantial value, even if each individual reader derived only modest benefit or enjoyment from viewing the photo. Thus, wirephoto could be cost-effective, even though it involved substantial cost.

Although wirephoto was widely used by newspapers, this initial user set did not provide significant bandwagon benefits to users in other industries. Few other users had a strong community of interest with the newspaper industry. Also, few other users shared the need of newspapers to get pictures immediately. Other industries were not positioned to profitably reproduce pictures for a mass audience. Wirephoto remained a niche market and never evolved to widespread use.

Fax technology continued to progress throughout the twentieth century. Until 1956, however, customer equipment could not be marketed, because the Bell System prohibited telephone users from connecting non-Bell equipment to their telephone lines. This prohibition ended with Judge Bazelon's landmark decision in the Hush-A-Phone case. A decade later, several firms began to sell customer equipment for fax. Figure 6.1 shows the growth of three successive generations of fax machines.

The earliest group 1 machines were introduced in 1966. The installed base of those machines peaked at 142,000 in 1979. Group 2 machines were first introduced in 1972. By 1978, they had surpassed group 1 in terms of annual increment to installed base, and by 1982, their installed

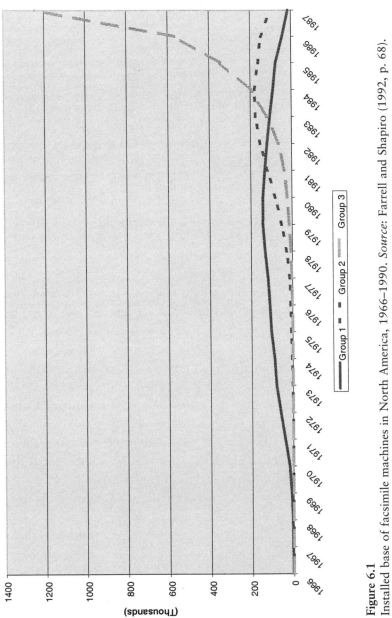

Figure 6.1
Installed base of facsimile machines in North America, 1966–1990. *Source:* Farrell and Shapiro (1992, p. 68).

base was greater. The installed base of group 2 machines peaked at 180,000 machines in 1984.

These levels of sales must be considered a success, since the machines cost on the order of $2,000 each through the early 1980s.[2] Nevertheless, the product showed no signs of taking off and heading toward widespread use. Many reasons explain why the fax did not grow more rapidly during this period; namely, the product was expensive, slow, and noisy, and the paper smelled bad. There can be no doubt that these shortcomings substantially lessened sales.

Nevertheless, the product did meet an important business need. It was by far the most convenient way to transmit written documents quickly to a distant location. Herein lies an important distinction between the fax of the 1860s and the fax of the 1970s. The former was useful primarily for transmission of pictures; the latter was also useful for transmission of words. The old Chinese proverb may apply to much communication, but for most business applications, 10,000 words are worth far more one picture. Furthermore, modern fax machines can transmit a high-quality picture, in addition to the 10,000 words.

The alternatives to the fax for rapid transmission of written documents were much inferior. Even overnight courier service (which had just recently been initiated) did not deliver documents until the next day. Dictation of long documents over the telephone involved substantial labor cost (at both ends) and the possibility of errors. Telegraph, a possible third alternative, was rarely used at that time. It involved the inconvenience of getting the document to the telegraph office, substantial cost for long documents, and the risk of loss of confidentiality.

If these alternatives were all regarded as unsatisfactory, the only remaining possibility was to make do with oral communication over the telephone. Such communication was, however, unsatisfactory for many purposes, such as discussing a long complicated contract that one of the parties had not seen.

In many cases, the advantages of the fax over all these alternatives was substantial. They would certainly seem to outweigh the fact that the fax machine was slow and noisy and the paper smelled bad.

A more fundamental problem was that the fax machines could be used only to communicate with a relatively small number of other fax machines. A large organization that deployed a fax could send faxes among all its various locations, but it could send them to only a limited number of locations outside the company. In this regard, we note that group 1 fax machines of different manufacturers used incompatible protocols and were therefore not interlinked. A technical standard for group 2 fax machines was not agreed upon until 1976. Thus, in the early period an organization could send faxes to only a small subset of the other fax users.

In terms of bandwagon theory, the initial user set included those organizations that could justify getting fax machines for internal communication. It also included small groups (mainly pairs) of organizations that could justify getting fax machines just to communicate with each other. The problem was that the demand-based equilibrium user set was not much larger than the initial user set.

This reasoning raises the possibility that the limited success of the fax during this period might be more accurately attributed to failure to solve the start-up problem than to inadequacy of the product. The issue can be framed as follows:

Suppose that the user set were 5 million to 10 million, instead of 112,000 in 1975 and suppose that all the machines were compatible. The user set would still have been relatively small and would have included only those users who highly valued the fax. Nevertheless, because of the larger user set with compatible machines, each user could have gotten many times as much value from fax as was possible in 1975.

The key question is, *Would such a user set have been sustainable?* If so, the limited success of the fax in this period was a failure to solve the start-up problem. If not, the limited success can be attributed to the inadequacy of the product at that time. In the latter case, the maximum equilibrium user set may not have been much larger than actual demand.

In any event, the start-up problem can be extremely serious where the industry structure is competitive. A bandwagon product must meet very high standards to succeed under these circumstances. Even if the product meets an important need in a cost-effective way, it may not reach a critical mass. The product has to be just about perfect—without any foibles, such as product odor (PO).

Group 3 fax machines were introduced in 1980. After their introduction, fax technology developed rapidly, spearheaded by the Japanese. They had a special need for the fax, because the telex was not very satisfactory for transmission of Japanese text. Technological progress dramatically lowered costs and improved product quality. The new machines were much faster. They could transmit a page in one minute, compared to six minutes with the group 1 machines. In addition, group 3 machines were quieter, and the paper did not smell bad. Prices of fax machines rapidly declined from $2,300 in 1982 to $185 in 1987.[3] A further impetus was that faxed copies were recognized as originals for official purposes, first in Japan, and later in other countries. As a result of these changes, the fax of 1987 can barely be compared to the fax of 1975.

A further constructive development was that in 1979, the major manufacturers of fax machines agreed on a compatible technological standard for group 3 fax machines. The conditions were ideal to reach such an agreement:

• No supplier had a dominant technological edge.

• The start-up problem was proving to be difficult. The product had been unable to reach a critical mass, and demand was not yet subject to positive feedback.

• The product had already achieved limited commercial success. With further technological improvements and interlinking, it seemed likely that the product would reach a critical mass and take off, allowing the suppliers to earn large transitory profits.

In reality, the combination of technological progress and the agreement on a technological standard did allow the start-up problem to be solved. With lower cost and improved product quality, many large organizations found the fax cost-effective for their internal use. Because the machines were compatible, many smaller users found the fax cost-effective to communicate with larger organizations that already had deployed fax.[4] By 1990, the installed base exceeded 5.7 million.

After 150 years, fax manufacturers finally built such a better mousetrap that the world beat a path to their door. More precisely, the product had finally become so good that many users could justify purchasing it to send/receive faxes within a small user set. Even with this small user set, the product's benefits exceeded its costs. The product was also good enough to stimulate sufficient growth to achieve a critical mass. The consumer benefits then became enormous after the bandwagon really got rolling and the user set expanded to ubiquitous deployment.

6.1   Lessons from Case Study

The history of the fax shows how good a bandwagon product must be in order to succeed. The fax in the 1970s was quite a good product (albeit far from perfect), and it met an important business need. Nevertheless, although the product enjoyed some measure of commercial success, it could not achieve a critical mass. It was only after the fax evolved into the truly wonderful and low-priced product of the 1980s that it reached critical mass and ultimately became ubiquitous.

The history of the fax also illustrates how lack of interlinking diminishes demand and makes the start-up problem more difficult. The early fax machines of various suppliers were not compatible. Consequently, since no supplier had a dominant market share, users could send faxes to (or receive faxes from) only a small part of the total user set. They therefore could enjoy only a small fraction of the potential benefit of the product. As a result, the growth of fax was substantially impeded in the 1970s.

7

Early Telephone

Consider the problem from Alexander Graham Bell's perspective. You have just made one of the greatest inventions of modern times. You want to ensure that in recognition of this feat, you live prosperously and die rich. How can you develop the telephone so as to achieve these laudable goals?

At first, Bell (and his business associates) simply offered telephones for sale. Users then assumed responsibility for stringing wires between telephones in order to use them.[1] Telephones could then provide intercom service at a single location or be used to connect nearby locations, for example, the office and home of the president of a corporation.

The sale of telephones in this way did not involve any bandwagon effects. Bell's problem was therefore simply to maximize profits during the period of his patents. There is no way to tell how close he came to this objective, but he clearly made substantial profits. He leased telephones for $14 *per year*, while the manufacturing cost was only $4.[2]

To be sure, telephones strung together by users had substantial value in some applications. But much greater value began to be realized a few years later, when exchange telephone service was introduced. Users of exchange service did, indeed, enjoy bandwagon benefits. Exchange service became more and more valuable to each subscriber as the user set expanded.

7.1 Pricing of Exchange Service

Before we review the actual history of the pricing of telephone exchange service, let us consider what one would have expected, on the basis of bandwagon theory. Bell had patents that extended well into the 1890s (though considerable resources had to be expended for legal defense of the patents).[3] Thus, he was well positioned to appropriate the gains from solving the start-up problem. He could extract rents from a protected monopoly for almost twenty years. Thereafter, he could anticipate a formidable first-mover advantage. As discussed in section 4.3.3, the first-mover advantage is especially valuable and enduring in bandwagon markets without interlinking (and Bell certainly had the right to refuse to interlink[4]). The first mover can offer its customers bandwagon benefits with respect to a much larger user set than can a new entrant.

Thus, on the basis of bandwagon theory, one would have expected Bell to sacrifice profits in the early years in order to develop exchange service rapidly. At the end of the period of patent monopoly, he should have had an unassailable first-mover advantage. Given the resulting enduring monopoly, one might have further expected that telephone service would ultimately come under government regulation of some kind. The end result would be an industry structure of regulated monopoly.

In reality, the early history of telephone exchange service differed remarkably from these expectations. Far from sacrificing profits, the Bell companies earned an average return on investment of 46 percent per year between 1876 and 1894—during a period of modest deflation.[5] Around the end of this period, the price of telephone service was over twice as high in the United States as in comparable European cities. In the nine-year period from 1885 to 1894, the number of Bell telephones in service grew by only 75 percent. By way of comparison, cellular telephone, a hot product a hundred years later, grew many times as rapidly. Cellular telephones, like wireline telephones, require substantial infrastructure investments. Nevertheless, in a comparable nine-year period (1990 to 1999), seven years after the service was first introduced, the number of cellular and other mobile-telephone subscribers grew by 1,646 percent.[6]

It is completely obvious that the pricing of the Bell companies during this period reflects blatant exploitation of monopoly power. The Bell companies had a perfectly legal right to exploit Bell's patent monopoly, and exploit it they did!

What is less obvious, but we would contend equally true, is that this pricing harmed the Bell companies, as well as consumers. By pricing too high in the early years, the Bell companies squandered a substantial part of the fruits of Bell's remarkable invention. The goal should have been to maximize sales, subject to reasonable financial constraints. After demand had grown substantially, the Bell companies would have been able to sustain high prices to a much larger user set. Even more important, they would have locked up the market during the period of the Bell patents.

As it was, large parts of the market were still unserved in 1898. In most cities, the Bell companies served few residents, and there were many smaller cities that they did not serve at all. Furthermore, there was latent demand by businesses that could not afford the Bell companies' high prices. The market was ripe for plucking by competitors, which is exactly what happened. By 1902—only a few years after the advent of competition—independents had over 75 percent as many telephones in service as did the Bell companies.

7.1.1   Pricing Prior to Competition

Bell began to offer exchange service shortly after the invention of the telephone switchboard in 1878. The provision of exchange service, unlike the simple sale of telephones, required large capital expenditures. The supplier of exchange service had to purchase wires and poles and install them throughout the entire serving area.

For Bell to build a nationwide telephone exchange company from scratch and manage it would have been a vast undertaking. He would have had to raise enormous sums of capital and hire a mammoth workforce in all parts of the country. He would have had to assemble a large cadre of trusted managers (from who-knows-where) to ensure that the enterprise was functioning properly.

Instead, Bell followed the more prudent course of licensing associated telephone companies. The companies were granted exclusive licenses to their serving areas. They, in turn, agreed to use only Bell telephones, whose lease price was usually $20 per year. Originally, Bell negotiated contracts wherein he had the option to buy the associated companies after five to ten years.

Bell withdrew from the active management of telephone operations shortly thereafter. The corporation that assumed ownership of the Bell patents and the rights under the contracts with the associated telephone companies became, after a few reorganizations and name changes, the American Bell Telephone Company (ABT).

ABT did not exercise the options to purchase the associated telephone companies. Instead, beginning in the early 1880s, it entered into new contracts wherein

• the lease price of telephones was substantially reduced, usually to $10 per year,

• ABT did not have an option to buy the associated companies but did obtain a substantial interest (usually 30 to 50 percent) therein, and

• ABT waived the right to some or all dividends for several years.[7]

From 1885 to 1894, the lease prices that ABT charged the companies for telephones were approximately $11.00 per year. Beginning in 1895, however, the lease prices began to drop sharply. They were less than $3.00 per year in 1898.[8]

In the early period, ABT's income consisted mostly of telephone rentals. Dividends from associated companies grew fairly steadily but did not surpass rental income until 1895.[9] ABT's dividends rose, at least in part, because of the gradual expiration of the waivers of its rights to receive dividends.

Table 7.1 shows the prices of telephone service in several major cities in the United States and Europe. Most of the U.S. prices apply to 1896–1897, while the European prices are from a few years earlier. This table clearly shows how much higher these rates were in the United States, compared to Europe.[10] Furthermore, several European countries used the public telephone monopoly as a source of revenue for other public purposes. Even so, prices in major cities were lower than in the United States.[11]

The high U.S. prices of telephone exchange service were *not* attributable to the high lease prices of telephones. By 1896, ABT had already lowered the lease price below $4 per year. But the prices in table 7.1 differ by $50 per year or more in many cases.

Table 7.1
Nominal Price of Telephone Service, Selected Years

Cities	Rates per Year
Washington (1890)	$35 to $135—average $100
Stockholm	$20 average
Zurich	$10 upward
Berlin	$36
Copenhagen	$41
Amsterdam	$50 to $100
Paris	$18
Greater London	$100
Greater New York	$90 to $240
Chicago	$60 to $175
Philadelphia	$60 to $250
Greater Boston	$25 to $150

Source: Excerpted from Stehman, p. 45.

It seems likely, on the basis of this evidence, that the associated telephone companies were charging far more than (reasonable) cost for their services. Several possibilities exist:

- the associated companies may have earned very large profits;
- they may have paid excessive compensation to their owner/managers;
- they may have incurred large expenses that benefited their owners in other commercial ventures; and/or
- they may have been lax about keeping (legitimate) costs down.

Whatever the reason(s), the high prices retarded the growth of telephone service. As a result, ABT was harmed in the short run (by leasing fewer telephones) and even more in the long run (by reduction of the first-mover advantage of the associated companies, in which ABT had a large interest). ABT, as well as consumers, would have been much better off if it had structured its contracts with associated companies so that the latter had contractual obligations and incentives to keep prices down and rapidly expand service.

Apparently, during this period the associated companies were optimizing short-run objectives at the expense of long-run goals. That policy may have been eminently reasonable from their perspective. Because ABT waived its rights to dividends in the early years, the companies had a greater interest in current profits than in future profits. Furthermore, they may have feared that ABT, having control over key inputs, would squeeze their profits in the future.

Perhaps most important, managing a rapidly growing enterprise is demanding and often unpleasant. Most of the employees at any time are new recruits. Things always go wrong—especially when the technology, as well as the employees, are new.[12] Strong incentives are required to induce managers to make the requisite effort, rather than being satisfied with a more comfortable pace of growth. In modern high-tech industries, such incentives often take the form of prospects of enormous wealth. In Bell's contracts with the associated companies, the incentives appear to go the other way.

Mueller provides some interesting insights about pricing during this period. He cites the minutes of the 1881 National Telephone Exchange Association Convention to show that only three or four of the three hundred exchanges were able to pay for themselves at then-existing rates. According to Mueller, the losses occurred because unit costs surprisingly rose as exchanges grew. In high-technology industries, one generally expects unit costs to decline, or at worst remain constant, as output grows. There are, however, good reasons for the opposite with respect to early telephone service. Consider the following example:

Suppose that the number of subscribers doubled. Each subscriber would then have approximately twice as many other subscribers that he or she could call. If he or she therefore made twice as many calls, the telephone company would have to employ twice as many operators *per subscriber* at the peak period. Thus, the unit costs of that component would double as the number of subscribers doubled. Total costs would quadruple.

To be sure, internal supply-side scale economies (rather than the opposite, internal supply-side scale diseconomies) apply to other cost components of telephone service. In particular, construction costs and the costs of telephone poles increase only moderately as the number of wires on a particular route doubles. Nevertheless, it appears that the diseconomies of scale dominated the economies as exchange telephone ramped up from 1878 to 1881.[13] Unit costs did, in fact, increase, and the increase was largely unexpected.

The associated companies dealt with this problem in an unsurprising way by raising prices. They also presumably put pressure on ABT to lower the lease prices of telephones (which it did in renegotiating new contracts).

The problem is that the price increases far overshot the mark. By the mid-1890s, such increases had led to U.S. prices that far exceeded European prices.[14] Those prices retarded the growth of telephone service and left the Bell companies unnecessarily vulnerable to competition.

Brooks attributes the high prices in this period, in part, to greed on the part of the managers of ABT. He contrasts the shortsighted policies of ABT President William H. Forbes with the far-seeing views of the traditional Bell System hero, Theodore Vail.[15] Vail resigned as General Manager of ABT in 1887, but returned twenty years later as President of AT&T (which in 1899 had succeeded ABT as the parent corporation of the Bell System).

7.1.2 Pricing after Competition

Many non-Bell firms entered the market between 1894 and 1898. They were primarily small firms that served areas unserved by the Bell companies. For the most part, they were not competitors of the Bell companies. Serious competition did not begin in earnest until after 1898.

ABT's large reduction in the rental price of telephones beginning in 1894 must be considered in this light. Such a large price reduction would not have been a reasonable response to the modest competition that the Bell companies faced at that time. It may be that ABT had explicitly or implicitly agreed to lower rental prices as it began to receive dividends from the associated companies.

In any event, the rental price reduction led to a relatively small reduction in the price of exchange service. Substantial reductions in the price of exchange service occurred only when Bell companies began to face competition in their serving areas. When that happened, they substantially reduced prices, often by 50 percent or more.

One does not need a bandwagon model to explain why a former monopolist would drastically cut prices when competitors first appear. What may be more surprising (but not to readers who have gotten this far in the book) is that the Bell companies substantially reduced prices in many areas in which they did *not* yet face competition, as well as in areas in which they did.

These reductions are rather difficult to explain in the context of standard economic models. In particular, the sunk costs of providing telephone service were low, compared to variable costs. Hence, Bornholz and Evans argue that the price reductions cannot reasonably be explained as a precommitment strategy to deter entry.[16] A precommitment strategy for an incumbent firm could be carried out as follows:

Lower price and when demand expands, make irreversible capital investments to meet that demand. If a competitor subsequently enters, the incumbent can be expected to treat the irreversible investments as sunk costs. Rather than lose a customer, the incumbent will find it profitable to offer that customer a price that recovers only variable costs plus a small markup. A potential competitor, understanding the incumbent's likely response, will probably choose not to enter.

This strategy is effective only if the irreversible investments are large relative to variable costs. If on the other hand, variable costs are large, the incumbent will lose money if it responds to competitive entry by substantially lowering price. Under those circumstances, a potential competitor may well believe that the incumbent will not choose to incur those additional losses. Bornholz and Evans observe that for early telephone service, variable costs were, indeed, large, relative to the irreversible investments. Thus, the precommitment could not be expected to have much of an entry-deterrent effect.

Viewed from the perspective of bandwagon theory, however, the price reductions of the Bell companies are easy to understand. They led to expansion of the user set and increased bandwagon benefits to consumers. As a result, the Bell companies could look forward to charging higher prices *in the future* and enjoying a greater first-mover advantage.

From the bandwagon perspective, competition appears as a wake-up call to the Bell companies. They finally began pricing and expanding the network the way they should have been for the previous ten years. As a result, the Bell companies retained their position as the industry leaders, but it was too late to stop the growth of independent telephone companies. Table 7.2 shows the growth of the independent companies through 1917. During the entire period from 1902 to 1917, they continued to grow rapidly.

Table 7.2
Growth of Independent Telephone Companies

Census Year	Number of Telephones in Use	
	Bell Telephone System	All Other Systems
1902	1,317,178	1,053,866
1907	3,132,063	2,986,515
1912	5,087,027	3,642,565
1917	7,326,858	4,389,662

Note: The figures are taken from "Growth of Telephone Industry, by Five-Year Periods from 1902 to 1917," citing U.S. Census, Special Report, 1917, p. 12.
Source: Excerpted from Stehman, p. 127.

Gabel characterizes the pricing of the Bell companies during this period as predatory. There is certainly some evidence of anticompetitive intent. In some areas, the Bell companies introduced "fighting prices." The goal of fighting prices was apparently to drive competitors out of the market. The expectation was presumably that after competitor(s) exited, prices could be raised again, because there would no longer be any need to fight. Such a strategy is precisely predatory pricing.

There is, however, another side to this story; namely, the strategy failed. Maintaining fighting prices was very costly for the Bell companies, which had a large customer base. It was much less costly for the new entrants. Furthermore, the fixed capital (e.g., telephone lines) of new entrants could not exit the market. That investment remained available for use by the entrant (or perhaps the well-funded successor that bought out the entrant) whenever the Bell companies tired of bleeding money. Eventually, they abandoned fighting prices.

To be sure, the Bell companies needed to defend their position as the bandwagon leaders. Where entrants competed in their territory by offering low prices, the Bell companies had to respond by lowering prices, though matching the competitors' low prices was surely unnecessary (because the Bell companies, with their larger bandwagon, offered a superior service). If the Bell companies did not respond at all, competitors could have displaced them as the market leader in bandwagon markets wherein they originally had the first-mover advantage.

That outcome would have led to enormous and unnecessary loss of long-run profits.

What the Bell companies did *not* need to do, and ultimately stopped doing, was attempt to drive competitors out of business. They needed only to enhance their positions as market leaders gradually over time. Doing so would have ensured a satisfactory outcome in which Bell customers enjoyed ever-greater bandwagon benefits, and the competitive advantage of the Bell companies continually increased. The entrants who would have been competing at an increasing disadvantage in Bell territory might eventually have withdrawn from that territory, but the Bell companies did not need to precipitate that outcome.

Nevertheless, because of bandwagon effects, the Bell companies may have profited by setting prices below what was required for a minimal defensive response. In general, lower prices increase demand and increase bandwagon benefits, which the supplier can share with customers. Expansion of demand also makes the supplier less vulnerable to competition in the future—not just with respect to the particular competitive threats it currently faces. Such pricing can be justified in bandwagon markets, even where the supplier does not yet face competition. It can be explained in terms of bandwagon theory, without reference to anti-competitive intent.

7.1.3 Ultimate Outcome

Telephone competition ultimately ended as a result of industry consolidation. The federal government originally resisted consolidation by threatening antitrust action. To avoid such action, AT&T President Vail agreed in 1913 to discontinue acquiring competing telephone companies (the Kingsbury Commitment). Ultimately, however, the federal government condoned consolidation with the Willis-Graham Act of 1921.[17] The quid pro quo was that AT&T acquiesced to government regulation.

Thus, at long last, the bandwagon arrived at its expected destination. There were, however, a few detours along the way. The pricing of the Bell companies in the early years did not conform to the expectations of the bandwagon theory. Thus, bandwagon theory is more useful for explaining how the Bell companies *should* have priced than how they actually priced. The actual history illustrates the penalties for not pricing according to the theory, since competitors captured a large share of the market. In later years, the Bell companies did price in accordance with bandwagon theory. That pricing helped them limit the losses from their previous lapses.

7.2 Interlinking

Before we review the actual history of interlinking, let us (as we did with respect to pricing) consider what one would have expected, on the basis of bandwagon theory. One would certainly have expected the Bell companies to interlink with noncompeting telephone systems. Interlinking increases bandwagon benefits and makes the services of both suppliers more valuable to subscribers. Both suppliers could then expect the demand for their services to increase. Such an agreement would be all the more lucrative for suppliers if it contained a covenant not to compete in each other's territories.

One would have expected the Bell companies to be reluctant to interlink with competing telephone companies. The Bell companies had a large first-mover advantage (albeit not as large as it might have been). In addition to having the largest local network in most sizable cities, ABT also had by far the largest long-distance network. Entrants were therefore competing at a substantial disadvantage in Bell territory. The Bell companies could offer their customers the bandwagon benefits associated with a larger local network, as well as the benefits of interlinking via the ABT long-distance network to other Bell local networks. Because of this competitive advantage, the Bell companies could enjoy some measure of monopoly profits—notwithstanding the existence of smaller competitors. After interlinking, the entrant would have been able to provide full bandwagon benefits to all Bell customers. The profits of the Bell companies would then have been very uncertain—depending on the vigor of competition in the resulting duopoly.

Many actual entrants competed with the Bell companies in some areas but also served areas in which the Bell companies did not operate. Under such circumstances, one would expect that interlinking agreements would *sometimes* be negotiated. The goal of the Bell companies would be to gain the bandwagon benefits of interlinking with the entrant where it did *not* compete, while minimizing the competitive impact where the entrant *did* compete. A plan that minimized competitive impact would be unattractive to an entrant that expected otherwise to be able to make substantial incursions into Bell territory. It would be more attractive to an entrant that was less optimistic about its prospects of competing in Bell territory.

In reality, ABT originally prohibited the Bell companies from interlinking with *any* entrants—even those that served separate territories and did not compete with Bell companies at all. The policy of not interlinking with noncompeting telephone companies does not seem rational. By refusing to interlink, the Bell companies forewent bandwagon benefits, and it does not appear that they gained any comparable value in compensation.

In any event, that policy was abandoned shortly after competition intensified. By 1901, AT&T was actively encouraging interlinking with noncompeting telephone companies. Those companies were offered agreements wherein they agreed to use Bell equipment. Also, both the Bell companies and the other companies agreed not to compete in each other's territories. The Bell companies generally continued (with a few exceptions) to refuse to interlink with competing telephone companies.[18]

By and large, the Bell interlinking policies—after the initial false start—are easily understandable in terms of bandwagon theory. They accord fairly well with the expectations stated at the beginning of this section.

7.3   Lessons from Case Study

The primary lesson from the early history of telephone is the folly of being too greedy during the start-up phase of a bandwagon service. Bell, because of his patents and his relentless enforcement of them, had what should have been an insurmountable competitive advantage. Much of that advantage was squandered through high prices and slow development of the market during the early years of telephone exchange service. As a result, the Bell companies were unnecessarily vulnerable to competition when the Bell patents expired.

After competition intensified, the Bell companies limited losses by lowering prices and accelerating the development of the market, but competitors continued to grow rapidly. The Bell companies' attempt at "fighting" (i.e., predatory) pricing failed, but the companies continued to maintain low prices both in areas that were already served by competitors and in those that were not—precisely the appropriate strategy in a bandwagon market.

The early history of the telephone also lends insight regarding interlinking from the perspective of an incumbent firm with a large first-mover advantage. Initially, ABT irrationally prohibited the Bell companies from interlinking with any other companies, but that policy was abandoned when competition intensified. AT&T then encouraged interlinking with companies that did not operate in the same geographic areas as Bell companies. The Bell companies did, however, continue to resist interlinking with competitors. In general, it is often prudent for an incumbent firm with a large first-mover advantage to refuse to interlink with competitors, because interlinking can greatly intensify competition.

8

Picturephone

After examining two success stories, we now turn our attention in this chapter[1] to a great fiasco. Albeit less uplifting, it provides balance to our discussion and illustrates how easily one can fail in high-technology industries. In the words of the chess grandmaster Bogoljubov, "The blunders are all there, waiting to be made."

Someday, a two-way video communications service is certain to win widespread acceptance. In science-fiction stories, the characters *always* use video communications, if not something even more advanced. The speed with which television supplanted radio demonstrates the great value of video communications. The only issue, it would seem, is timing. When will technology drive costs down far enough so that people can afford a two-way video service?

In the early 1970s, the Bell System thought that the time had come. They developed Picturephone Service and offered it on a trial basis in Chicago. The service was offered for $86.50 per month, which included one-half hour of free usage (which few users exceeded). Demand saturated at about two hundred sets—far less than minimal expectations. Shortly thereafter, the service was withdrawn. The state regulator (the Illinois Commerce Commission) disallowed all costs associated with Picturephone; so the losses were borne solely by AT&T stockholders. The extent of AT&T's hopes afterward was that people would soon forget about this embarrassing episode.

The above paragraph provides a succinct description of the corpse. Let us now conduct a postmortem. Like any new product, Picturephone had some technological shortcomings. The original Picturephones did nothing to facilitate the transmission of written or graphical materials.

The only way to transmit such material was to hold it in front of the camera. Shortly after the product was introduced, it became apparent that users would appreciate a more convenient way to transmit writing and graphics. Bell Labs engineers quickly designed a fix. A horizontal frame was attached to the bottom front of the Picturephone. The user inserted the written or graphical material in the frame and flipped the camera lens to the alternate position. The material was then on camera and in focus. Another technological problem was that users had to remain relatively stationary or they would go outside the range of the camera. That problem could have been fixed by using a wider-angle lens, but then picture quality would have suffered.

Notwithstanding these shortcomings, it does not appear that Picturephone failed because the technology was inadequate. Indeed, Picturephone was, in many respects, an impressive technological achievement. Costs had been driven down through innovative use of narrowband technology. For transmission of video images, Picturephone used the same copper wires that were used for telephone service. Most users did not complain about the picture quality, though it was not as good as commercial television. The product worked without major mishaps in the field.

Wish and Rohlfs investigated preconceptions, perceptions, and opinions about Picturephone by conducting a questionnaire study of 173 randomly chosen respondents. The respondents were invited to a market research firm, and the interview was conducted by Picturephone. In that way, respondents had some basis for evaluating communication via Picturephone.

Respondents were asked to evaluate the effectiveness of telephone, Picturephone, and face-to-face communication for eighteen general business situations. Respondents almost invariably ranked telephone the lowest and face-to-face communication the highest. On average, Picturephone was in between, but somewhat closer to telephone (on the subjective scale) than face-to-face communication.

Respondents were also asked to evaluate telephone, Picturephone, and face-to-face communication in a variety of dimensions other than effectiveness. By and large, Picturephone ranked in between the other two modes of communication. It did, however, get the highest ranking for the questions "How prestigious?" and "How conducive to sticking to the point and avoiding tangential discussions?" It got the lowest rating for the question "How relaxed?"

There was great variation in how respondents evaluated Picturephone. Some responded very favorably, while others regarded Picturephone as an invasion of their privacy. In this regard, we note that Picturephone had no analogue to the mute button on a speakerphone; users had no way unobtrusively to get off camera. An interesting anecdote in this regard is that the president of Bell Labs kept a black cover over his Picturephone. If someone called him on Picturephone, he answered the telephone. The average questionnaire responses cited above are the means of very diverse responses.

Wide variation in tastes does not necessarily diminish market demand. Indeed, it may be helpful in getting a new product started. In chapter 3, we noted that small user sets can embody substantial value, contrary to Metcalfe's Law, if there is wide variation in tastes. Thus, variation in tastes is probably not the explanation for Picturephone's failure.

The Wish-Rohlfs study, like any analysis based on customer surveys, was far from conclusive. It did, however, yield evidence that Picturephone can provide significant value to many consumers. Two-way video communication does appear to be a viable product concept.

Picturephone does, however, require users to change the way that they perform the basic function of business communication. Customers are generally reluctant to make such fundamental changes unless the benefits are clear-cut—and then only after substantial delay. In this regard, the benefits of Picturepone were far from clear-cut, and new users bore substantial risk. Their bread-and-butter communications with their customers and suppliers could suffer if Picturephone turned out to be unsatisfactory for some unexpected reason. Picturephone was therefore a hard sell. Developing the market required skillful sales technique (perhaps beyond the capability of the Bell System) and the patience to wait for users to experiment with the product before they accepted it.

There is also the issue of whether the price was right. In this regard, we note that business managers spend a substantial part of their workday in telephone communications. If they could have been convinced (or learn through experiment) that Picturephone provided a significant improvement over telephone for most business communication, the price of $86.50 does not seem excessive. Picturephone would be all the more cost-effective if it could (because of its superiority over telephone) substitute for some face-to-face meetings and thereby save travel time. This reasoning does, however, presume that Picturephone could be used for all the manager's business communication. Therein lies the rub.

The most common user complaint, by far, was that there was virtually no one to talk to over Picturephone. Each of the two hundred users at the peak level of demand knew relatively few of the other users. For that reason, Picturephone usage was low, and the service offered commensurately little benefit to users. Given the small diverse user set, it was not worth $86.50 per month to potential subscribers to join the network; so the user set did not grow. In short, the start-up problem was not solved.

It may seem that AT&T was in an excellent position to invest in solving this start-up problem. It had a monopoly franchise in Chicago, as well as rights to the proprietary technology. It could therefore appropriate all the gains if the product were successful. Furthermore, if the Chicago trial were successful, it could reap similar gains in other cities, as well.

In reality, the regulatory regime provided strong disincentives for AT&T to incur initial losses to solve the start-up problem. If the service had been successful, AT&T's profits would have been limited by rate-of-return regulation. Apart from regulatory lag, such regulation would have limited AT&T to a return on investment commensurate with what a competitive enterprise could expect to earn. On the down side, it is clear that Picturephone costs would be disallowed (as, indeed, they were in Illinois) if the service were unsuccessful. The odds were, "Heads, I gain a little; tails, I lose big time." Given these odds, it is understandable that AT&T made only a half-hearted effort to solve the start-up problem and fairly quickly cut its losses.

Even so, it must be said that AT&T's actual strategy was an almost certain loser. To all appearances, AT&T introduced the bandwagon service, Picturephone, with no consideration of the start-up problem. The guiding principle appeared to be, "Build it; they will come." That principle does not work for bandwagon products. It has to be, "Build it and reach a critical mass; the rest will follow."

AT&T had no good answer to the question, "Why should I pay $86.50 per month for Picturephone, given that I would have virtually no one to talk to?" In retrospect, it is clear that AT&T should have chosen between incurring much larger costs to make a serious effort to solve the start-up problem or not offering Picturephone at all.

Two approaches (possibly among others) might have been considered to solve the start-up problem: (1) initially marketing Picturephone primarily as an intercom service, or (2) trying to construct a self-sufficient user set with a substantial community of interest within itself.

8.1   Picturephone as an Intercom Service

AT&T could have tried to sell systems of, say, thirty Picturephones to large corporations for intracompany communications. The Picturephones might, for example, have resided in the offices of top corporate officials. If the price were $86.50 per month per set, AT&T would have been trying to make sales of approximately $30,000 per year in annual revenues to each corporation (equivalent to over $100,000 per year in current dollars).

To say that such sales would be difficult to make is a massive understatement. The customer corporation would have had no previous experience with Picturephone. It would have had no way to make an informed judgment that the value of improved communications was worth $30,000 per year.

Furthermore, even apart from perceptions, it is far from obvious that improved intercom communication really *would* have been worth $30,000 per year. Telephone is fully satisfactory for handling most short communications, and persons working in the same building have the easy alternative of arranging a meeting if telephone would be inadequate. For these reasons, Picturephone may have been worth $30,000 per year only after it could be used for substantial intercompany, as well as intracompany, communications.

All in all, it seems quite likely that AT&T would have been able to make substantial sales only if it deeply discounted the service below $86.50 per month per set. To solve the start-up problem, AT&T would have had to offer these subsidies at many corporations in order to achieve a critical mass for intercompany communications.

The strategy of offering discounts raises some additional concerns. Firstly, no one knew what user set would constitute a critical mass. There was a real possibility that after expending considerable resources, AT&T would have had to abort the subsidy program because a critical mass had *still* not yet been achieved.

A second concern was that users might unsubscribe when prices rose in the future, as AT&T attempted to recoup its initial losses. A substantial price increase would certainly be the occasion for many users to evaluate whether Picturephone was really worth the cost.

This latter problem could have been ameliorated through usage-sensitive pricing, as recommended by Oren and Smith in 1982 and earlier by Rohlfs and Wish. As discussed in section 4.3, usage-sensitive pricing allows the price to increase automatically as the value of service increases. With such pricing, there would have been no specific occasion for customers to evaluate their purchase decision. Nevertheless, it is quite possible that customers would have found the high usage charge (which would probably have been at least $0.25 per minute) to be excessive.

8.2   Constructing a Self-Sufficient User Set

An alternative strategy is to try to construct a self-sufficient user set for intercompany communication. For example, AT&T could have asked actual Picturephone users for the names of the persons with whom they communicate the most. It could then have attempted to make sales to those other persons. They might have named the service "Friends and Family."

Many firms market their products, in part, by offering customers inducements to recruit their friends as customers. This strategy can be especially effective in a bandwagon market, because the original customer enjoys bandwagon benefits if one of his or her principal contacts joins the user set. Consequently, the supplier may not need to offer any additional inducements to get the customer to be a recruiter. It may need only to focus its marketing efforts to take advantage of such recruiting.

Constructing a user set in this manner can ensure that the user set embodies a substantial community of interest. In particular, it can ensure that the user set contains an average of at least two principal contacts for every subscriber. (See the mathematical appendix.)

This approach to solving the start-up problem has the advantage of requiring a relatively small dollar commitment from each company to which a sale is made. The companies could therefore try Picturephone out without taking sizable risks. Nevertheless, it is not clear how much customers would be willing to pay to communicate with two (or even three or four) of the persons with whom they have the most communication.

8.3 Actual Outcome

After the initial disappointing sales of Picturephone, AT&T seriously considered trying the approach of constructing a self-sufficient user set to solve the start-up problem. Ultimately, however, AT&T decided to withdraw Picturephone instead.

It is hard to fault AT&T's decision to withdraw Picturephone. Given the regulatory regime, trying to solve the start-up problem was probably a poor risk. It may have been a poor risk (too hard a sell), even apart from regulatory considerations.

In any event, the utter failure of Picturephone has been determinative. More than twenty-five years later, the science-fiction vision of a pervasive two-way video telecommunications service is nowhere in sight. Recently, low-cost add-ons to personal computers have been offered for two-way video communications, but they are still far short of solving the start-up problem. It may be quite a while longer before the science fiction vision becomes a reality.

8.4 Lessons from Case Study

Picturephone illustrates the disastrous consequences of introducing a bandwagon product with no consideration of the start-up problem. Typical market-research analyses can be misleading for such products unless bandwagon effects are taken into account.

As the case study of the fax illustrates, it is not enough for a bandwagon product to be good; it must be *extremely* good to reach a critical mass. A product such as Picturephone, which is not that good, may still succeed if the supplier successfully undertakes a campaign to solve the start-up problem. Such a campaign is, however, both costly and risky. The expected returns may not justify these costs and risks—in addition to all the other costs and risks associated with introducing a new product. In that case, the product should not be brought to market at all.

9

Compact-Disc Players

The history of CDs is a picture-book model of how to start up a product that involves complementary bandwagon effects. The performance of the leading supplier, Philips NV, resembled that of a virtuoso who makes a very difficult piece seem easy. The outcome was highly beneficial for both suppliers and consumers.

Philips's performance does, however, create problems for those writing about bandwagon effects. Readers may seriously underestimate the difficulty of the start-up problem for CDs. They may think that CDs succeeded solely on the basis of the quality of the product. In reality, things do not work that way in bandwagon markets.

CDs were, indeed, a great product advance in recorded music. They provide a high level of fidelity of sound reproduction and are far more durable than vinyl records and cassette tapes. In addition, they allow random access to music selections on compact discs.

Nevertheless, CDs faced serious start-up problems. In particular:

1. There was no unique technological standard for CDs.

2. There were initially no CDs available for sale.

3. Even when CDs became available, the selection was inevitably limited. Furthermore, users already had substantial libraries in the old technology and would not necessarily want to upgrade. For these reasons, users could be expected to have only small libraries of CDs for some time; and the benefit they could derive from a CD player would be commensurately small.

Solving these problems constituted a three-step parlay that CD suppliers had to win if they were to achieve commercial success.

Although these problems were serious, we note that suppliers did *not* have to surmount two other potential start-up problems that have arisen with respect to some other high-technology products:

• There was no need for upward compatibility; in this case, for CD players to be able to play vinyl records or cassette tapes. CD players were small. It was reasonable to expect users to include CD players in their home stereo systems, *in addition to* turntables and/or cassette players.

• There was no need to establish any new distributional channels. Retail stores that sold records and cassettes could also sell CDs. Indeed, CD packages were originally designed to fit (two for one) in the same display cases as phonograph records.

The sound-recording industry had made several similar transitions in the past, for example, to 45 RPM, LPs, and (analog) cassettes. Philips undoubtedly benefited by drawing upon this base of previous industry experience. Many of the other innovations discussed in this book had no such base of similar past experience, and the innovators had to make it up as they went along. It is hardly surprising, therefore, that many of them managed the transition far less well than Philips.

9.1   Technological Standard

In 1979, Philips had the lead in developing the technology for CDs, but several other firms had viable alternatives.[1] Sony, like Philips, had a laser-based technology. Philips was closer to having a marketable product, but the Sony technology for correction of errors was better. Telefunken was developing a technology in which information was engraved in grooves, similar to conventional phonograph records. JVC was developing a technology based on magnetic, rather than optical, scanning.

If Philips had simply rushed its product to market, it would have enjoyed a first-mover advantage, but other producers would probably have entered the market shortly thereafter. A standards war would then have ensued. Because the technological standards of competing suppliers would not be interlinked, each user would enjoy bandwagon effects only with respect to products of a single manufacturer. The start-up problem, which was already difficult, would have become much more difficult and perhaps insurmountable. Furthermore, all suppliers would lose from the price cutting that would likely accompany a standards war.

Instead, Philips chose the path of trying to establish a single technical standard for all manufacturers. In that way, consumers could enjoy bandwagon effects that applied to the total customer base—not just the customers of a single supplier—and the start-up problem would therefore be far easier to solve. Moreover, Philips's technology enjoyed patent protection; so Philips profited from license fees paid by other producers. The license fees did, however, have to be moderate to induce other suppliers to pay the fees rather than push their own technological standards.

The downside of this approach for Philips was that it allowed all suppliers—even those with inferior technology—to compete on equal terms (apart from the license fees). Philips gave up its chance of leveraging its technological advantage to become the dominant supplier in a bandwagon market without interlinking.

Adam Smith observed, "People of the same trade seldom meet together, even for merriment and diversion, but the conversation ends in a conspiracy against the public, or in some contrivance to raise prices."[2] That observation is generally a reliable guide, but it does not necessarily apply to meetings in which business leaders try to agree on technical standards. As discussed in section 4.6, the establishment of such a standard and the subsequent interlinking can substantially benefit consumers. In this case, CD players (at any given price) would have initially been far less attractive to consumers if a standard had not been agreed upon. Consumers would have had fewer choices of CDs (fewer bandwagon benefits), and they would have faced the risk that their CD player and all their CDs would ultimately be orphaned. Quite possibly, no supplier would have succeeded in solving the start-up problem. If the start-up problem were solved, one supplier would likely have won the standards war and would thereafter have been able to price as a monopolist. The theoretical discussion in section 4.3.3 suggested that the consumer harms in this scenario are unlikely to be outweighed, in terms of expected value, by consumers' transitory gains from low prices during the period of the price war.

With an agreed-upon standard, CD players became a much more attractive product. Consumers could derive the full bandwagon benefits, and there were fewer risks that their products would be orphaned. Consumers benefited from competition in production, if not with respect to standards. Prices were, however, presumably elevated to include Philips's license fees.

In section 4.3.3, we discussed three possible drawbacks that might result from interlinking. None is of concern here:

• *Increased costs.* Interlinking was not very costly in this case. It did, however, require Philips to educate other suppliers in how to use the technology.

• *Reduced incentives to innovate.* To be sure, Philips could have enjoyed some competitive advantage by declining to interlink, but it placed greater value on the gains from interlinking. It follows that interlinking enhanced, rather than diminished, Philips's incentives to develop the technology in the first place.

• *Reduced incentives to solve the start-up problem.* Philips had the incentive to do what was required to solve the start-up problem. Again, interlinking probably increased, rather than decreased, that incentive.

All in all, the outcome with an agreed-upon standard was almost surely better for both consumers and producers.

Philips implemented its plan to establish a single technical standard by first reaching an agreement with Sony. The negotiations with Sony led to some product changes. At Sony's request, the technology was changed from 14 bits to 16 bits, and the playing time was increased to seventy-four minutes (long enough to play von Karajan's recording with the Berlin Philharmonic of Beethoven's Ninth Symphony). These changes improved the performance of CDs for playing music. The trade-off was that the compact disc became somewhat less compact.[3] Nevertheless, two rows of CDs still fit into one rack for LPs in a retail store. The negotiations with Sony also achieved their original objective; namely, they led to an improved technological standard that embodied Philips's advanced technology, together with Sony's better technology for error correction. Philips and Sony planned to bring the product to market in four years in summer of 1983.

Once Philips and Sony had reached an agreement, they invited other suppliers to join in supporting their technical standard. Other suppliers were quick to do so. By the end of 1981, thirty suppliers had agreed to the Philips/Sony standard. Telefunken and JVC had withdrawn their competing technologies. This outcome was largely driven by the superior technology of Philips and Sony, but it also indicates that reasonable licensing terms were offered to participating suppliers.

A single technical standard was now established: step 1 of the parlay.

9.2   CDs Not Available

At the beginning of part II, we described the chicken-and-egg problem, which applies in some markets involving complementary bandwagon effects. It applied overwhelmingly to the initial offering of CD players and CDs. There would have been little or no initial demand for CD players if they were offered before CDs. CD players have value only for playing CDs and therefore had no value until CDs became available. At the same time, there would have been little or no initial demand for CDs if they were offered before CD players. CDs can be played only on CD players and therefore had no value until CD players became available.

This problem would have been extremely difficult to solve without coordination among producers of CD players and producers of CDs. It was partially solved through vertical integration. Philips had a 50 percent interest in Polygram, a major producer of recorded music, though by no means the largest. It remained to work out cooperative arrangements with the other producers of recorded music.

Affiliates of Philips and Sony undertook the manufacture of CDs. In particular, a West German plant of Polygram was manufacturing 25 million CDs per year by 1985. At that time, a plant in Terre Haute, Indiana, owned jointly by Sony and CBS Records was producing 450,000 per month, with production scheduled soon to increase to 600,000 per month.[4]

Philips and Sony offered the record companies access to their technology and manufacturing capability at reasonable prices. In return, record companies agreed to make a substantial inventory of recordings available to consumers at the time that CDs were introduced.

These negotiations took place in a high-technology bandwagon context. The issues involved were, however, the same issues involved in any business deal. Philips and Sony controlled key inputs and were the entrepreneurial leaders. They were therefore looking for large profits if the venture turned out to be successful. They did, however, need to recruit other participants for the venture, or they would come up empty. As a result, they had to offer sufficiently favorable terms of trade to induce the record companies to participate.

CBS Records was a key participant in this process. Sony already had an arrangement whereby it distributed CBS records in Japan. It was therefore well positioned to recruit CBS Records for this venture. CBS Records, because of its key role, was apparently able to negotiate favorable terms. In particular, it negotiated substantial equity participation through its joint manufacturing venture with Sony.

Many other record companies were also induced to participate. In 1983, the year that CDs were launched, approximately 650 titles were available at a cost of about $22.00 each.[5] Thus, there was an adequate supply of CDs available to get the bandwagon rolling: step 2 of the parlay.

9.3 Small Libraries of CDs

An early purchaser of a CD player usually concurrently bought some of the 650 CD titles that were available. Even so, however, he or she initially had only a small library of CDs. The benefit that consumers could derive from CD players was therefore initially limited to playing selections from that small library.

Under these circumstances, most consumers were unlikely to purchase a CD player unless they believed that the number of other purchasers was going to grow substantially in the future. If and only if this happened could they look forward to purchasing more CDs from an ever-widening selection of titles.

Given that a consumer had faith in the future growth of CD players, the trade-off was as follows:

1. *The consumer could purchase the CD player now.* He or she could then immediately benefit from playing selections from a small library of CDs. Over time, the consumer could expand his or her library of CDs. Ultimately, the larger library would justify the initial purchase of the CD player.

2. *The consumer could delay the purchase.* He or she would then not have to make an immediate outlay. Ultimately, he or she could purchase a CD player, together with a large number of CDs from the wider selection that would then be available. Because of technological progress and scale economies, the price of CD players would likely be lower at that time. A disadvantage of this option is that new music recordings bought prior to the CD player would be in the old technology.

In order for the start-up problem to be solved, a large number of consumers must choose the first option rather than the second.

This third step of the parlay relates to the dynamic considerations discussed in section 3.4. Potential purchasers of CD players not only had to consider the bandwagon benefits offered by the current user set; they also had to assess what the equilibrium user set was likely to be and how quickly it could be reached. The larger that equilibrium was likely to be and the more quickly it was likely to be reached, the more favorable the product was for immediate purchase.

These dynamic considerations do not require a particular start-up strategy by suppliers. They do, however, require an exceptionally good product. The product must provide substantial benefits, even when the user set is small. In addition, it must be good enough to inspire consumers to believe that user set will expand rapidly in the future.

Let us consider what the start-up problem for CDs would have been absent bandwagon effects. That is, suppose that record stores always carried a full line of recordings in all formats. In that case, assuming that CDs offered even a moderate quality improvement and the price was right:

• A music lover who highly valued the better quality of CDs would purchase a CD player and replace his favorite selections from his music library with CDs. The changeover could be quite expensive, but it could provide great value to a music lover.

• A consumer (with no music library) purchasing her first stereo system would purchase a CD player.

• A consumer who made frequent purchases of recorded music would purchase a CD player to avoid making continued purchases in the old technology.

These purchases would suffice to define a market niche for CDs, which would grow over time as more and more new consumers came of age and purchased their first stereo systems.

In reality, record stores did not initially stock a full line of CDs. They stocked only 650 titles. Thus, the music lover could not replace all his or her favorite selections but rather only those that were among the 650 available titles. All purchasers had to gamble on a greater selection's being available in the future. In these important respects, CD players initially provided less value to consumers than they would in a market without bandwagon effects. Under these circumstances, the product had to be extraordinary to induce consumers to purchase it.

The CD player actually was an extraordinary product. It offered substantial benefits, both in terms of quality of music reproduction and ease of use. The quality of the product supported the expectation that the number of users and the selection of available CDs would grow. It sufficed to induce initial purchases, even when only 650 selections were available: step 3 of the parlay.

9.4   Subsequent Developments

Having pulled off the three-step parlay, Philips and Sony proceeded to the cashier's window. Both firms benefited from the rapid growth of demand for CD players and CDs. But their policy of interlinking, which stimulated that growth, also led to the rapid growth of competition. When introduced in March 1983, CD players sold for $1,300 and CDs sold for $22. By mid-1985, these prices had fallen to $300 and $12, respectively.[6] These price reductions obviously limited the profits of Philips and Sony.

Nevertheless, Philips and Sony did quite well. Philips benefited from its interest in Polygram, as well as from its manufacturing of CD players.

The proliferation of CD players greatly stimulated sales of CDs. In addition to purchasing new recordings, users of CD players bought many older recordings that were re-released.

Before the introduction of CDs, Polygram Records had been doing poorly. In 1984, *The Wall Street Journal* reported that in the previous six years, Polygram had lost $255 million on U.S. sales of $974 million.[7] The value of the company around that time was estimated at about $100 million.[8] In 1985, Philips purchased the remaining 50 percent of Polygram Records from Siemens. In 1989, it sold a 20 percent stake for $500 million.[9] This price corresponds to a market value of $2.5 billion for the company. Thus, Philips (paper) capital gain from its holdings in Polygram Records was probably around $2 billion.

During the same period, Sony used its great skill in product innovation to differentiate itself from its competitors. In the fall of 1984, it introduced the Discman portable CD player, which was an instant and lasting hit in the market.

9.5   Other Digital Players of Recorded Music

Not long after the great success of CDs, the industry followed Hollywood's example and brought out several sequels. As is often the case, however, the sequels did not do well at the box office.

9.5.1   Digital Audiotape Players

The first sequel was the digital audiotape (DAT) player, which was introduced by Sony in Japan in 1987. At that time, record companies were afraid that DATs would spawn illegal copying of their music. They were therefore reluctant to make their music available on DATs. With no music (or even an inadequate supply of music) available on DATs, DAT players had little value to consumers and could not possibly succeed.

Progress on the copying issue was made in 1989, with the development of the Serial Copy Management System (SCMS). SCMS allows any number of copies to be made from an original tape, but copies cannot be made of the copies.

SCMS was an important technical advance. It permits most "fair-use" copying but prevents large-scale chain copying. Nevertheless, SCMS does not prevent illegal copying altogether. Consequently, the record companies still did not support DATs. The following statement, by the president of the Recording Industry Association of America, reflects the view of the record companies on this issue: "The beauty, value, and greatness of CD has been, in addition to being a wonderful product, that if people wanted to enjoy it they had to go out and buy it."[10] They could not simply obtain an illegal copy of it. As this statement indicates, the record companies were quite satisfied with the status quo and saw no reason to embrace the new technology.

Ironically, CDs in the past few years have evolved into the most effective vehicle of all for piracy of copyrighted music. Read-only CD drives are standard equipment on modern PCs. The additional cost for the capability to write ("burn") CDs is moderate, and many PCs have that capability. Given these capabilities, PC users can easily pirate copyrights by uploading and downloading music to and from the Internet. Copyright owners have naturally taken legal actions in the hope of preventing such piracy; suits against against Napster and MP3 are two examples. Nevertheless, it is extremely difficult to stop this kind of piracy.

In any event, agreement between the record companies and player manufacturers was finally reached in 1992. Both supported the passage of the Audio Home Recording Rights Act, which imposed royalties on blank tapes and required DAT players to install SCMS.

At this point, Sony could conceivably have tried to organize a coalition of record companies to bring out recordings on DAT, but the product was by then obsolete. Almost immediately after the act was passed, Philips announced plans to introduce a more advanced technology, namely, digital compact cassette (DCC) players. Furthermore, Sony had itself already developed a new technology: the minidisc (MD), discussed below.

The failure of DAT players is easy to understand. The hardware was virtually worthless if record companies did not provide the complementary products. The record companies refused to do so, because they believed that DATs compromised their intellectual property. They were not concerned that the user set was too small to make the supply of DATs profitable. From their perspective, the optimal user set for DATs was the null set. The whole fiasco of DATs can be fully understood without any recourse to a bandwagon model.

9.5.2 Digital Compact Cassettes

We can examine the introduction of DCC players in terms of the same three-step parlay that Philips/Sony pulled off earlier in the decade. The issue was whether Philips/Matsushita could win the same bets with DCCs.

The first step of the parlay was to reach agreement on a single technical standard. That bet was lost, because Sony's MDs came on the market shortly after DCCs. Because there were two incompatible competing products on the market at the same time, both products had less value to consumers than they would have had were there no competing products. It was less likely that either product would reach a critical mass. Thus, consumers faced the very real prospect (actually realized) that the selection of available DCCs would not grow substantially. Indeed, the product might be discontinued. Furthermore, a consumer faced the risk that even if one of the two products succeeded, it might be the one that he or she did not choose. Thus, DCCs (actually both products) were off to a bad start.[11]

Philips and Matsushita, not surprisingly, did much better on the second step of the parlay. They secured commitments for an adequate supply of recordings. Philips's subsidiary Polygram and Matsushita's subsidiary MCA could, of course, be relied upon to provide DCCs. Further commitments were secured from EMI, Warner, and even CBS Records (which was by then owned by Sony).[12] Thus, the second step of the parlay was won.

The third step of the parlay is to have a sufficiently good product. First of all, DCC players had to provide sufficient consumer value to compensate for the drawback that consumers could initially have only small libraries of DCCs. This consumer value must be figured on an incremental basis—over and above the value that consumers could derive from preexisting technology. In the case of DCCs, the most important preexisting technology was CDs. Analog cassettes were also available for making recordings, though the recordings were of lower quality than DCCs.

We previously observed that CDs did, indeed, provide sufficient incremental value. Let us consider whether DCCs offered comparable incremental value. In this regard,

• CDs, when they were introduced, provided a substantial improvement in quality of sound reproduction. DCCs provided about the same quality as the preexisting technology.

• CDs did not have recording capability, while one of the preexisting technologies (analog cassettes) did, albeit of inferior musical quality. DCCs did offer recording capability.

• CDs offered random access to selections on the disc. DCCs did not offer this capability.

• CDs were not backward-compatible. DCCs were able to play but not record analog cassettes.

This list is a combination of pluses and minuses, so the comparison is not clear-cut. Nevertheless, there are adequate reasons to believe that the innovation of CD offered more incremental value to most consumers:

• The improvement in quality of sound reproduction was the key selling point for CDs.

• CD players that play multiple CDs can be used to construct customized programs—one of the important recording applications of cassette recorders (whether digital or analog). Indeed, CD technology is much easier to use for this purpose.

• Although the backward-compatibility feature of DCCs was convenient, it did not improve the sound quality of analog cassettes. It therefore did not provide a lot of incremental value to users who already had an analog cassette recorder.

• Finally, users who planned to save money by obtaining illegal copies of DCCs would have had to record an enormous number of them to recover the purchase price, which was initially close to $1,000.

All in all, DCC players appear to have won only one step of the three-step parlay. One out of three is not good enough for this game. Indeed, two out of three would probably not have been good enough. The product therefore did not reach a critical mass and must be regarded as a failure.

9.5.3 Minidiscs

MDs have capabilities that are very similar to those of DCCs. They both offer high-quality sound reproduction (comparable to CDs) and also have recording capability. The main differences are that MDs have no capability for backward compatibility but do allow random access to selections on the disc.

The reasons for the failure of MDs are almost the same as for DCCs. There was no single technical standard, and the product did not offer sufficient incremental value over preexisting technology, primarily CDs. MDs, like DCCs, did not achieve a critical mass and must be considered a failure.

9.5.4 Likely Outcome Absent Bandwagon Effects

As we have seen, DATs failed, apart from bandwagon effects. It is interesting, however, to consider how DCCs and MDs would have fared if they were not subject to bandwagon effects. Suppose that record stores carried a full line of recordings in all formats. What would have happened, assuming that DCCs and MDs were offered at competitive prices?

Under these circumstances, consumers purchasing a first stereo system would tend to purchase either a DCC or MD player rather than a CD player if they wanted to be able to make or play recordings. Moreover, if a full line of recordings were available, consumers might purchase a DCC or MD player, in addition to the CD player that they already owned. Ultimately, DCC and MD players would have captured a significant part of the market. Indeed, they might eventually have surpassed CDs in popularity.

This outcome was not, however, possible in the actual bandwagon context. A full line of recordings was not available in either of these formats. Furthermore, consumers could not realistically expect that a full line would ever be available—especially since a single technical standard was not established. Consequently, for the great majority of consumers, purchasing either a DCC or MD player did not make sense.

Put another way, DCC and MD players were good products. They were not, however, extraordinary enough to succeed in a bandwagon market.

9.6   Lessons from Case Study

The introduction of CDs is a model of effective solution to the start-up problem for a product involving complementary bandwagon effects. Philips and Sony pooled their technologies and developed a truly superior product. They next licensed other firms to establish a single technological standard; so the products of all manufacturers were inter-linked. They then solved the chicken-and-egg problem by working out agreements with the major suppliers of complementary products (viz., the record companies) to ensure that an adequate initial supply of complementary products was available. The result was a spectacular success.

DATs failed for reasons unrelated to bandwagon effects. In contrast, DCCs and MDs would probably have enjoyed some commercial success, but for bandwagon effects. The products embodied competing technical standards, and the resulting lack of interlinking reduced the attractiveness of both products to consumers. In addition, although the products were good, they were not extraordinary enough, relative to the pre-existing technology of CDs, to achieve a critical mass in a bandwagon market. Put another way, CDs had a first-mover advantage that (as is often the case in bandwagon markets) turned out to be insurmountable.

10
VCRs

The history of VCRs is a colorful and exciting saga. The extremely rapid growth of the product is an interesting story in itself. In addition, the standards confrontation between Sony (Beta) and Matsushita/JVC (VHS) was a dramatic clash. Finally, a legal attack by Hollywood put the whole industry at risk. Incredibly, the U.S. Supreme Court came within one vote of (in effect) declaring the VCR to be an illegal device.

Bandwagon effects have played an important role in shaping the VCR industry. Nevertheless, their impact is less than meets the eye. By carefully examining the history of VCRs, we can distinguish the real bandwagon effects from other effects.

10.1 Early Developments

In the early 1970s, Sony and Matsushita jointly developed the U-Matic VCR and agreed to a single technical standard. To develop the product, the two companies signed a patent-sharing agreement. The U-Matic enjoyed some measure of success in commercial applications. It was, however, too expensive for the home market. In addition, it used commercial $3/4$-inch tape, which made the product inconveniently large for home use.

Apparently, both firms were dissatisfied with that joint arrangement. Sony believed that Matsushita (which was originally farther from bringing a product to market) had caused Sony to delay its entry and lose competitive advantage.[1] Matsushita believed that the joint arrangement favored Sony and led to Sony's making most of the profits.[2] Both firms were determined to avoid making the same mistake again.

When Sony developed a home VCR with a ½-inch tape, it invited Matsushita to join in supporting the technical standard (Beta). Matsushita, which was again farther from bringing a product to market, delayed in responding to Sony's offer. Sony was unwilling to be held back again and rushed its product to market in 1975. Matsushita brought out its own VCR with the incompatible VHS format the following year.

10.2   Early VCR Use

To understand the early history of VCR, one must recognize that the original intended use of the VCR was solely to record television programming and watch it at a different time ("time-shifting"). Prerecorded videocassettes were not on the market, and there was no reason to assume that Hollywood would make them available. Indeed, as we shall see later, Hollywood fought the introduction of VCRs. Certainly, neither Sony nor Matsushita made any plans to coordinate the availability of pre-recorded videocassettes with the introduction of the VCR. There was no activity analogous to Philips's lining up of record companies to produce CDs. Furthermore, no retail outlets were in place to distribute the nonexistent prerecorded videocassettes.

In later periods, VCRs have been purchased largely, often primarily, to view prerecorded videocassettes. This application involves complementary bandwagon effects—the same as CDs. In contrast, time-shifting, the predominant early use of VCRs, was a stand-alone application that did not generate substantial bandwagon effects. The utility of time-shifting is not much affected by how many others use VCRs with the same format.

For this reason, the VCR was not a bandwagon product when it was introduced. The suppliers did not have to deal with a bandwagon start-up problem. Instead, they simply had the usual (though by no means trivial) problem of winning market acceptance for a technological innovation.

Because bandwagon effects were absent, the benefit of a single technical standard was not especially great. There was no issue of increasing bandwagon benefits through interlinking. Users were not greatly inconvenienced by using incompatible formats for time-shifting.

It is probably precisely for that reason that Sony and Matsushita did not struggle harder to agree on a technical standard. To be sure, the companies bore ill will from their negative experience with the U-Matic. Furthermore, according to Lardner that experience simply compounded the ambient ill will between the upstart (Sony) and the traditional Japanese industry leader (Matsushita).[3] Nevertheless, if the VCR at the time of introduction had been a bandwagon product (like the CD player), it seems likely that Sony and Matsushita would, indeed, have reached an agreement. Each company may have had contempt for the way that the other operated, but business is business.

10.3   Beta versus VHS

Beta and VHS are not really very different. They both evolved from the same technology used in the U-Matic. That technology was available to both Sony and Matsushita (and Matsushita's affiliate JVC) through their patent-sharing agreement. Both technologies were apparently far superior to any alternatives. Nevertheless, the products based on the Beta and VHS formats differed in some respects. In some ways, Beta was better; in other ways, VHS was superior.

10.3.1   General Product Design

The design of Beta VCRs was more compact than that of VHS VCRs. Beta also had some other advantages. Lardner quotes a columnist in a 1980 issue of *Video* as saying, "In my opinion, the Sony-developed Beta format is superior to VHS in several ways, including better cassette design, superior tape handling, and overall better video engineering."

10.3.2   Picture Quality

Cusumano, Mylonadis, and Rosenbloom state, "Differences in picture quality are more difficult to assess, but VHS did not have a reputation as being superior to Beta, and the truth may indeed have been the opposite." They support this view by citing a 1984 issue of *Time*, a 1983 article in *The New York Times*, and a 1981 issue of *Home Video*. Picture quality may, however, be in the eye of the beholder. Klopfenstein

Table 10.1
Recording-Playing Time Comparison Selected Months/Years, May 1975–
September 1982

Month/Year	Beta Format	VHS Format
May 1975	1 hour (Sony)	
November 1976		2 hours (JVC)
March 1977	2 hours (Sony)	
October 1977		4 hours (Matsushita)
October 1978	3 hours (Sony)	
March 1979	4.5 hours (Sony)	
August 1979		6 hours (Matsushita)
August 1979		4 hours (JVC)
December 1979		6 hours (JVC)
March 1982	8 hours (Sony)	
September 1982	5 hours (Sony)	

Source: Excerpted from Cusumano, Mylonadis, and Rosenbloom, p. 77.

cites technical experts and some product reviews in *Consumer Reports* to support the view that Beta's picture quality was *not* superior to VHS's.

10.3.3   Playing Time
A key issue in the contest between Beta and VHS was playing time. Table 10.1 gives a timetable for the introduction of VCRs of different playing times. As the table shows, VHS had longer playing times during much of the early period. That advantage had critical importance in the contest between Beta and VHS. Ultimately, Beta had sufficiently long playing times for virtually all applications, but it had already fallen behind in the bandwagon race.[4]

10.3.4   Features
The suppliers competed in bringing out new features. Table 10.2 shows the timing of introductions of various features. As the table shows, sometimes Sony was first; sometimes the VHS suppliers were first. In all cases, the features were quickly matched in the other format.

Table 10.2
Special Effects Comparison by Introduction Date (Year/Month)

	Sony	Matsushita	JVC
Wireless Remote	March 1977*	June 1977	June 1979
1/2-Speed Machine	March 1977*	June 1977	August 1979
Slow/Still	March 1979	July 1978	December 1977*
Portable VCR	September 1978	February 1980	February 1978*
1/3-Speed Machine	March 1979*	August 1979	December 1979
Scan/Slow/Still	March 1979*	June 1980	August 1979
Stereo Recording	July 1980	August 1979*	August 1979*
Hi-Fi	April 1983*	May 1983	November 1983
One-Unit Camera- Recorder	July 1983*	January 1985	March 1984

* Marks the first to introduce the feature.
Source: Excerpted from Cusumano, Mylonadis, and Rosenbloom, p. 78.

10.3.5   Price

The suppliers naturally competed on price. Prices always ranged widely, depending on the VCR's features. During much of the early period, starting in mid-1977, Matsushita and/or JVC had models priced substantially below Sony's least expensive model. Thus, VHS had a price advantage, at least in the low end of the market. This price advantage reflected a cost advantage of the VHS suppliers.[5]

10.3.6   The Outcome

VHS quickly took the lead in the standards contest. Table 10.3 shows market shares of the two formats. In 1978, two years after VHS entered the market, it pulled ahead of Beta in annual sales. The following year, VHS also had the larger installed base.[6]

Nevertheless, Beta still had a large, loyal following. Sony could reasonably have expected to retain a sizable share of the market, although it had lost the market lead. But then came the bandwagon.

10.4   The Bandwagon

As previously discussed, complementary bandwagon effects sometimes involve a chicken-and-egg problem. With VCRs, the stand-alone

Table 10.3
Beta-VHS Annual Production and Cumulative Shares, 1975–1988 (thousands of units)

	Beta Format		VHS Format	
Year	Annual Production	Cumulative Shares	Annual Production	Cumulative Shares
1975	20	20	—	—
1976	175	195	110	110
1977	424	619	339	449
1978	594	1,213	878	1,327
1979	851	2,064	1,336	2,663
1980	1,489	3,552	2,922	5,585
1981	3,020	6,572	6,478	12,063
1982	3,717	10,289	9,417	21,480
1983	4,572	14,861	13,645	35,125
1984	6,042	20,903	23,464	58,589
1985	3,387	24,290	40,977	99,566
1986	1,106	25,396	29,553	129,119
1987	669	26,065	39,767	168,886
1988	148	26,213	44,761	213,647

Source: Excerpted from Cusumano, Mylonadis, and Rosenbloom, p. 54.

application of time-shifting of television programs (call it "the chicken") solved this problem. Once VCR penetration reached a certain level, natural market forces led to the creation of prerecorded videocassettes ("the egg").

In terms of bandwagon theory, the initial user set resulted from purchases of VCRs for time-shifting. That user set was sufficiently large that the demand-based equilibrium user set exceeded a critical mass for the product.

A critical mass for VCRs was achieved in the late 1970s. At that time, an independent supply of prerecorded videocassettes spontaneously appeared—notwithstanding the opposition to the VCR by many Hollywood interests.

The bandwagon created strong pressures for a single technical standard. As long as two technical standards existed, videocassette rental stores had to maintain inventories in both formats. Consumers of each format then had fewer titles from which to choose. The reduced variety was the loss of the bandwagon benefits of interlinking.

Rental stores obviously had an incentive to maintain a larger inventory of videocassettes in the more popular format, which was VHS. Consequently, VHS had an additional advantage over Beta—over and above the advantages that led to its being more popular in the first place. As the VHS market share grew as a result of these advantages, the less popular format (Beta) had an ever-greater disadvantage in the market. By the late 1980s, Beta had disappeared entirely from the home market. The winner, VHS, had taken all.

10.5 The Hollywood Assault

In 1976, Universal Studios filed suit against Sony. It claimed that Sony, by marketing the VCR, had infringed on its copyrights as a producer of television programming. Thus, Universal aimed a thrust at the heart of the VCR industry. It remained to be seen whether Sony could parry the thrust.

Sony won the first round at the District Court, but in 1981, the Ninth Circuit Court of Appeals found Sony guilty of copyright infringement. That decision was, of course, immediately appealed in the U.S. Supreme Court.

The U.S. judiciary system operates at glacial speed, and sometimes that slowness leads to anomalous results. In this case, the VCR industry metamorphosed between the time the MCA suit was filed and the time of the Ninth Circuit Court decision. Hollywood may have regarded time-shifting as an ugly caterpillar to be stomped on. By 1981, however, it had good reason to regard prerecorded videocassettes as a beautiful butterfly that could bring Hollywood enormous profits. Ironically, even Universal had begun to license prerecorded videocassettes before the Ninth Circuit decision. As early as 1986, videocassette revenues exceeded box office revenues.[7] They are now several times box office revenues.

In any event, after the Ninth Circuit Decision, the battle shifted to the political arena. Legislation was introduced in Congress to modify the copyright laws to undo the court decision. Hollywood countered by proposing legislation under which manufacturers of VCRs and blank tapes would pay royalties to copyright owners.

Congress did what it usually does when strong political forces are arrayed on both sides of an issue. It passed no legislation, but it did hold extensive hearings and collected large campaign contributions from both sides. Thus, the issue remained to be decided by the courts.

In 1984, the Supreme Court reached a decision. By a 5-to-4 vote, it overturned the Ninth Circuit ruling. It decided that the marketing of VCRs does not constitute copyright infringement. Thus, after eight years of legal wrangling, the Hollywood assault on the VCR came to nothing.

If one vote in the Supreme Court had gone the other way, the VCR would have essentially been declared an illegal device. The whole VCR industry would have been thrown into chaos. For starters, Sony (and other VCR manufacturers) may have had to pay considerable damages to copyright holders after some further legal wrangling.

Nevertheless, it seems unlikely that the VCR industry would have been shut down. Congress, notwithstanding its penchant for passing no legislation when powerful interests are arrayed on both sides, would have been forced to act. The Supreme Court decision would, of course, have changed the political dynamics. VCR manufacturers would have been desperate for legislation. They would probably have acquiesced to a plan under which they paid royalties to Hollywood.

10.6   The Videocassette Business

The story of the origin of the videocassette business is remarkable.[8] The big guys completely missed the boat. An enormous cadre of local entrepreneurs then created a multibillion dollar business out of whole cloth. The story could almost make one believe political rhetoric about the importance of small business to the economy.

It all began in 1976 with Andre Blay, a video-equipment entrepreneur in Farmington, Michigan. Blay had worked with the U-Matic and appreciated the potential of the VCR. He knew of Hollywood's opposition to the VCR. Nevertheless, he had the chutzpah to write to the CEOs of all the Hollywood studios except Universal to request licenses to sell pre-recorded videocassettes of the studios' movies.

His letter arrived at the right time on the desk of the right person at Twentieth Century Fox. Fox licensed Blay to sell fifty (not too valuable) titles, and a new industry was born. Blay constructed a factory to manufacture the videocassettes. He made the big time when he successfully gambled $65,000 on an ad in *TV Guide* and got an overwhelming response.

Shortly thereafter, George Atkinson, an entrepreneur from Los Angeles, began to rent videocassettes. The Hollywood studios initially claimed that such rentals infringed on their copyrights. That view, however, turned out to have no legal merit (much to the benefit of the studios). Rentals quickly became the primary videocassette business.

Small local entrepreneurs all across the country rushed to take advantage of this new opportunity. As expected, many failed but some made sizable fortunes. In 1980, the production of prerecorded video-cassettes already exceeded 3 million. By 1987, it was 68 million. These were purchased, primarily by rental stores, for about $2.4 billion in total.[9]

The VCR and videocassette markets after 1980 illustrate how rapidly demand can grow in a bandwagon market that has achieved a critical mass (in this case, largely because of initial demand for time-shifting) and is subject to positive feedback. Growth was stimulated to some extent by the decline in unit costs and prices. In this regard, the lowest-priced VCR cost about $200 in 1977 and $100 in 1985.[10] More important, however, the growth was fueled by the demand growth itself. As more VCRs were sold, more prerecorded videocassettes became available, and the product became more valuable.[11]

10.7 Videodisc Players

The videodisc player (VDP) was an alternative technology to the VCR. Unlike the VCR, however, the VDP cannot be used to time-shift television programs. It has no stand-alone application and its value derives entirely from playing prerecorded videodiscs. Consequently, the VDP, like the CD player, is a pure bandwagon product.

If the VDP had been introduced before the VCR, it could conceivably have succeeded in the market, but it could not have traveled the VCR's easy road to success. In order to generate any demand at all, the proprietors of the VDP would have had to solve the start-up problem. The most important part of the solution would have been to coordinate the availability of the complementary products (videodiscs) with the introduction of the VDPs themselves. The VDP proprietors could have attempted to carry out the same strategy that Philips carried out with respect to CDs. The start-up problem would, however, have been more difficult for VDPs, because appropriate retail outlets did not exist for VDPs (before the introduction of the VCR). Retail outlets could not be expected to appear spontaneously. They appeared in the VCR market only *after* the user set for VCRs was sizable. Small entrepreneurs would have been very unlikely to rush in to provide complementary products until there was a significant base of VDPs already in place. Moreover, VDP suppliers would have had the additional problem of putting an adequate retail distribution network into place.

Only a technological behemoth could have succeeded with the VDP under these circumstances. Philips was a potential candidate. We have already observed the exceptional skill with which it carried out the three steps of the parlay with respect to CDs. In reality, Philips was scratched before the start of the race. It was unable to make sufficient technological progress to introduce the VDP before the VCR hit the market.

RCA introduced the VDP much later, in 1981. At that time, videocassette rental stores were already beginning to proliferate; and they could have provided a satisfactory retail distribution system for videodiscs. VDPs also had the advantage of somewhat better picture quality than VCRs. Nevertheless, the odds were decidedly stacked against RCA in this venture:

• VCR producers had a big headstart in the bandwagon race; a far greater variety of prerecorded titles were available on videocassettes than RCA could reasonably hope would be available on videodiscs.

• VCRs had the additional advantage of being able to time-shift television programming.

• Although VDPs had an inherent long-run cost advantage, VCR producers had gone farther down the learning curve and had a short-run cost advantage over RCA.[12]

RCA tried to make up for the above disadvantages by offering VDPs at lower prices than VCRs and thereby accepting short-run losses. This strategy seems doomed to failure against formidable, aggressive, and well-financed competitors such as Matsushita and JVC (not to mention Sony, which was not yet out of the race). The VCR producers lowered prices in response to the competition from VDPs.[13] It seems inconceivable that the VCR producers (especially Matsushita) would have stood by and let RCA, with its inferior product and high costs, steal the bandwagon market from them. RCA's strategy can be likened to going into the ring against a champion Sumo wrestler with one arm tied behind one's back. Not surprisingly, RCA was pushed out of the ring in short order.

10.8   Lessons from Case Study

The history of VCRs illustrates the great value of a stand-alone application for starting up a bandwagon product. The stand-alone application of time-shifting allowed VCRs to attain a critical mass. The subsequent rapid proliferation of videocassette rental stores, in turn, shows how effective competitive markets can be in providing complementary products—but only after a sizable user set is in place.

The standards battle between Sony (Beta) and Matsushita/JVC (VHS) clearly illustrates the winner-take-all tendency of bandwagon markets without interlinking. Beta was not a bad product, but there was no second prize.

11

Personal Computers

Young readers will not have had the character-building experience of using the computers of the 1950s and 1960s. We therefore provide some background. It sounds like Grandpa telling of his long walk to school in the snow.

Computers of the 1950s and early 1960s were primarily "mainframe" computers. They were huge and expensive, and a single computer often served all of a large organization. They were operated by computer departments, which were often viewed with deep suspicion by other departments in the organization.

An important technological advance that began to flourish in the late 1960s was the minicomputer. Minicomputers were often operated by individual departments within an organization. The department was thereby freed from the central computer department. Individual users, however, were still dependent on departmental computer experts.

Both mainframe and minicomputers were used for all sorts of tasks, including

• those that required numerous repetitions of calculations, such as payroll;
• those that involved large databases, such as inventory control; and
• those that involved serious number crunching, such as engineering applications.

Regardless of the application, the direct users of computers were primarily professional programmers. Computers were generally not practical for applications that did not justify the cost and inconvenience of getting a professional programmer involved. The usual alternative was for an army of clerks to do the job manually, using ledger sheets and electric calculators.

Personal computers (PCs) revolutionized computing. They allowed individuals to worship the Computer God on their own, without the intermediation of the priestly class of professional programmers.

The result has been phenomenal. Computers have become ubiquitous. They facilitate the production of documents, routine calculations, and a thousand other tasks. They are found not only in major corporations, but also at the local gas station and the corner liquor store. They are used by the quantitatively challenged, as well as by math whizzes. Young children can be seen operating computers before they have the coordination to form letters with a pencil.

Many major product innovations were required to get from there to here. Bandwagon effects had a lot to do with determining which innovations and innovators were successful, and which came up empty.

Computer systems require both hardware and software in order to be useful. Manufacturers of mainframes and minicomputers generally provide systems software. The user organization then writes most of the applications software that it uses. This industry structure embodies large internal scale economies on the supply and demand side. Large firms can produce mainframe and minicomputers more efficiently, and large organizations can use them more efficiently. The industry structure does not, however, involve substantial (external) bandwagon effects.

In contrast, most users of PCs write relatively little of the applications software that they use. Rather, they depend upon outside firms to supply applications software. Manufacturers of PCs generally provide little applications software. Thus, the value of the hardware depends largely on the supply of software by independent software vendors (ISVs).

The supply of software by ISVs embodies complementary bandwagon effects. The more computer systems of a particular type there are, the more software that ISVs tend to write for that type of system. The more applications software that is written, the greater is the value of, and demand for, the computer system. Once a critical mass is reached, this process is subject to positive feedback.

PCs began to be offered in the early 1970s, but commercial success did not arrive until 1977, when Apple Computer Company introduced the Apple II computer. That same year, Commodore and Radio Shack announced PCs. Atari announced PCs the following year.[1]

PCs then began to grow rapidly in the 1980s. Sales were approximately $2 billion in 1981. They grew to approximately $31 billion in 1987 and to approximately $60 billion in 1990.[2]

11.1 Early Application Software

The early growth of PCs was fueled by two general-purpose software applications: word processors and spreadsheets—the original "killer applications." Word processors were available earlier for larger computers. They began to be available for PCs in the mid-1970s. The first spreadsheet, VisiCalc, was introduced in 1979. It was an enormously important innovation and has profoundly affected computing practice. Video games are a third killer application that fueled the growth of home computers. Atari diversified from the production of video game machines and was a leading supplier of home computers during the early period. In addition, numerous ISVs, such as Electronic Arts and Sierra, supplied computer games. Video games were initially the number one use of home computers.[3]

These applications allowed PCs to achieve a critical mass. They were so valuable that many customers purchased PCs for the sole purpose of using those applications. In terms of bandwagon theory, these users constituted the initial user set, which was sufficiently large to achieve a critical mass. Given that user set, ISVs found it profitable to write a wide range of applications software—both general-purpose and special-purpose. The availability of this additional software led to positive feedback by stimulating additional demand for PCs, which stimulated the writing of additional applications software, and so forth.

11.2 The Rise of the IBM PC

For decades preceding the advent of PCs, IBM had dominated the computer industry, but it was late in offering PCs. Nevertheless, the belated entry of IBM in August 1981 had a profound effect on the PC market.

Before the entry of IBM, PCs were mainly based on 8-bit micro-processors. The most widely used operating system was CP/M, which had been developed in 1974. Intel developed a 16-bit microprocessor (the 8086) in 1978. In 1979, it developed the 8088, which used 16 bits internally but supported 8-bit device-controlling chips. A 16-bit upgrade of CP/M was not, however, available and did not become available until April 1982.[4]

The IBM PC was a 16-bit computer based on the 8088. Compared to an 8-bit computer, a 16-bit computer can accommodate larger applications and run many applications faster. At the time of IBM's initial offering, few applications programs had been written for 16-bit computers, but a 16-bit computer was forward-looking. A user who purchased an 8-bit computer in 1981 faced the prospect that the computer would need to be replaced before very long. A user who purchased a 16-bit computer was prepared for the future.

The IBM PC was not the first 16-bit computer available on the market. Texas Instruments had introduced one in 1979. But the IBM PC, in conjunction with its operating system PC-DOS, had the great advantage of being largely upward compatible from CP/M. That is, programs written for 8-bit CP/M computers could be easily modified to run on the IBM PC using PC-DOS.

The IBM PC had the additional advantage of an open architecture. The only proprietary IBM hardware was the keyboard and the ROM-BIOS chip. The latter linked the operating system to input and output devices. The open architecture allowed users of IBM PCs to take full advantage of competitive offerings of software and peripheral hardware.

When IBM entered the PC market, Apple and several smaller firms had a big headstart. IBM therefore had to play catch-up. To be sure, it had a good product, but users had to be concerned that a late entrant might not prosper, or even survive. Hence, there might be little new software written for that computer in the future.

In this regard, the IBM brand name was a valuable asset. Both users and writers of applications software expected that because of IBM's good reputation as a supplier of computers, the IBM PC platform would survive and prosper. As discussed in section 3.4, such expectations tend to be self-fulfilling in bandwagon markets. In this particular case, the expectations were indeed fulfilled. Users who bought IBM PCs were rewarded through the availability of a wide range of applications software. Writers of applications software for the IBM PC were rewarded through the rapid growth of the base of potential customers.

Although the IBM PC became the standard for most of the PC industry, other standards survived. Apple has carved out a niche for itself. It has had a user set with a strong community of interest within itself. This set includes many users associated with educational institutions. Apple developed this niche through a combination of giving away some computers and selling some at discounted prices. This type of strategy is precisely what is called for in bandwagon markets. It has definitely redounded to Apple's benefit.

Apple has also brought out a number of successful products over the years. Nevertheless, one has the impression that Apple has been a strong swimmer going against the swift current of bandwagon effects. Apple has had some commercial success, but not at all commensurate with the scope and quality of its innovations.

Computer workstations running various versions of Unix form another niche that has continued to grow. Workstations have higher performance than PCs and sell for considerably higher prices. They are used primarily for engineering and scientific applications. Users of workstations enjoy bandwagon benefits from the large number of programs written for Unix. In terms of bandwagon theory, the users of workstations constitute a community of interest that is largely separate from PC users.

11.3   The Decline of the IBM PC

For a while, it looked as if IBM had hit the jackpot. Sales of IBM PCs soared. It appeared that IBM was well on its way to dominating the PC market, as it had dominated the markets for larger computers.

Then, a funny thing happened. The IBM clones hit the market. Since the IBM system was so open, the clones had only to design their own keyboards and reverse engineer the ROM-BIOS chip. That turned out to be a trivial challenge for Silicon Valley (and slightly later, for Asian electronics firms). Clones using their own keyboards and reverse-engineered

ROM-BIOS chips were on the market less than a year after the introduction of the IBM PC.

Of course, consumers did not immediately rush to purchase clones. The compatibility claims of the clones had to be tested, but it soon became clear that the clones were performing as advertised. Thereafter, they rapidly found market acceptance.

Because of intense competition from clones, IBM's position in the PC market declined substantially and rapidly. Columbia Data Products released the first clones in June 1982. By 1986, IBM's market share dropped to 25 percent. It was only 12 percent in 1993.[5]

This sequence of events can be easily understood in terms of bandwagon theory. IBM's brand name was probably necessary to give credibility to its original PCs. It substantially contributed to the bandwagon effects by stimulating the production of applications software. Unfortunately for IBM, manufacturers of clones were also in a position to benefit from these bandwagon effects. In bandwagon terms, IBM's open architecture had the effect of interlinking the IBM PC and its clones.

One should understand that the importance of IBM's brand name did *not* lie primarily in giving customers confidence that the product was reliable and durable. To be sure, the IBM PC was expected to be, and indeed was, reliable and durable. But many other companies could and did make durable and reliable computers. The key contribution of the IBM brand name was rather in creating the expectation that the IBM PC platform would attain industry acceptance. That self-fulfilling expectation started the bandwagon.

The salient events in the history of the IBM PC are thus as follows: IBM entered the industry and lent its prestigious name to a particular platform. It thereby started up the bandwagon—a feat that the clones could never have accomplished by themselves. Then, IBM lost control of the technology and was overtaken by the clones.

The obvious question is, "How could this have happened?" One would certainly not have expected, a priori, that a firm of IBM's caliber could lose out in such a manner.

The answer lies in IBM's misjudgment in underestimating the potential of the PC until it was almost too late. IBM was nowhere in terms of developing a marketable PC in the late 1970s and had to play a desperate game of catch-up. The players that IBM assigned to this game were highly capable. They salvaged billions of dollars of profits from what could have been a complete write-off. In doing so, however, they gave up most of IBM's potential for the future.

The 1980–1981 timeframe offered a unique opportunity for IBM's entry because Digital Research had not yet upgraded CP/M to 16 bits. That window could, however, close at any time, and IBM had not yet developed either the hardware or the software to put forth a product.

The IBM team turned that liability into an asset. They bought almost all the hardware and software components from others, assembled a product, and put the IBM name on it. Because the product embodied virtually no proprietary hardware or software, the architecture was fully open. Users could take advantage of a variety of vendors for whatever hardware and software that they needed, over and above the basic PC and its operating system. The open architecture clearly contributed substantially to the success of the IBM PC.

Nevertheless, one cannot help but wonder if there was a way for IBM to have done better and won the future as well as the present. Could IBM somehow have kept sufficient control over the technology to prevent widespread cloning and still have offered a sufficiently open architecture to win consumer acceptance?

The most obvious possibility would have been to retain proprietary rights to the operating system. The architecture would then have been somewhat less open, but customers would still have been able to use a variety of hardware and software vendors. It seems quite possible, in retrospect, that the product would have won consumer acceptance.

The problem with this strategy is that the owner of the operating system that IBM needed did not want to give IBM sole proprietary rights. Apparently, IBM was so desperate to get into the PC business that it caved in on this key bargaining issue—and there went the future. To all appearances, IBM—the premier computer company, a legend in the management of high technology—was thoroughly outmaneuvered by the young proprietor of a small start-up company in Seattle, a fellow named Bill Gates. Gates had just bought the rights to DOS for approximately $100,000 and then bargained to make one of the best business deals in history.

In any event, the loss of IBM's future potential should not be blamed on the PC development team. They were in a desperate situation and operating under great pressure. They had to make momentous decisions in real time or else lose for sure. They managed to salvage a great deal. The fundamental problem was IBM's getting into that desperate situation in the first place.

IBM continued to participate in the PC market—even after the deluge of the clones. In 1990, its PC revenues were $9.6 billion, and it had the second highest profit margin (after Apple) in the industry.[6] These revenues and profits are certainly substantial. IBM thus benefited considerably from its entry into the PC market. Nevertheless, the ultimate outcome must be regarded as disappointing, given that IBM had started the whole PC bandwagon.

11.4   The Role of Apple

Richard Schmalensee, in his testimony for Microsoft, argues that Microsoft's success was largely attributable to good products and sound business judgments. In discussing Apple, he says, "Many industry students of the personal computer industry have commented that Apple blundered in failing to unbundle its operating system from its hardware and from maintaining high prices—both of these business decisions impeded Apple from achieving network economies [i.e., bandwagon benefits for its customers]." Let us examine these two issues in light of bandwagon theory and the history of the industry.

11.4.1   Unbundling the Operating System from the Hardware
We have previously observed the positive and negative effects of IBM's strategy of having virtually no proprietary hardware or software. Apple could, of course, have emulated this strategy. The result would have been to usher in a raft of Apple clones. Apple's market share, like IBM's, would then have rapidly declined. Unlike IBM, however, Apple had sole proprietary rights to the operating system. It could reasonably have hoped to reap compensatory profits in its role as a producer of operating systems. Microsoft's subsequent success demonstrates the viability of this strategy. Furthermore, Apple had obvious strengths in the produc-

tion of operating systems. Who knows what the computer industry would look like today if Apple had adopted this strategy?

Apple's actual strategy—the strategy of Steve Jobs, who was Apple's chief executive officer at the time—was exactly the opposite of IBM's. Apple manufactured and sold end-to-end computer systems, including peripheral equipment, such as disk drives, keyboards, and monitors. Jobs sought to produce as much of the computer system in-house as possible.

Jobs's strategy in this regard is reminiscent of another industrial genius, namely, Henry Ford. Ford's goal was to control all the productive processes that went into the production of his automobiles. He was not satisfied with merely producing most of the components of the automobile itself. He also owned a steel mill that produced the steel that went into his automobiles. Further, he owned a coal mine that produced the coal that was used by the steel mills. Still further, he owned the railroad that transported the coal from the mine to the steel mill. (The Pennsylvania Turnpike now uses the right of way of that defunct railroad.)

As a general matter, this philosophy of end-to-end production has now been largely discredited. Today, manufacturing firms almost always rely on other firms to produce a sizable part of the total value of their products.[7] By doing so, they benefit from the sharp efficiency incentives that characterize competitive supplier markets.[8]

Jobs justified his policy by claiming that under his leadership, Apple could produce "insanely great" personal computer products.[9] Such a claim could normally be dismissed as hubris, but it must be taken seriously when made by Steve Jobs. A large number of insanely great products were indeed developed under his leadership. Even so, the policy of end-to-end production did not work well and was an important factor in Jobs's being demoted in 1985.

An apparently inevitable side effect of the end-to-end philosophy is that consumers get insufficient choice of features and options.[10] The original IBM PCs had a number of slots wherein users could insert cards of their choice, supplied by IBM or by others. By doing so, they could configure their PCs to have the capabilities they desired. Apple computers did not have such capability until much later. By then, Apple had fallen hopelessly behind in the bandwagon race.

In retrospect, it seems clear that Apple should have opted for an intermediate policy between IBM's complete reliance on outside suppliers and the fully closed architecture that Apple actually chose. The goal should have been to retain sufficient proprietary technology to inhibit cloning, while giving users maximum flexibility. By focusing on its core product line, Apple could also have concentrated more resources on what should have been its prime objective—namely, building market share to win the bandwagon race.

We note that this strategy does not require that clones be eliminated altogether. It may suffice to ensure that clones cannot be designed until each new product of the "clonee" comes out. Then, by the time the clones can reach the market, the clonee can be introducing a new product, embodying the next generation of technology. As we shall see later, this strategy has worked extremely well for Intel and Microsoft.

11.4.2 Pricing

Schmalensee suggests that Apple may have blundered by charging excessively high prices. Let us now examine that suggestion.

The critical period in which excessive prices would have been especially damaging was during the early 1980s, when the bandwagon race was being run. Table 11.1 shows Apple's revenues and net income for the period 1981–1985. Net income was over 10 percent of revenues in 1981 and 1982. After the clones hit the market, Apple's net income became a smaller and smaller fraction of sales. Indeed, net income declined after 1983. In 1985, Apple's net income was only 2.4 percent of revenues.

Table 11.1
Apple's Revenues and Net Income, 1981–1985

Year	Revenues	Net Income
1981	$334.8	$39.4
1982	$583.1	$61.3
1983	$982.8	$76.7
1984	$1,516.8	$64.1
1985	$1,905.5	$45.8

These data suggest that Apple (unlike the early Bell System, for example) was *not* excessively greedy for short-run profits. To offer substantially lower prices to be more competitive, Apple would have had to sustain negative net income during this period. Operating in that manner would have added substantial additional risk to what already was an extremely risky environment. Thus, one can easily understand Apple's reluctance to embark on that course.

Nevertheless, voluntarily accepting such losses may have been the only winning strategy for Apple. Unlike IBM and the producers of IBM clones, Apple was in a position to appropriate the benefits of bandwagon effects from expanded use of Apple computers in the future. It might therefore have been profitable for Apple deliberately to incur some level of losses to increase its market share.

This strategy would have been more effective in conjunction with making Apple's design more open (though still retaining some proprietary technology). Without an improvement in Apple's design, it is quite possible that (reasonable) price reductions would not have sufficed to win the bandwagon race. IBM's fully open system set a high competitive standard that Apple had to meet.

11.4.3 Perspective on Apple's "Blunders"

The preceding sections suggest that Apple could have done much better in exploiting its initial first-mover advantage in the computer industry, together with its impressive product developments. Nevertheless, one can easily go too far in condemning Apple's performance. Apple did participate in the growth of the PC business. In 1992, its market share was 9 percent, and it had the highest profit margin on sales in the industry.[11] Thus, Apple's performance can be compared to that of a golfer who squanders an early lead and finishes third in a tournament, winning only $300,000 instead of $1 million. It cannot be compared to the player who loses everything in a poker game and leaves the table wearing a barrel.

11.5 The Rise of Intel and Microsoft

Chess players are familiar with the concept of a "won game." It is an advantage that *should* prove decisive. By playing even reasonably well, an ordinary player with a won game can defeat a very strong opponent. Nevertheless, many "won" games have been lost through careless or passive play.

In precisely this sense, bandwagon effects have given Intel and Microsoft won games in the PC business, that is, a decided edge over their opponents. The play of Intel and Microsoft has been the opposite of careless and passive. Hence, the bandwagon edge has turned out to be decisive.

The ultimate goal of a competitor that seeks to displace Intel or Microsoft should be to attract a large customer base that can enjoy its own bandwagon benefits. To succeed, the competitor must initially offer products that are upward compatible from the current Intel microprocessors or Microsoft operating systems. Only if it does so will customers be able to switch to the products of the competitor without forfeiting the bandwagon benefits that they currently enjoy.

If Intel or Microsoft stood still, many potential competitors could achieve this goal. Intel does not have a monopoly on the ability to produce good microprocessors, and Microsoft does not have a monopoly on the ability to write good operating systems. Given enough time, competitors could offer products that were better and less expensive than current products and fully upward-compatible. For Intel or Microsoft to allow this to happen would be analogous to losing a won chess game through passive play.[12]

In reality, Intel and Microsoft have not stood still. Intel continued to innovate through upgrades in its 8086 line of microprocessors and made a timely upgrade to 32-bit technology. Microsoft made several upgrades of MS-DOS and then introduced and upgraded Windows. It made a timely upgrade to 32-bit technology with the introduction of Windows 95.

Given that Intel and Microsoft continue to move forward, they have a great advantage over their rivals in developing new products that are upward compatible. Even before an upgrade comes out, they can be well under way to develop the next upgrade. Other firms cannot make progress until the upgrade has come out and they have had substantial time to study it.

An alternative strategy for competitors of Intel and Microsoft is to be a clone. That strategy involves playing a continual game of catch-up. AMD, in particular, has played this game quite well and kept pressure on Intel to innovate rapidly.

A clone of Intel or Microsoft can be compared to an understudy in a Broadway play. The job may suffice to make a living, but no one takes it (solely) for that reason. The real hope is that the star will get sick or (literally) break a leg. Then, the understudy gets his or her chance. So far, neither Intel nor Microsoft has gotten sick or broken a leg in the marketplace (though Microsoft has not fared so well in antitrust court).

11.6 Microsoft's Pricing

11.6.1 Essential-Component Model
One could conceivably model Microsoft as having a virtual monopoly of the operating system, an essential component of IBM-compatible (or more accurately, Intel- and Microsoft-compatible) PCs. Microsoft's share of this market exceeds 90 percent.[13] This model describes reasonably accurately the substitution possibilities open to most users in the short run. They have no reasonable choice but to use Microsoft operating systems.

Reddy, Evans, and Nichols demonstrate that a static variant of this model (which does not take account of future bandwagon benefits) cannot explain Microsoft's pricing behavior. In particular, if there were no substitute for Windows, Microsoft could greatly increase its short-term profits by jacking up the price. In particular, it would profit in the short term by setting the price of Windows far above the current level of $45 to $65 per copy. To be sure, such a price increase would raise the total price of PC systems and thereby repress demand for them. But the price of Windows constitutes only a small fraction of the total price of PC systems. Thus, even a substantial percentage price increase by Microsoft would (when passed along to consumers) lead to only a moderate percentage increase in the total price of PC systems. It would therefore only moderately repress demand for PC systems and the resulting demand for Windows. On net, Microsoft would come out way ahead *in the short term*.[14]

It follows that the static essential-component model is untenable; it completely fails to explain Microsoft's pricing. The problem lies in two of the key assumptions of the model:

• the assumption that Microsoft maximizes short-run profits, without regard to future bandwagon effects; and

• the essential-component assumption.

In reality, both these assumptions are suspect. In the next section, we examine how Microsoft's pricing behavior *can* be explained if we relax these two assumptions.

11.6.2   History of Microsoft's Pricing

The low price of MS-DOS in the early 1980s can be easily explained. During that period, the goal was to expand market penetration to be in a position to enjoy bandwagon benefits in the future. This goal was shared by Microsoft and IBM, which owned the rights to PC-DOS, a variant of MS-DOS.

This same explanation applies to Windows, when it was first gaining market acceptance. It was profitable for Microsoft initially to price low to ensure adoption. By so doing, it had the prospect of profiting from future bandwagon effects.

A similar explanation applies to the introduction of Windows 95. Microsoft wanted to ensure that users quickly made the transition to 32-bit technology using Windows. If Windows 95 were too expensive and were not rapidly adopted, Microsoft could have eventually become vulnerable to competitive challenge from an alternative operating system for making the transition to 32 bits.

The preceding three paragraphs explain why Microsoft had an incentive to charge low prices during much of the historical period. But Microsoft actually charged low prices for the *entire* historical period. Thus, we need a further explanation.

Microsoft offers the latest version of Windows to computer manufacturers for a price of $45 to $65 per copy. This price is contingent on the manufacturer's paying for Windows on *all* its computers. The vast majority of manufacturers accept this deal. There is greater demand for a computer with the latest version of Windows than for a computer that costs from $45 to $65 less but has no operating system.

This strategy by Microsoft probably would not work if the price were much higher, say $300 per copy. In that case, many manufacturers would indeed opt to sell computers without operating systems. Users would then have two options: they could use an illegal copy of Windows or a legal copy from an old computer that is to be retired.

These user alternatives make demand for Windows more sensitive to price changes than is implied by the essential-component model. In particular, Microsoft would get, say, $300 from each user who bought the latest version of Windows. It would get zero from users who opted to use illegal copies or older versions of Windows. These latter possibilities are not envisioned in the essential-component model.

Charging higher prices would also have made Microsoft vulnerable to competitive challenge. If many older versions of Windows were running on new computers, a competitor could ultimately offer consumers an operating system that was better than what they were using but cost less than Microsoft's newer operating systems.[15]

In summary, Microsoft has made enormous profits through skillful exploitation of bandwagon effects. It became the world's most valuable firm, in terms of market value. With regard to pricing, it made these remarkable achievements by not being too greedy to earn short-run profits.

11.7 Recent Applications Software

Applications software has been the primary source of bandwagon effects for computers and operating systems, but historically it was not subject to substantial bandwagon effects itself. Users could choose their applications software without much regard for the choices that other users made.

This situation has changed dramatically with the growth of the Internet (discussed in chapter 13). It is now commonplace for users to exchange files generated by applications programs. Consequently, a real advantage exists to using the same applications programs as other users. Users who employ the same applications programs enjoy bandwagon benefits.

Among software suppliers, Microsoft has been the primary beneficiary of these bandwagon effects. It has the leading word processor (Word), the leading spreadsheet (Excel), and the leading database program (Access). These programs are generally sold as packages ("office suites"). In 1999, Microsoft had an 83 percent share of the market for office suites.[16] As a result of bandwagon effects, competitors in the future will find it harder and harder to dislodge Microsoft from its dominant position in applications software.

11.8   Linux

In 1991, Linus Torvalds put his version of Unix on the Web. He named it Linux, after himself. He invited users to post improvements to Linux on his Web site. Torvalds has remained the arbiter of which contributions become part of the official Linux. Many users have responded with contributions that have been accepted. As a result, Linux has been vastly expanded and improved.

Linux is used primarily for network servers that run Internet applications. It has become a serious competitor to Microsoft in that market. The Linux market share in 1998 was approximately 25 percent of the market share of Windows NT, Microsoft's network server product.[17] Windows operating systems are generally used for LAN file servers, which must be compatible with other Windows computers on the network. It follows that the Linux share of *other* network servers (in particular, those used in conjunction with Internet applications) must have been substantially greater than 25 percent. The popularity of Linux is largely attributable to its operating stability, resulting from many years of constructive user contributions. Linux, unlike Microsoft's network products, has the reputation of rarely crashing.

Linux has been able to make the inroads that it has because network servers are not subject to substantial bandwagon effects. Network servers do not generally run applications software. Those who use Linux as a network server are not significantly disadvantaged because far less applications software has been written for Linux than for Windows.

Linux could conceivably challenge Microsoft for the PC market other than network servers, but users of Linux cannot enjoy the bandwagon benefits that users of Windows enjoy. Some ISVs, most notably Corel, have adapted their programs to run on Linux. Not surprisingly,

Microsoft has not written versions of Word, Excel, or Access that run on Linux. Since the Microsoft applications programs have become industry standards, it will be difficult for Linux to make much progress in displacing Windows for PCs other than network servers.

11.9 Java

Java is a computer language for writing applications programs. It was developed by Sun Microsystems and released in May 1995.[18]

Java has become the industry standard for Internet applications. It has the great advantage of being able to run on multiple operating systems, including Microsoft Windows, Unix, and Apple. Programs written in Java can therefore be used by the great variety of computers and operating systems that access the Internet.

In bandwagon terms, Java has the advantage of interlinking operating systems. That is, users of multiple operating systems enjoy the full bandwagon benefits from programs written in Java. This interlinking has contributed significantly to the growth of the Internet.

If applications programs were primarily written in Java, both Microsoft and Intel would lose much of their market power. It would no longer be necessary to purchase products from these two companies in order to enjoy the bandwagon benefits associated with availability of applications software. Users could enjoy the same bandwagon benefits by using any microprocessor and any operating system that ran Java.

The U.S. Department of Justice (DOJ) and nineteen state attorneys general alleged that Microsoft engaged in exclusionary practices in the market for Internet browsers, largely for the purpose of avoiding the above outcome. Discussion of those practices is outside the scope of this book. Interested readers are referred to Fisher and Schmalensee's testimonies, which constitute a high-level debate of the issues.

We do note, however, that Microsoft is itself the major producer of applications software. It obviously has no incentive to write its own applications programs in Java and thereby destroy much of its market power in operating systems. By declining to write applications programs in Java, Microsoft can prevent operating systems from being interlinked with respect to those programs. Since Word, Excel, and Access are the industry standards and benefit from their own substantial bandwagon effects, the potential interlinking of operating systems through Java is severely limited. It follows that Microsoft's declining to write applications programs in Java may well have sufficed to meet the competitive challenge of Java. Microsoft probably did not need to engage in any allegedly exclusionary practices in the Internet browser market.

The DOJ proposed that Microsoft's operating system and applications businesses be split into separate companies. We do not purport to evaluate the costs and benefits of that proposal. We do note, however, that under this arrangement, the applications business would no longer have any incentive to protect the operating system business. Instead, its goals would be to earn short-run profits, while maintaining (or possibly even enhancing) its position as bandwagon leader in applications markets.

11.10   The Role of Misjudgments

In 1980, the conventional wisdom was that one could not make big bucks by producing semiconductors or writing software. The most successful computer firms—including IBM, the most profitable by far—produced computer systems. In contrast, profits in the semiconductor industry were limited by intense competition. Software was subject to illegal copying and was too customized to allow substantial profits to be made from any single program.

A modern Rip Van Winkle, who fell asleep in 1981 and awoke in 2001, would be astounded at the structure of the computer industry. He would have found that the two most successful firms in the computer industry were a software firm (Microsoft) and a semiconductor firm (Intel). How can that be?

The answer is that it could not be—if all firms had acted rationally in the past. On the contrary, the current industry structure is a low-probability outcome that could only have come about through spectacular misjudgments.

The far more likely outcome, a priori, is that the manufacturers of computer systems would use sufficient proprietary technology to remain in control. By playing one supplier of semiconductors off against the others, they could severely limit the profits of that sector. They would write their own systems software, including the operating system.

Obviously, this "expected" result did not occur. Instead, IBM, after some initial success, lost out to the clones. This outcome is an anomaly, engendered by IBM's early misjudgment in underestimating the potential of PCs and later having to play a desperate game of catch-up. That misjudgment has shaped the entire PC industry.

Schmalensee, in his testimony for Microsoft, cites Apple's blunders. To be sure, Apple did make some serious misjudgments. Nevertheless, Apple may have been harmed more by IBM's misjudgments than by any blunder on its own part. IBM earned large short-term profits before losing out to the clones. Apple was substantially harmed, in both the short term and long term, by the proliferation of low-priced clones.

The major beneficiaries of IBM's misjudgments were Microsoft and Intel. They could sell their products to an ever-growing market of low-priced PCs. At the same time, their products were much harder to clone.

Consumers also greatly benefited from the proliferation of low-priced clones. Indeed, consumers may be far better off than if IBM had gotten its act together earlier. In most markets, consumers benefit from the actions of the "invisible hand" that directs competitive firms that are acting rationally. In this case, consumers benefited from the fumbling hand.

11.11   Lessons from Case Study

The history of PCs illustrates the tendency of bandwagon markets without interlinking to gravitate toward a single supplier. The bandwagon leaders have been Intel in the production of microprocessors and Microsoft in the production of operating systems. These firms have had a great competitive advantage over their rivals, because they can offer their customers bandwagon benefits from a huge user set. They have skillfully exploited bandwagon effects to maintain their dominant market shares for over fifteen years.

The history also shows that smaller firms can survive by serving niche markets, based on communities of interest among their users. In particular, Apple has survived largely by serving users with special interests—especially those in educational institutions. For such users, the applications software written for Apple is adequate (in some cases, superior), and they often enjoy better user support than do users of computers that run Microsoft Windows.

The history of Microsoft is the obverse of the early history of telephone. The latter illustrated the costs of being too greedy for profits during the start-up phase of a bandwagon product. Microsoft's success illustrates the great potential rewards of *not* being too greedy.

The history of PCs also illustrates the unforgiving nature of bandwagon markets. A supplier who makes misjudgments during the critical start-up phase may be seriously harmed (e.g., by falling behind in the bandwagon race) and gets no second chance. Such misjudgments can have enduring consequences on industry structure. Indeed, the whole structure of the PC industry was largely determined by early misjudgments of IBM and Apple.

The histories of IBM and Apple illustrate the adverse consequences of too little or too much vertical integration, respectively. IBM vertically integrated hardly at all. It may have had no choice, because it was so late in entering the PC market. In any event, because the IBM PC had very little proprietary hardware and software, it became interlinked with its clones. The clones ultimately overwhelmed IBM, because they offered customers a low-cost way to enjoy the full bandwagon benefits of IBM-compatible PCs. At the other extreme, Apple internally produced almost all the components of its computer systems. This excessive vertical integration contributed substantially to Apple's loss of market leadership. Apple could have saved money and offered customers greater flexibility by relying more (though not wholly) on independent producers of components, such as keyboards, disk drives, and modems.

12
Television

The year is 1945. World War II is winding down, and people are beginning to think beyond the war. The returning GIs will soon have to find jobs in the civilian economy, and the huge wartime industrial effort will be turned to peaceful applications. In this year, the FCC is resuming the process it began before the war of setting policies for a new service—television—that will substantially change life in America and across the globe.

12.1 The Emergence of Television

The period at the end of World War II was one of optimism. No one at that time could be certain of the success of television, but it offered the potential for enormous profits on risk capital. Before any such profits could be realized, however, a difficult start-up problem had to be solved.

Three components were necessary for the start-up of television. Programming had to be produced, it had to be broadcast, and viewers had to have television sets to receive it. None of the three components—programming, broadcasting, or sets—had any significant value without the other two. The metaphor of the three-step parlay, which we used to describe the start-up problem for CD players, is perhaps unseemly where governmental decision making is involved. Let us therefore say that the start-up of television was a stool that needed three legs to avoid collapsing.

There was also the problem of establishing a technical standard. With a single standard, each television set would be able to receive all broadcasts, and viewers could thereby enjoy the full bandwagon benefits. With multiple standards, different sets would have been required to receive different broadcasts. Consequently, no viewer would have been able to enjoy the full bandwagon benefits without purchasing multiple sets.

Solving the start-up problem for television would have been extremely difficult had the producers of the three components acted independently. In reality, the start-up problem for television was solved through extensive government intervention. National governments across the globe have generally assumed responsibility for the allocation and assignment of electromagnetic spectrum within their borders. The FCC in the United States was involved in television from the start by allocating spectrum for television and then assigning it to individual broadcasters.

12.1.1   Technical Standard

Technical standards and spectrum allocation/assignments are intertwined. In the case of television, the technical standard determines how much spectrum each broadcaster needs in order to generate a usable signal. A related consideration is the power at which various stations are allowed to broadcast. With higher power, a station can reach a wider audience. But increased power increases interference with other broadcasters; so fewer channels can be assigned in any geographic area. The technical standard, together with the allowed power, defines limits on the geographic spacing of stations broadcasting on the same channel.

For these reasons, efficient spectrum allocation requires that the spectrum-management authority (usually an agency of the national government) first determine which technical standard or standards would be best for the intended use. Then, spectrum can then be allocated and assigned, consistent with that standard or those standards.

12.1.1.1   Standard-Setting Process for Television   In 1939, NBC began television broadcasting from its experimental station W2XBS in New York.[1] The FCC ordered the station to stop broadcasting until the FCC had time to develop a technical standard for television.

The following year, the Radio Manufacturers' Association (RMA) formed the National Television Standards Committee (NTSC). The NTSC was commissioned to develop recommendations for technical standards for television. Nine months later, it recommended the "NTSC standard" to the FCC. That standard was a compromise between standards proposed by RCA (NBC's parent) and Philco. One month later, the FCC adopted the NTSC standard.

This process of standard adoption was extremely rapid. It contrasts sharply with the lengthy process for determining the technical standards for digital television half a century later. The rapid adoption of the NTSC standard was largely attributable to the unimportance of proprietary technologies. All the major manufacturers were capable of making sets that conformed to the NTSC standard.

12.1.1.2 Mandating the NTSC Standard   Having determined that the NTSC standard was the best practical choice for television, the FCC mandated that television broadcasters use the NTSC standard. Mandating the standard is not, however, a necessary part of this process. The FCC could alternatively have done the following:

• optimized spectrum allocation, assuming the NTSC standard would be deployed;

• established appropriate standards for radio interference, assuming that broadcasters used the NTSC standard;

• then let broadcasters use any technical standard they desired, subject to the interference standards.

The general advantages and disadvantages of mandating a technical standard were discussed in section 4.6. The principal advantage is to maximize bandwagon benefits and thereby to facilitate the solution of the start-up problem. In this case, after the FCC mandated the NTSC standard, broadcasters knew for certain which type of equipment to purchase and manufacturers knew which kind of sets to produce. An outcome in which all viewers could enjoy full bandwagon benefits was ensured.

Governmental standard setting often has the drawback of requiring long procedural delays. In this case, however, delays were not a problem.

The NTSC standard was developed and adopted very rapidly. In any event, the United States entered World War II seven months after the standard was approved. The development of television was then delayed until the end of the war.

Even apart from this particular case, the procedural delays in setting mandatory technical standards are often relatively unimportant for spectrum-based services. The government needs to determine the likely technical standard in any event in order to allocate and assign spectrum efficiently. It may then be possible to mandate that standard without significant additional delays.

Another potential disadvantage of mandating a technical standard is that the governmental decision maker may choose the wrong standard. In this case, the FCC had already chosen to optimize allocation/assignments, assuming the NTSC standard. If the NTSC standard were the wrong one, the allocation/assignments might have been far from optimal. Nevertheless, under these circumstances, broadcasters and set manufacturers could conceivably limit the damage by adopting the right standard.

The danger of a flexible approach to standard setting is that market participants may generate economic waste by pushing their own proprietary standards. Users would then lose bandwagon benefits from interlinking. The loss of bandwagon benefits could conceivably prevent the start-up problem from being solved.

In this particular case, the adoption of the NTSC standard, which was a consensus of the major manufacturers, was probably inevitable. If the FCC had played no role in setting the standard, the industry would probably have agreed to the NTSC standard on its own.

12.1.1.3 Mandating Technical Standards for Other Spectrum-Based Services   The case for mandating the technical standard does not apply uniformly to all spectrum-based services. In particular, bandwagon effects have much less importance for mobile telephone service. Most of the benefits of mobile service derive from local calls to and from wireline subscribers.[2] These benefits are ensured if each mobile telephone provider uses a single technical standard throughout its local calling area. A mobile supplier with national or international coverage can addition-

ally offer the benefits of roaming throughout its entire serving area. External bandwagon effects that depend on the number of mobile subscribers are therefore limited.[3] Thus, what is usually the primary benefit of mandating a technical standard is largely absent. For this reason (among others), the FCC has now adopted a flexible approach to technical standards for mobile telephony. Alternative technical standards therefore fight it out in the market.

12.1.2   Television Station Assignments

In 1945, the FCC resumed its policymaking with regard to television. It set aside spectrum for channels 2 to 13 in the VHF frequency range. According to the FCC plan, only a subset of these channels could be used in any geographic market. More channels were set aside in large markets than in small markets. Even so, a large number of channels were set aside in small markets.

The FCC then began the process of awarding licenses to broadcast on specific channels in specific areas. Many of the most valuable licenses were awarded outright, without any procedure for evaluating alternatives. By 1948, it had become apparent that the licenses were valuable properties and that the FCC process did not even meet minimal standards of due process. At that time, 123 licenses had been awarded (though 15 of them never went into operation). There were over 300 pending applications. On September 20, 1948, the FCC put a freeze on further station assignments. After four years of deliberations, the FCC lifted the freeze and set aside spectrum for channels 14 to 83 in the UHF frequency range.[4]

In the case of multiple applications for the same station assignment, the FCC awarded licenses on the basis of "comparative hearings." Under this process, each competing applicant argued why the public interest would best be served if he or she were awarded the license. The FCC then decided on the basis of purely subjective standards which party had the best argument. That party was then awarded the license.

Needless to say, such a process is highly susceptible to political influence and corruption.[5] It also involves regulatory procedures that may last for years and delay the service's reaching the market. It generates economic waste by encouraging applicants to incur large costs to construct filings that they believe will be effective. For these reasons (among others), comparative hearings are rarely used any more to assign spectrum.

12.1.3   The Start-Up Problem

Although the FCC process for awarding licenses has been justly criticized, it did go a long way toward solving the start-up problem. The licenses had a "use it or lose it" proviso. Broadcasters were awarded valuable spectrum property for free. To retain their rights to that property, however, they had to broadcast television programming— irrespective of whether anyone wanted to watch it or whether the population had sets with which to view it. The "use it or lose it" proviso ensured that one of the three legs for solving the start-up problem was in place.

The second leg, programming, was put in place through vertical integration. The FCC rules allowed television networks to own VHF stations in up to five metropolitan areas. The major television networks, CBS and NBC, acquired VHF stations in the largest metropolitan areas. They then negotiated affiliation agreements with stations in smaller metropolitan areas. As a result of ownership and affiliation agreements, the networks could make investments in programming with the assurance that the programming would be aired (though not necessarily watched).

A second sort of vertical integration also helped establish the second leg. RCA, the parent of NBC, was vertically integrated into the manufacture of television sets. By broadcasting programming, RCA stimulated demand for the television sets it manufactured.[6]

The third leg was put in place through competitive market forces. Programming that people wanted to watch (e.g., *The Howdy Doody Show* and *Kukla, Fran and Ollie*) was being broadcast. Strong demand for television sets was created. Competitive market forces are fully adequate to deal with this kind of problem. There was no start-up problem from the perspective of set manufacturers. The demand was already there. They needed only to produce sets (of sufficiently high quality at sufficiently low prices) to satisfy that demand.

This competitive market response is analogous to the market response by which videocassette rental stores proliferated thirty years later. In general, once demand is in place, competitive firms waste no time in meeting that demand. No governmental intervention or vertical integration is required.

Thus, the start-up problem for television was solved through a combination of government intervention, vertical integration, and competitive market forces. The overall result, at least in terms of solving the start-up problem, was an unqualified success.

12.2 Color Television

The year is 1949. It has only been four years since the FCC set aside the VHF spectrum for television. Yet, it is a different world. The United States and the Soviet Union have emerged as the dominant world powers, and the Cold War has begun. There was an unexpected period of inflation after the war, but the economy is prosperous. Harry Truman is serving his first year as president, after his unexpected victory over Thomas Dewey. On the social front, the United States has entered a period of "normalcy," and the Baby Boom is underway.

In this year, the FCC has begun developing policies for color television.

12.2.1 Technical Standard

The first order of business was to set a technical standard. CBS and NBC proposed standards based on very different technologies. Compatibility was a key issue in choosing between these two standards.

The NBC standard was downward-compatible. That is, existing black-and-white televisions could receive color signals in the NBC format, though the resulting picture was, of course, black and white.[7] The CBS standard, on the other hand, was not downward compatible. After a year of deliberation, the FCC chose the CBS standard. An important factor in this decision was that the NBC prototype was still experiencing technical problems. Shapiro and Varian (p. 215) quote David Sarnoff, "The monkeys were green, the bananas were blue, and everyone had a good laugh."

Color television then got off to a very bad start. CBS began broadcasting in color several hours per week from its New York station. Unfortunately, viewers with black-and-white television sets could not watch CBS at all during this period. Besen and Johnson quote one observer as saying, "Any black-and-white receiver in the New York area which happened to be tuned to Channel 2 produced either sixteen little black-and-white pictures moving rapidly upward in unison or a batch of hash depending on the particular model of the receiver." CBS lost all revenues attributable to the great majority of viewers during the period it broadcast in color. Furthermore, many viewers probably did not immediately switch back to CBS when it resumed black-and-white broadcasting.

It goes almost without saying that these initiatives by CBS were doomed to failure. The episode bears resemblance to the introduction of the Picturephone twenty years later—the introduction of a bandwagon service with no advance consideration of the start-up problem. Indeed, one must wonder what CBS was thinking of when they embarked on this misadventure. Obviously, only a small fraction of the viewing audience could be expected to buy expensive color television sets, given that color programming was available only for several hours per week on one network. In light of this virtually certain response, it made no sense for CBS to forego revenues from the great majority of viewers in order to broadcast in color. The inevitable outcome was that CBS would eventually tire of bleeding money and abort the whole venture. One must also wonder what the FCC could have been thinking of when it went along with this fiasco. A likely explanation is that the start-up problem for black-and-white television went so smoothly that no one focused on how difficult it might be for color television.

In any event, the Korean War intervened. The National Production Authority issued an order to stop production of color television receivers. This decision is attributed by some to Sarnoff's relationship with Secretary of Defense Wilson. In any event, CBS was then, for all practical purposes, forced to discontinue color broadcasting and thereby to stop inflicting injury on itself.

The story of color television picks up again after the Korean War. In July 1953, a second NTSC approved a color television technical standard that was compatible with black-and-white television. The technical problems that plagued the RCA prototype in 1950 had largely been solved. The new standard embodied contributions from Philco, Hazeltine, Sylvania, General Electric, and Motorola, as well as RCA. The FCC approved that standard in December 1953.[8] For some years thereafter, NBC voluntarily shared its technology with other manufacturers.[9]

A compatible standard was probably essential for solving the start-up problem. Even with such a standard, however, the start-up problem for color television, like that for original (black-and-white) television, had three components. Programming had to be produced in color, it had to be broadcast, and viewers had to have color television sets. All three of these components had to be present in order for color television to succeed. Again, the stool needed three legs to avoid collapse.

12.2.2 Solving the Start-Up Problem

The first step in solving the start-up problem was for television stations to deploy the technology that allowed them to broadcast in color. NBC and CBS stations deployed the technology very rapidly. Most of them deployed it in 1954, and most of the remainder deployed it in 1955. ABC and independent stations, however, deployed the technology much more slowly.[10]

Thus, the broadcasting leg of the stool was constructed quite early. CBS and NBC were the dominant networks at the time; ABC was much weaker. Color broadcasting by CBS and NBC certainly sufficed to enable the start-up of color television, once the other two legs of the stool were constructed.

Table 12.1 shows the amount of programming broadcast in color by each of the three networks. It is clear from the table that NBC was driving the process—no doubt largely because of its manufacturing interests. Both NBC and CBS broadcast about one hour per week in color in 1954. Thereafter, NBC rapidly expanded its color broadcasting to approximately seventy-seven hours per week in 1965. CBS, however, stood pat and even discontinued color broadcasting for a few years. ABC did not even start color broadcasting until 1962.

Table 12.1
Yearly Hours of Network Color Broadcasts

Year	NBC	CBS	ABC
1954	68	46	0
1955	216	46	0
1956	486	74	0
1957	647	53	0
1958	668	24	0
1959	725	10	0
1960	1,035	5	0
1961	1,650	0	0
1962	1,910	0	0
1963	2,150	4.5	120
1964	2,135	4.0	200
1965	4,000*	800	600

* Estimated. (NBC Color Information Department as cited in *Advertising Age*, November 29, 1965, p. 109.)
Source: Excerpted from Ducey and Fratrik, Table 2, p. 75.

Thus, the programming leg of the stool was in place, but it was a little wobbly. Early adopters of color television had a good selection of NBC programming to view in color, but there was little color programming other than NBC's.

The third leg of the stool was the purchase of color television sets by consumers. That leg was constructed quite slowly. Even in 1965, well under 10 percent of households had color television sets. Then, sales of color television sets took off. Ten years later, over 60 percent of households had color television sets.

After the sales of color television sets took off, the supply of color programming *by all broadcasters* also increased dramatically. That start-up problem was then solved, but the solution came a decade after color broadcasting had started.

12.2.3 Incentives
Let us now examine the incentives that led to this slow adoption of color television. The easiest question is, Why did consumers delay so long before buying color television sets? The answer is that the price was too

high. During the 1960s, the price of color television sets was three to five times that of black-and-white television sets.[11] The price difference was even greater in the 1950s. In 1954, the price was $1,000—equivalent to over $4,000 in current dollars.[12] Consumers were unwilling to pay that much to watch color television on NBC.

What about the incentives of programmers? It seems strange that after broadcasters spent so much to gear up to transmit color broadcasting, programmers were so slow to adopt it. In this regard, we note that the incremental costs of producing color programming are not exceptionally large. Nor are they insignificant. It does cost significantly more to maintain production values in color programming.

These significant costs had to be weighed against the trivial fraction of households that had color television sets. On balance, there may have been little incentive to expand production of color programming. Most programmers other than NBC certainly saw it that way.

NBC's incentives were, however, very different than those of other programmers. At the time, NBC was owned by RCA and therefore vertically integrated into television set manufacturing. The proliferation of color television was very profitable for NBC's parent. In this regard, we note that sales of a million color television sets at $1,000 each makes little impact on the television viewing audience. It does, however, yield $1 billion in revenues for television manufacturers. This arithmetic makes plain why NBC was the driving force in the adoption of color television. The profits from television sales could easily outweigh the moderate costs of producing color programming. Even the slow pace of sales of color television sets before 1965 sufficed to drive this process.

We note that this strategy was profitable only because the color television technology was downward-compatible. To broadcast in color, NBC had to incur a moderate increase in programming costs. It did not, however, have to forego revenues from the great majority of its viewing audience that had black-and-white television sets. Consequently, color television could be profitable for RCA-NBC, even though it was adopted slowly.

Where complementary bandwagon effects are present, the production of the complementary products generates benefits that are external to the producers of those products. As discussed at the beginning of part II, vertical integration is one way to internalize these externalities. That is precisely what happened here.

The vertical integration was, however, only partial. NBC did not monopolize television broadcasting. On the contrary, CBS was the most popular network. Also, RCA did not monopolize television set manufacturing. Nevertheless, this degree of vertical integration sufficed to start up color television.

Quite possibly, color television would have started up more quickly if there had been more vertical integration between programmers and television set manufacturers. Adoption would undoubtedly have been more rapid if CBS, as well as NBC, rapidly expanded its production of color programming. As a result, profits from manufacturing color television sets could have increased, and consumers would have derived more benefit from the purchase of color television sets.

It seems unlikely, however, that demand for color television could have taken off much before 1965. Most consumers would probably have been unwilling to pay the high prices of color television sets in the 1950s and early 1960s, no matter how much color programming was available. Rapid adoption had to wait until technology drove down the costs.

12.3   High-Definition Television

The year is 1987. Ronald Reagan is nearing the end of his second term as president of the United States. There has been a prosperous, non-inflationary economy for several years, and the recession of 1990 has not yet arrived.

Since 1954, the Japanese economy has made an astonishing recovery. The words "made in Japan," which used to denote cheap shoddy construction, have come to be a guarantor of high product quality. The United States now has a huge international trade deficit, largely with respect to Japan. The success of Japanese companies, often at the expense of U.S. competitors, has spawned a raft of articles that admiringly describe Japanese-style management.

The Japanese now dominate the consumer electronics industry. The only remaining U.S. television manufacturer is Zenith, which makes most of its televisions in Mexico. RCA has divested NBC and this year is being acquired by the French firm Thomson.

Television has become the dominant form of entertainment in America. Television viewing averages about seven hours per day. In addition to broadcasting, cable television has now become a major factor in the market. Approximately 50 percent of households subscribe to cable.[13] Fox has initiated its operations as the fourth television network. The market shares of the big three television networks have begun a long, steady decline, losing ground to cable programming, as well as to Fox (and subsequently, other networks, as well).

By this time, video games (often using television sets as monitors) and PCs have taken off. The Internet, however, is in a relatively early stage of its development. Convergence of these technologies is on its way, but as of yet, they are still largely separate.

It was in this year that the FCC began to develop policies with regard to "high-definition television" (HDTV). HDTV offered the promise of improved quality for the picture, as well as the sound.[14] It posed yet another start-up problem for television.

In order to understand the FCC proceeding, we need to recognize the wide range of parties to the proceeding and their diverse economic interests:

Television set manufacturers were the largest potential beneficiaries of this process. They stood to reap enormous profits if the American public changed out their old television sets for newer sets with advanced capabilities. The manufacturers did, however, have diverse interests with respect to the choice of technical standard. Several of them had competing proprietary standards.

Viewers were also potential beneficiaries of this process. If the process were successful, they would have the *option* of purchasing more expensive televisions to get improved quality of picture and sound. Surely, the FCC would not repeat its mistake of 1950 and create an outcome in which viewers were unable to continue receiving television programming with their old television sets.

Broadcasters and television networks, considered as a whole, stood to gain relatively little from the adoption of these new technologies. Their revenues depended on the size of the viewing audience. They could not realistically expect HDTV to increase television viewing much above the preexisting level of seven hours per day. There are only so many hours in a day.[15]

Although HDTV may have little effect on aggregate television viewing, it definitely has the potential to affect viewing of individual stations. The choice of viewing one station versus another would obviously be affected if one station broadcast in HDTV, while the other broadcast in the NTSC standard.

The problem, from the perspective of broadcasters and networks, was that they could not hold back the adoption of the new technologies. The new technologies would at some time be adopted by cable television companies, by direct broadcast satellites (DBS), and for videocassettes. Broadcasters and television networks would then be at a serious competitive disadvantage if they could not use the new technologies themselves. For this reason (among others), broadcasters and television networks favored the FCC's opening of the inquiry into HDTV.

The proceeding became timely, because the FCC was considering allocating some of the upper end of the UHF spectrum to uses other than television. The broadcasters and television networks argued that the spectrum was needed for HDTV.

Cable television companies would have been best off if the whole regulatory process failed. If it did, the cable companies' competitors, the broadcasters and television networks, would have been less able to use the advanced technologies. The competitors would not have any additional spectrum available, and the start-up problem would have been more difficult in the absence of an agreed-upon technical standard.

In contrast, cable television companies did not need the FCC to determine a technical standard for use by cable. The board members of the NCTA, who did not have sizable financial interests in competing proprietary technologies, would probably have been able to agree on a single technical standard that was best for cable (but perhaps less satisfactory for broadcasting). The FCC was unlikely to adopt a better standard for cable than the cable industry could decide for itself.

In addition, cable companies would have been unambiguously worse off if broadcasters began to use the new technologies:

• If cable companies did not then adopt the new technologies themselves, cable programming would been at a competitive disadvantage relative to over-the-air programming, which many viewers could obtain without cable.

• If cable companies did adopt the new technologies, they would have incurred additional cost. After doing so, demand for cable service would probably not have been significantly greater than the status quo ante, prior to broadcasters' using the new technologies.

• Additional cable capacity would be required for a cable company to carry the new signals, as well as the old signals, of local broadcast stations. Yet, if a cable company did not do so, its offerings would be less attractive (relative to the status quo ante) to one group of viewers or the other—that is, those who had television sets that received the new signals or those who did not. Furthermore, broadcasters were certain to argue before the FCC that cable companies should be *required* to carry both signals. The cable industry could not be certain of prevailing in its resistance to such a requirement.

Computer manufacturers originally opposed the introduction of HDTV, because they feared competition in computer graphics.[16] After the FCC had decided upon a digital standard, the goal of the computer industry was to ensure that the new technical standard for television was compatible with the technical standards used by computer monitors. If it were, monitors could (without substantial additional cost) double as television sets and provide more value to computer users. Computer manufacturers could hope thereby to participate in the potential bonanza in which consumers changed out their old televisions for models that embodied the new technologies.

The outcome of this confluence of diverse economic interests and strong political forces converging on Washington was a regulatory process destined to become a virtual three-ring circus, with the FCC serving as ringmaster. It was not the greatest show on Earth, but it was a spectacle that will long be remembered by those involved in communications public policy. No one could be sure of the outcome of this process. All that was certain is that it would last a long time.

Indeed, the process did last a long time. The FCC appointed a committee to research the issue and make recommendations. The committee then appointed several subcommittees to research specific areas. At each level, it was necessary to let all interested parties muster their arguments and have their say. It was ten years before the FCC approved a technical standard.

12.3.1 Hi-Vision

The original HDTV technology was Hi-Vision. It was developed by the Japanese state broadcaster Nippon Hoso Kyokai (NHK), in collaboration with the major Japanese electronics manufacturers. Hi-Vision's picture has approximately four times the resolution of NTSC's and has far superior sound quality. In addition, it supports a screen aspect ratio of 16:9, compared to NTSC's 4:3. The higher aspect ratio allows movies to be shown in their original wide-screen format.

These product advantages are quite considerable. Unfortunately, however, Hi-Vision also had some important disadvantages:

Hi-Vision requires a lot of bandwidth. A television picture embodies a set of information, namely, the colors of each of numerous points on the screen. The picture is regenerated fifty to sixty times per second. That regeneration requires that new information be continually provided. The new information can be transmitted either over the air (broadcasting) or via cable.

The more information that is transmitted (per second), the higher must be the "bandwidth" of the transmission medium. Higher bandwidth for broadcast transmission means the use of additional spectrum. Use of spectrum, in turn, incurs opportunity costs because the spectrum cannot be used for other valuable applications, such as mobile telephony. Higher bandwidth also leads to higher costs if the signal is transmitted by cable. If the programming has higher bandwidth, fewer channels can be transmitted on any given cable.

The bandwidth required to transmit television signals can be substantially reduced through video compression techniques. One such technique is to transmit only changes in the picture. The television set must then have the intelligence to insert the changes, while regenerating the part of the picture that did not change. Other compression techniques can further reduce the bandwidth required.

Without video compression, Hi-Vision would require approximately four times as much bandwidth as the NTSC standard in order to generate a picture with four times the resolution. This multiplier can be substantially reduced through video compression. Indeed, by using the Multiple Subnyquist Sampling Encoding (MUSE) system, Hi-Vision can be transmitted using the same bandwidth as the NTSC. This video compression does, however, somewhat reduce the picture quality, relative to uncompressed Hi-Vision.

Hi-Vision is not downward-compatible. Existing NTSC television sets cannot receive Hi-Vision signals. Thus, Hi-Vision is analogous to CBS's technology for color television. As we have seen, incompatibility makes the start-up problem much more difficult. In particular, the CBS experience demonstrated the folly of trying to use the spectrum that is currently used for the old technology. NHK dealt with this problem in Japan by using DBS to transmit HDTV. That solution is workable, but it is quite costly. Costly satellite capacity and scarce spectrum are tied up during the lengthy period in which consumers switch over to HDTV sets. During the start-up period, the satellite capacity and spectrum generate little (current) economic value.

Hi-Vision is an analog standard. This is not a disadvantage relative to the NTSC, which is also analog. Nevertheless, analog technology is giving way to digital throughout the entire high-technology world. Virtually any analog technology is likely to be displaced by digital in the not-too-distant future.

Hi-Vision was expensive. In 1990, the price of a HDTV was $43,000. This price dropped to a little over $6,000 by 1993.[17] Further price reductions were certain, as the technology developed, but the price would have had to decline *considerably* below $6,000 if the technology were to be widely adopted. It is always difficult to predict in advance how rapidly such price reductions will occur.

Hi-Vision was invented in a foreign country. This "disadvantage" is, perhaps important enough to have been listed first. Foreign products can, of course, provide fully as much value to consumers as can domestic products. Nevertheless, in setting technical standards, national governments often pursue protectionist objectives to benefit domestic industry. They do not generally announce that protectionism is their goal. Nevertheless, a cynic who believed that protectionism was the driving force worldwide in television standard setting would not have been surprised by any of the actual events. The Japanese were the technological leaders and quickly adopted their own technology as the standard. European governments, however, were impressed by the technical merits of a standard developed by European firms. The U.S. process led to the adoption of a system architecture that was developed largely by U.S. interests (though the technology MPEG-2 was based on an international standard).

12.3.2 Europe

European governments rejected Hi-Vision, citing its incompatibility with existing television sets.[18] European electronics firms, primarily Thomson and Philips, then developed the downward-compatible Multiplexed Analog Components (MAC) system for HDTV.

European governments had previously rejected the NTSC standard for color television. Instead, they adopted Phased Alternate Line (PAL) and SECAM.[19] These standards were adopted thirteen years after the FCC adopted NTSC. Because the existing European standards differed from NTSC, a separate European technical standard was required if HDTV was to be downward compatible.

Like (uncompressed) Hi-Vision, MAC required more bandwidth than did existing television technology. Indeed, no version of MAC was ever developed that could be transmitted in the bandwidth assigned to broadcasters. DBS was the intended transmission medium.

This plan seemed workable (albeit costly) in the European context. Programmers could use DBS and reach the wide audience that had television sets in the old technology. In 1988, European governments committed to using MAC for national DBS services. The plan was for viewers gradually to switch to HDTV as the prices of MAC television sets came down.

The plan was elegant, but even elegant plans often go awry in the high-technology world. MAC suffered a serious setback when Rupert Murdoch launched Sky Television in February 1989. It was critically important for Murdoch to get a head start on the government's British Satellite Broadcasting (BSB), and MAC equipment was not ready in time. Furthermore, even if the equipment were ready, broadcasting in MAC would have not have benefited Murdoch, because no viewers had MAC television sets. Murdoch could conceivably have struck a deal whereby manufacturers compensated him for broadcasting in MAC, but negotiating such a deal would have used up valuable time. Furthermore, the manufacturers might have used the occasion of the negotiations to bring political pressure to bear on him. Murdoch's decision to use the old technology and rush the service to market is, thus, very understandable. It also turned out to be highly successful.

By the time that BSB finally launched in April 1990, Sky already had 1.5 million subscribers and an unassailable first-mover advantage. BSB was forced to merge with Sky in November 1990, and the combined enterprise became BSkyB. Thereafter, there were no U.K. broadcasts in MAC. This development completely upset the European plans. DBS was supposed to be the domain of MAC. Instead, the largest and most successful DBS broadcaster was using the old technology. Furthermore, the U.K. government, a key member of the MAC coalition, no longer had any reason to support MAC, particularly since none of the major MAC manufacturers were U.K. firms.

From then on, MAC began to unravel. It was abandoned in 1993. The whole effort turned out to be a huge waste of resources.

12.3.3 Japan

Not surprisingly, relatively few Hi-Vision television sets were sold in Japan at the high prices of the early 1990s. By 1993, the installed base was only 10,000 sets.

Seeking a technology that would win consumer acceptance more rapidly, the Japanese developed the downward-compatible system Enhanced Definition Television (EDTV). The original EDTV used advanced technology to make incremental improvements to the NTSC standard. The screen retained the same aspect ratio as the NTSC, but the picture quality was significantly improved. By the mid-1990s, EDTV sets sold for as little as $600.

The Japanese at that time planned an orderly transition from NTSC to EDTV to EDTV-2 and finally to HDTV. EDTV-2 had the wider 16 : 9 aspect ratio and improved picture quality, but the picture quality was still not as good as HDTV's. This transition plan seems quite sensible.

Such planning was possible because of the close cooperation between the state-owned NHK and the major Japanese electronics manufacturers. This close cooperation internalized the externality between broadcasters and television set manufacturers. It played a role analogous to the vertical integration between NBC and RCA when color television was introduced in the United States.

12.3.4   United States

The FCC HDTV sweepstakes began in 1987.[20] The FCC formed an Advisory Committee on Advanced Television Service to study alternative technologies for providing HDTV. Electronics manufacturing firms were invited to enter the race by putting forth their technologies for consideration.

12.3.4.1   Compatible Standards   Since the FCC had such a disastrous experience with CBS's incompatible technology for color television, one would certainly have expected it to adopt a downward-compatible standard for HDTV. The FCC did initially specify that the standard had to be downward compatible. But it modified this position in 1988 and required only that all programs broadcast in HDTV also be made available to NTSC television sets for an interim period.

The FCC could conceivably have adopted EDTV as the technical standard. EDTV was developed in 1989, before any U.S. technologies for HDTV. By adopting that standard, the United States would have bought into the Japanese plan for gradually transiting to higher definition television. The transition to full HDTV might have taken as long or longer than the transition to color television, but viewers would enjoy considerable benefits in the meantime.

EDTV did, however, have the serious "disadvantage" of having been invented in a foreign country. This disadvantage was especially serious, because of concern about the U.S. trade deficit, particularly with respect to Japan. For this reason, the adoption of EDTV by the FCC may have been politically impossible.

A homegrown alternative to EDTV was SuperNTSC, developed by Yves Faroudja. Like EDTV, SuperNTSC offered significant improvements to NTSC at low cost. Another homegrown entry that was downward-compatible was Advanced Compatible Television (ACTV), developed by Zenith. Sarnoff, in partnership with Thomson, Philips and NBC, developed a variant of ACTV. The performance of ACTV was comparable to that of EDTV-2. If EDTV and EDTV-2 were unacceptable for protectionist reasons, one would certainly have expected (a priori) that SuperNTSC or ACTV would be favored to win the race.

All these technologies had the disadvantage of being analog systems. This advantage inheres in downward-compatible systems. The technologies allowed an easy transition to considerable improvements in picture and sound quality. They did, however, portend that a further transition to digital would be required in the future. The choice was between (1) a difficult transition to digital now, or (2) an easy transition now and a difficult transition to digital some time in the future. Since the quality improvements of EDTV and ACTV were considerable, the difficult transition to digital might have been delayed a long time.

Let us suppose (contrary to fact) that the FCC had adopted one of these compatible standards. How would the start-up problem then have been solved? The FCC could have chosen between two general approaches to this problem: the market approach and the regulatory approach.

The market approach would have been for the FCC to set a standard (or perhaps multiple standards; e.g., EDTV and EDTV-2) and let it go at that. Broadcasters would then be free to broadcast in the new standards if they chose to do so. This approach leads to the chicken-and-egg problem. Broadcasters have no incentive to broadcast in HDTV, because no one has television sets to receive the broadcasts (in HDTV). Consumers have no reason to buy HDTV television sets, because no one is broadcasting in HDTV.

The chicken-and-egg problem was solved for color television by the vertical integration of RCA and NBC. The integrated company could produce both the chicken and the egg. Now, however, NBC was an independent company, and none of the major television networks were integrated into television set production.

Quite possibly, the HDTV chicken-and-egg problem could have been solved through joint ventures between one or more television networks and manufacturers of television sets. For example, the manufacturers whose standard was chosen might have induced NBC to broadcast in HDTV. NBC would thereby gain a competitive advantage over the other networks until the latter began also to broadcast in HDTV. The arrangement could additionally allow NBC to share in the profits from sales of HDTV television sets.[21]

Pulling off this deal would obviously require some skillful negotiating. But that is precisely what top corporate leaders are supposed to be able to do to justify the large salaries that they pay themselves.

This solution relies primarily on market forces, rather than regulation. We note, however, that the start-up problem would be far more difficult (in this hypothetical scenario) if the FCC did not first set the technical standard. Both broadcasters and purchasers of television sets would then have had to bear the risk that the technology they adopted would ultimately be orphaned. (See section 4.6.)

If the FCC did not have confidence in market forces (and regulators rarely do), it could have opted for the regulatory approach. That is, it could have compelled large television stations (within a year or two) to broadcast in one of the compatible HDTV standards. This requirement would not be onerous if the standard were EDTV or SuperNTSC. The cost for a station to broadcast in SuperNTSC was only about $300,000.[22] That cost is only a small fraction of annual revenues for a large television station. In this scenario, the FCC could wait for costs to decline considerably before mandating the next transition, for example, to EDTV-2 or ACTV.

Both the regulatory and the market solutions to the start-up problem seem workable. In either case, downward-compatible technology would provide a rapid and inexpensive way to produce significant improvements in the quality of picture and sound for television.

12.3.4.2 Transition to Digital Television In reality, the FCC rejected downward-compatible technologies in favor of a digital technology. That technology requires viewers to have digital television sets; the signals cannot be received on existing analog television sets.[23] This kind of digital technology may well be the best long-term solution to HDTV. It does, however, have much higher costs, and the start-up problem is far more difficult.

According to the FCC plan, broadcasters get additional spectrum to broadcast in HDTV, while retaining their current spectrum to broadcast the same signal in the NTSC standard. By assigning additional spectrum in this way, the FCC avoids the debilitating problem of the CBS standard for color television. Television stations can broadcast in HDTV without cutting back on their broadcasts to viewers who do not have HDTV sets.

In exchange for being assigned the additional spectrum for free, television stations must agree to use that spectrum to broadcast in digital format. The stations are supposed to return the spectrum that they use for NTSC broadcasting when the transition is complete, that is, when the great majority of consumers have bought digital televisions.

This plan, at least in principle, provides a solution to the start-up problem. As with the original television licenses, broadcasters are given spectrum with a "use it or lose it" proviso. Television stations are required to broadcast in digital format, irrespective of whether anyone has digital television sets. Given that there will be digital broadcasts, manufacturers can be relied upon to produce digital television sets. The key question then is whether consumers will buy the sets at the high prices at which they will be offered. Consumers could conceivably purchase digital television sets in addition to their existing analog sets. Alternatively, they might wait until their existing sets wear out and must be replaced. Even then, however, they might regard digital televisions as too expensive.

The FCC plan can succeed in making the transition to digital television, even if that transition takes a long time. If the transition is long, however, the costs of the plan may well exceed its benefits. In particular:

• The stations' investments in HDTV equipment will generate little benefit for either viewers or the stations until the user set becomes sizable.

• The additional spectrum used for digital television (in addition to the analog spectrum, which continues to be used) will also generate little social benefit for either viewers or the stations so long as there are relatively few viewers.

Meanwhile, consumers who cannot afford digital television sets will always be worse off than if less expensive analog HDTV were available.

Some economists have been quite skeptical of the FCC's plan. Farrell and Shapiro (1992) characterize it as "gold-plating."[24] Noll asks, "Why did any nation (or, for that matter, any company) bother sinking so much effort into a technology that seems to hold so little commercial prospect?"[25] Nothing has happened so far to call these economists' views into question. Nevertheless, the FCC's plan may still be vindicated by future events.

In any event, it seems fair to say that the FCC plan was extremely risky and that fully acceptable, less-risky alternatives were available. We need to ask, therefore, why the FCC embarked on this course. The answer lies in the political constraints under which the FCC operated.

Broadcasters vigorously argued that the best use of the upper end of the UHF spectrum was for HDTV. They had great influence on the FCC, which ultimately accepted the broadcasters' view.[26] The FCC was, however, under strong political pressure to auction the spectrum for other purposes. In Congress's budget reconciliation process, auction revenues are counted as negative expenditures. Thus, each dollar of auction revenues provides one dollar more that Congress can spend and still have a balanced budget. The FCC had recently been highly successful in auctioning the Personal Communications System (PCS) spectrum. Extremely high estimates of spectrum values were being bandied about. The FCC's auctions of the A and B bands of PCS had yielded $6 billion for 60 MHz of spectrum. At that rate, the spectrum for a 6 MHz television channel was worth $600 million (on a nationwide basis). Estimates were even higher after the FCC auction of the C band PCS spectrum, but those estimates declined after widespread defaults by bidders. Jackson and Haring argued that for a variety of economic and technical reasons, the spectrum packaged as ATV station licenses was at that time worth less at auction than the PCS spectrum. In any event, the high estimates themselves, regardless of whether they turned out to be accurate, sufficed to enable additional congressional spending. There was no true-up process.

All that was required was to get the Congressional Budget Office (CBO) to sign off on the estimates, and strong pressure could have been applied to coerce CBO to do so.

In this regard, we note that although consumers may get enormous pleasure from viewing television seven hours per day, broadcasters do not charge them for doing so. Moreover, broadcasters have no practical way to charge viewers for any part of the additional value that the viewers may derive from viewing HDTV broadcasts. On the contrary, broadcasters make money primarily from advertising. Even if HDTV were highly valued by viewers, broadcasters would likely enjoy only a modest increment in advertising revenues. The amount that broadcasters could profitably bid for the spectrum is the capitalized value of this modest increment. That amount may be far lower than the value that consumers would derive from viewing HDTV broadcasting.

In contrast, higher consumer benefits from other spectrum-based services (e.g., mobile telephony) translate directly via a two-step process into higher spectrum bids by suppliers of those services:

1. The higher consumer benefits first lead to higher prices of the spectrum-based services—given that the supply of spectrum is limited.

2. The higher prices of spectrum-based services then allow suppliers of those services profitably to bid higher prices at spectrum auctions.

For this reason, broadcasters would likely lose out to other uses in a spectrum auction, even if the spectrum had more value to broadcast viewers than to consumers of other spectrum-based services. Consequently, "letting the market decide" whether broadcasting is the best use of spectrum is not a reasonable decision process. Doing so is equivalent to deciding "no" without any justification. Of course, the FCC could make a *reasoned* decision that broadcasting was not the best use of the spectrum and then announce (disingenuously) that it was "letting the market decide."

In any event, because of Congressional pressure, the FCC would have been hard-pressed to save the spectrum if it adopted a more gradual plan for HDTV; for example, by first adopting a downward-compatible technology. In that scenario, by the time the FCC got around to making the transition to digital, the best spectrum would probably already have been auctioned off. Reclaiming the spectrum for digital television at that time would cause serious dislocations and would probably be impractical.

Thus, the most prudent course of action for the FCC was probably foreclosed by political considerations. The FCC instead had to choose between two second-best alternatives: (1) The (arguably) reckless gamble of rapid adoption of digital television; or (2) Losing forever the best spectrum for digital television. The FCC decided that the first option was the lesser evil. It may well have been right. Nevertheless, one can certainly question the efficacy of a political process that narrows down the choices to these second-best alternatives.

12.3.4.3   Technical Standard   The policies discussed in the preceding section derive largely from the FCC's responsibilities for spectrum management rather than its role as a setter of technical standards. The FCC decided that digital television was the best use of the upper end of the UHF spectrum. It then implemented policies to use the spectrum for that purpose.

At the same time, however, the FCC undertook to set a specific technical standard for digital television. We now turn our attention to the setting of that standard.

The FCC did not evaluate the alternative technical standards itself. Instead, it delegated that responsibility to the Advanced Television Testing Committee (ATTC), a private committee of broadcasters, manufacturers, and programmers. Four digital standards were submitted to ATTC for consideration. General Instruments and MIT submitted two versions of Digicipher; Zenith and AT&T submitted Spectrum Compatible HDTV (SC-HDTV); and Philips, Thomson, Sarnoff, and NBC submitted Advanced Digital Television (ADTV).

ATTC declined to choose among these standards and suggested that the proponents collaborate on a single standard. The proponents did so and developed the "Grand Alliance" standard. This process of competitive firms' collaborating on a technical standard is analogous to Philips and Sony's collaboration in CD technology. The process allows the technical standard to embody valuable contributions from multiple proponents.

At that time, the technology for digital television was only a few years old. The first digital system (Digicipher) was not revealed until June 1990. In the mid-1990s, no one could really be sure what the best technical standard would be. Nevertheless, the FCC had to adopt a standard to define the obligations of the broadcasters.

Under these circumstances, a flexible standard has great advantages. Recognizing these advantages, the Grand-Alliance designed substantial flexibility into its standard. The standard allows several options for broadcasting of HDTV signals. The manufacturers supporting the standard agreed to build sets that would receive broadcasts using any of the options. Thus, the standard can evolve in several directions, depending on future technological developments.

The FCC ultimately adopted the Grand Alliance standard. That action was far less controversial than the spectrum policies described in section 12.3.4.2.[27] The process took a long time, but the result was a good technical standard (though it subsequently developed some problems in the field).

Still, it remains to be seen whether digital over-the-air television will win consumer acceptance in a reasonable period of time. The standard-setting operation was a success, but the patient may die.

12.3.5   Comparison of Governmental Decision Processes

Opinions can, of course, vary as to the relative effectiveness of the governmental decision processes. In this case, it seems reasonable to conclude that the Japanese process worked best. It developed a sensible gradual transition path to HDTV. The U.S. process provided a transition path to digital television, but the policy involved unnecessary risk. The European process to establish MAC as the industry standard failed.

The Japanese process bears resemblance to the process by which Philips and Sony coordinated the introduction of CDs. Hi-Vision involved cooperation between hardware and software suppliers. There was sharing of technology among multiple equipment suppliers to develop a single technical standard. The process for HDTV worked far bètter than the process for VCRs, in which Sony and Matsushita could not agree on a standard, and Japanese government intervention was ineffective.

The U.S. standard-setting process worked well, albeit slowly, to develop a good standard for digital television. The U.S. process, like the Japanese process, involved collaboration among hardware and software suppliers and technology sharing among manufacturers.

Apart from technical standards, political pressures regarding spectrum allocation skewed U.S. policies and led to what may be premature deployment of digital technology. Congressional pressure on the FCC to generate auction revenues, together with FCC resistance to that pressure, turned out to be wholly counter-productive. It led to sub-optimal policies for HDTV and no auction revenues. That outcome is certainly second best or worse. It may, however, be superior to Congress's preferred alternative of auctioning the spectrum for some use other than television in order to get maximal budget offsets.

The European process failed because the EU could not hold the coalition together. This has been a recurrent problem for the EU in many areas. It does not relate to standard setting, in particular.

12.4 Lessons from Case Study

The history of television illustrates the wide range of possible outcomes from governmental standard setting—from effective action to utter failure. The process works best when government emulates the best practices of standard setting in the private sector. These practices include pooling of technologies by the technological leaders and licensing agreements for other producers to use the selected technology.

Sharing of technology is a desideratum for standard setting, whether done by private interests or the government. If the technologies are not shared, the technological achievements that are not embodied in the losing standards are wasted. The waste is all the greater, because technical standards tend to persist for a long time.

Sharing of technology can have the drawback of diluting incentives to be the technological leader. That drawback is ameliorated if the technological laggards pay royalties to the technological leaders. The governmental standard-setting process should certainly not discourage the exacting of such royalties.

The history of television illustrates many of the substantial defects that inhere in government decision-making; for example, the role of political influence/corruption and the pursuit of unworthy protectionist goals. Nevertheless, in bandwagon markets, government standard setting is sometimes superior to the alternative inefficient competitive process.

13

The Internet

As an information resource, the Internet is mind-boggling. It has over 100 million hosts. A lot of these hosts make many megabytes of information available to users. Several lifetimes would be required to download all the information that is currently available for free.[1] By the time it was all downloaded, many more lifetimes would be required to download the additional information that had become available in the meantime. And this is the time required just to retrieve the information with a high-speed modem. Countless additional lifetimes would be required if the user wanted to have even the most superficial knowledge of the content of the information.

The breadth and depth of available information certainly contributes to the value of the Internet. Even more important, however, is the availability of computer tools for convenient access to that information. By using those tools, a user can quickly obtain a wealth of information on a particular narrow topic of interest.

How and why did this resource come into being? Several articles have provided answers to this question from a technological perspective.[2] We attempt here to answer the question from an economics perspective. In particular, what were the *economic* incentives that led to the development of this novel means of communication?

The Internet is extremely complex. Indeed, some writers have likened it to an organism. Like any complex entity, it can be understood only as part of the physical environment in which it evolved and now resides (lives?), that is, telecommunications and computer networks. We therefore begin our discussion of the Internet by providing some background, largely technological, on telecommunications and computers. After doing so, we are better able to conduct an economic analysis of the development of the Internet and the role of bandwagon effects.

13.1 Size and Growth of the Internet

The Internet is a huge information resource, but how large is it in economic terms? How rapidly is it growing? Let us compare the telecommunications assets (primarily switching and transmission facilities) of the Internet with those of the voice networks of the traditional networks of local telephone companies ("telcos") and long-distance carriers (LDCs) in the United States.

13.1.1 Size
The largest set of telecommunications networks is that of the telcos. In the United States, these include the Bell operating companies—that is, those owned by BellSouth, Qwest, and SBC. Verizon is a hybrid company, formed from a Bell company (Bell Atlantic) and a non-Bell company (GTE). U.S. telcos also include over one thousand smaller companies. The telco networks carry:

• most local traffic,

• some short-haul long-distance traffic,

• traffic between end users and LDCs, and

• traffic between end users and Internet service providers (ISPs).

At the end of 1998, the book value of the physical plant of U.S. telcos amounted to $320 billion.[3]

The second largest set of networks is that of the LDCs. These include those of AT&T, WorldCom, Sprint, and over one thousand smaller LDCs. These networks carry traffic between cities, apart from the short-haul traffic that is carried end-to-end by telcos. At the end of 1998, the book value of the physical plant of LDCs amounted to approximately $70 billion. This estimate is derived in table 13.1.[4]

Telcos and LDCs comprise most (but not all) of the traditional telecommunications sector.[5] Their combined assets are huge—almost $400 billion. Telcos and LDCs, which were largely integrated before the AT&T divestiture, constituted a large corporate sector for most of the twentieth century.

Table 13.1
Physical Plant of LDCs (dollar amounts in billions)

(1) 1994 Physical Plant of AT&T	$26.5
(2) Adjustment for four years' growth at 8% [= (1)*(1.08)^4]	$36.1
(3) Market Share of AT&T	51.5%
(4) Physical Plant of LDCs [= (2)/(3)]	$70.1

Sources:
(1) FCC, Statistics of Common Carriers: 1994, Table 2.7—Communications Plant of Telephone Carriers Reporting Annually to the Commission Year Ended December 31, 1994. Figure is taken from account number 210 (Total Plant) less account 2007 (Goodwill), and reflects the balance at the end of 1994.
(3) FCC's Long Distance Market Shares: Fourth Quarter 1998, March 31, 1999, Table 1.1—Interstate Switched Access Minutes.

The Internet is a relatively recent phenomenon, but it has been growing extremely rapidly. It consists primarily of ISPs and the Internet backbone. These components have now become a significant part of the telecommunications sector. At the end of 1998, the book value of the physical plant of ISPs amounted to approximately $4.3 billion. This estimate is derived in table 13.2.[6] This estimated book value is, of course, only a small fraction of the market value of ISPs. Market values additionally reflect the expected future growth of the Internet.

At the end of 1998, the physical plant of the Internet backbone amounted to about $7.8 billion. This estimate is derived in table 13.3.[7]

13.1.2 Growth

The networks of the telcos and LDCs were designed for voice communications and are still used primarily for that purpose. The Internet carries primarily data traffic and has become the primary medium for transmission of data traffic. Thus, the rate of growth of data traffic provides a good proxy for the rate of growth of the Internet. As shown in figure 13.1, the amount of data traffic has grown extremely rapidly. Note that the vertical axis of figure 13.1 has a logarithmic scale. Data transmission has grown by nine orders of magnitude in the past thirty years. Over the past decade, the amount of data transmission has more than doubled each year.[8]

Long-distance voice traffic has long enjoyed rapid growth—approximately 8 percent per annum in recent years.[9] This is considerably higher

Table 13.2
Physical Plant of ISPs (dollar amounts in billions)

(1) Total Property and Equipment (AOL)	$0.99
(2) AOL Market Share	23%
(3) Physical Plant of ISPs [= (1)/(2)]	$4.3

Sources:
(1) AOL 10-K (1999). Figure reflects the total of land, buildings, equipment and related improvements, leasehold and network improvements, furniture and fixtures, computer equipment and internal software, and construction in progress excluding depreciation and amortization at the end of 1998.
(2) Figure is AOL's estimated market share for the overall ISP market.

Table 13.3
Physical Plant of the Internet Backbone (dollar amounts in billions)

(1) 1994 transmission plant of AT&T	$14
(2) Adjustment for four years' growth at 8% [= (1)*(1.08)^4]	$19
(3) Market share of AT&T	51.5%
(4) Adjustment to include LDCs other than AT&T [= (2)/(3)]	$37
(5) Downward adjustment to reflect smaller Internet capacity	21%
(6) Total Physical Plant of the Internet Backbone [= (4)*(5)]	$7.8

Sources:
(1) FCC, *Statistics of Common Carriers*: 1994, Table 2.7—Communications Plant of Telephone Carriers Reporting Annually to the Commission Year Ended December 31, 1994. Figure is the sum of accounts 2230 (Total Central Office Transmission) and 2410 (Total Cable and Wire Facilities) at year-end 1994 levels.
(3) FCC's *Long Distance Market Shares*: Fourth Quarter 1998, March 31, 1999, Table 1.1—Interstate Switched Access Minutes.
(5) Figure is derived from Coffman and Odlyzko [1998] estimates of the bandwidth of the U.S. long distance voice network and the Internet. To adjust plant size to reflect smaller capacity, we took the ratio of the Internet to the U.S. voice network, or 75 Gpbs divided by 350 Gpbs, or 21 percent.

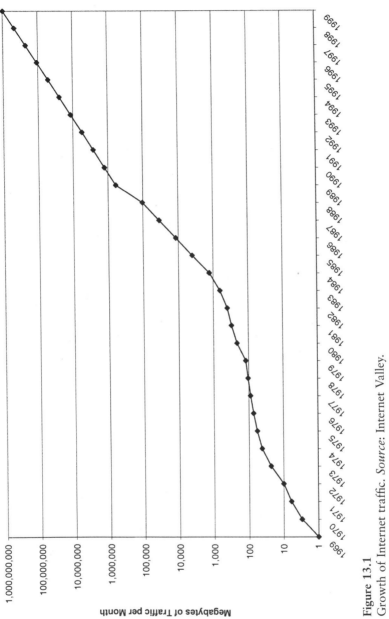

Figure 13.1
Growth of Internet traffic. *Source*: Internet Valley.

than the economy-wide growth rate. Telcos have also enjoyed significant growth—4.5 percent per annum in recent years.[10] While sizable, these growth rates cannot even be compared to the extremely rapid growth of the Internet.

At the end of 1998, the size of the Internet was only one-sixth that of the voice networks of the LDCs and one-thirtieth that of the networks of the telcos. Nevertheless, assuming that the Internet's enormous rate of growth persists, it will soon be larger than the voice networks of the LDCs. Indeed, it may already be larger by the time this book gets into print. Before too long, the Internet may be as large as the combined voice networks of the telcos *and* the LDCs.

13.2 Telecommunications Technology

The Internet was designed to carry data traffic—not voice communications. In this respect, the Internet is the opposite of the networks of telcos and LDCs. The Internet can be used for voice communications, but the quality of service (QoS) is substantially lower than that of voice services provided by LDCs and telcos.[11]

The networks of LDCs and telcos existed long before the Internet. A key question, therefore, is why these existing networks could not, or at least did not, meet the needs of data users. Why was a different network developed for data transmission? To answer these questions, one needs a basic understanding of the technologies of the LDCs and telcos, and of how those technologies differ from that of the Internet. In this regard, the key technology of the Internet is packet switching. The raison d'être of the Internet revolves primarily around the cost characteristics of packet switching, as compared to circuit switching, the dominant technology of voice networks.

13.2.1 Circuit Switching
Figure 13.2 is a diagram of a local telephone call. The call originates when user *U* dials user *V*'s telephone number. The call lasts until *U* and *V* hang up.

The transmission links *UO* and *TV* are dedicated links that connect *U* and *V* to the telephone network. The link *OT*, between the two telco switches, is shared by many users.

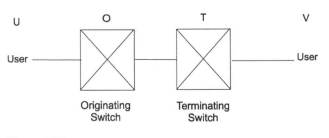

Figure 13.2
Switched local call.

The call in figure 13.2 goes through two telco switches (O and T).[12] They are called circuit switches, because they switch calls from one circuit to another. In the figure, the call is switched from circuit UO to circuit OT and again from OT to TV. (The same switches also transfer calls to/from a large number of other circuits.)

Most of the costs of modern telco networks depend on the number of lines connected to the network rather than amount of usage. Nevertheless, traffic-sensitive costs are significant. In figure 13.2, traffic-sensitive costs are associated with the switches O and T and with the transmission link OT.

Some switching costs relate to processing of calls. Call-processing capacity is used only when a call is initiated and terminated. While the call is continuing, that capacity can be used to process other calls. Call-processing costs depend on number of call attempts. These costs are the same, irrespective of the duration of the calls. They are also approximately the same for calls that are not completed, for example, because the line of the called party is busy. With modern digital technology, the costs of call processing are quite small.[13]

More important are the traffic-sensitive costs associated with minutes of use. In figure 13.2, these costs are associated with the transmission link OT and the switching ports connected thereto. The transmission link itself is generally a large facility that may be shared by thousands of simultaneous users. Nevertheless, the communication between U and V uses a channel that is dedicated to that particular communication for the duration of the call. Similarly, the switching ports connected to OT are dedicated to that particular communication for the duration of the call.

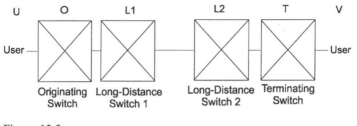

Figure 13.3
Switched long-distance call.

Figure 13.3 is a diagram of a long-distance call. As compared to figure 13.2, the call involves two additional switching occurrences (*L1* and *L2*) by the LDC.[14] *L1–L2* is an intercity transmission link, which may go all the way across the country.

The traffic-sensitive costs of long-distance calls are considerably higher than those of local calls. For a long-distance call, call-processing costs (per call attempt) are incurred with respect to more switches. More important, higher costs (per minute of use) are incurred with respect to more and longer transmission links, as well as the switching ports connected to them.

13.2.2   Packet Switching

Packet switching is a new technology that was developed in the 1960s and 1970s for data communications. It involves dividing the "message" (e.g., a data file that is to be downloaded) into "packets" of approximately two hundred bytes each. As each packet arrives at a switch, it is switched and sent on its way. Transmission paths are individually established from one switch to the next for each packet—not for the entire message of many packets and not for end-to-end communication through many switches.

With packet switching, not all packets from the same message go on the same path. They do not necessarily arrive at their final destination in order. Some packets may get lost along the way and have to be retransmitted.

This method of switching and transmission is especially suitable for data. With voice communications, no value whatsoever derives from transmitting information after a delay of more than a few tenths of a second. For example, if a partial syllable from a conversation gets lost in transmission, there is no utility in having it arrive several seconds later. On the other hand, errors are not a serious problem for voice communication, so long as they are infrequent. Voice communication can still be easily understood.

The opposite obtains with respect to data communications. Lengthy delays for individual packets are tolerable, so long as the average transmission speed is satisfactory. The data must, however, be transmitted without error, or the entire transmission may be worthless. Indeed, it may be far worse than worthless if the error is not detected. Packet switching (e.g., using the Internet protocol TCP/IP) meets these specific requirements of data communications.

The cost characteristics of packet switching differ considerably from those of circuit switching. With packet switching, traffic-sensitive costs (apart from the LAN) depend on number of packets—not on call attempts and not on minutes of use.

For packet switching, unlike circuit switching, call-processing costs are incurred throughout the call. Each packet must be individually processed. Call-processing costs are therefore higher for packet switching than for circuit switching, but they are still fairly low with modern digital technology.

Packet switching is very economical in its use of transmission channels and the switching ports connected thereto. These facilities are dedicated to a particular communication only while packets are actually being sent. Packets from other communications can be interspersed between the packets for any single communication. Thus, the costs of these transmission channels and switching ports depend on number of packets—not on minutes of use. Packet switching greatly economizes these costs, relative to circuit switching. Packet switching is *far* less costly for the typical pattern of data communications in which the user is on line for a long time but sends and receives relatively few packets. It is most cost-effective for long-distance and international traffic, for which transmission costs are highest.

13.3   Evolution of the Computer Industry

The development of the Internet depended on the evolution of the computer industry, as well as on telecommunications technology. The key developments, in this regard, were the growth of time-sharing in the 1960s and the 1970s, followed by the proliferation of personal computers in the 1980s and 1990s.

13.3.1   Time-Sharing

In the late 1960s and early 1970s, batch processing, whereby users handed decks of punched cards across a counter and waited (often several hours) for a thick printout to be generated, was a common practice. (This is Grandpa again, walking to school in the snow.) Time-sharing was, however, becoming more and more popular. It was the only way that organizations too small to justify purchasing a minicomputer could do computing. Such businesses subscribed to time-sharing services, which they accessed via telephone, using "dumb" computer terminals in their offices.[15] In addition, large organizations at the time were using internal time-sharing for more and more purposes. Terminals in many offices in a building were often connected to a mainframe or minicomputer.

As compared to batch processing, time-sharing allowed a more interactive approach to computer usage. The programmer could try something and (if it did not involve too much number crunching) could get a quick response from the computer. After examining the response, he or she could then try something else.

13.3.2   Personal Computers

The proliferation of PCs has profoundly affected the development of the Internet. In this regard, the Internet benefited from the previously discussed complementary bandwagon effects between PCs and applications software. A similar complementary bandwagon effect has occurred in recent years with respect to PCs and the Internet. The proliferation of PCs stimulated the development of Internet applications. Those applications, in turn, stimulated sales of PCs *with modems*. That development led to positive feedback and further stimulated the development of Internet applications, and PCs with modems.

13.4   Telecommunications Prices

Packet-switching technology was originally developed as a cost-effective means of data transmission. To understand this development, we need to examine telecommunications prices. Those prices determined how much money could be saved through the use of packet switching.

Long-distance telecommunications prices in the late 1960s and early 1970s were quite high, compared to today's prices. In 1998, the average price of interstate calls was approximately $0.14 per minute.[16] In contrast, the price in 1970 was $0.23 per minute (see AT&T), which corresponds to approximately $0.97 per minute in current dollars. Furthermore, this average included substantial residential calling at discounted rates. The average cost for a business customer, who made most of his or her calls during the business day, was considerably higher.

These high prices, in part, reflected high costs. The digital revolution in telecommunications had not yet occurred. Analog technologies were used for both switching and transmission. Fiber optics had not yet been deployed on any significant scale. These developments, and their associated cost reductions, had not yet occurred.

High long-distance prices also partly reflected a deliberate policy of the FCC and state telecommunications regulators. Regulatory policy was to price long-distance services far above cost and use the revenues to keep prices of local residential services low—in many cases, below costs.[17]

Rohlfs (1978) estimated that long-distance prices in 1975 were more than twice their costs. Rohlfs obtained similar results using top-down estimates, based on historical data, or bottom-up engineering estimates of costs. At the same time, prices of local services were below costs—especially local usage, for which the most usual (usage-sensitive) price was zero.

The rationale for this regulatory policy was to promote universal telephone service. In principle, such pricing might have been justified by the bandwagon benefits that accrued to existing telephone subscribers as new residential subscribers were induced to join the network (see section 4.8). In reality, however, that pricing probably substantially lessened the productivity of the telecommunications sector—notwithstanding the bandwagon benefits.[18] Nevertheless, the policy of keeping local residential rates low (albeit at the cost of high long-distance rates) had, and indeed still has, strong political support.

Furthermore, the FCC, in consultation with a board of state regulators (and with the acquiescence of AT&T), agreed in 1970 to the "Ozark Plan," whereby interstate long-distance services were to bear an ever-increasing share of the costs of local telephone services. In consequence, the average price of interstate services rose from $0.23 per minute in 1970 to $0.33 per minute in 1981—even though the 1970 price substantially exceeded cost.

This trend sharply reversed after the AT&T divestiture. The FCC viewed the preexisting subsidy scheme as unsustainable with vertical disintegration and the onset of long-distance competition. AT&T had a clear incentive to "bypass" the artificially high-priced services of the divested telcos. AT&T could lease lines and provide its own switching rather than purchase switched services from the telcos. It could self-provide the transmission facilities, and/or use transmission facilities provided by the telcos' competitors where such competitors existed. Indeed, failure to use bypass could have put AT&T at a competitive disadvantage relative to other LDCs.

The FCC made a concerted effort to make the prices of long-distance services better reflect their costs. These policies were supported by both AT&T (which stood to benefit from demand stimulation, if its input prices were lowered) and telcos (which feared loss of revenues through bypass). The policies did, however, face strong political opposition from Congress and state regulators. Nevertheless, the FCC persevered, and its pricing policies led to substantial reductions in charges for long-distance telephone calls. In addition, competition put further pressure on long-distance carriers to reduce their prices—especially in pricing plans designed for large, price-sensitive customers. All in all, long-distance prices have fallen to well under half their 1981 levels in nominal terms. Real price reductions were even larger. The productivity of the telecommunications sector sharply increased.

The run-up of long-distance charges during the 1970s and early 1980s (before the FCC's reversal of this policy) generated billions of dollars of economic waste by inhibiting productivity growth of the telecommunications sector. It did, however, stimulate the development of packet technology, which in turn led to the development of the Internet. It's an ill wind that blows no good.

13.5   The Development of ARPANET

The Internet bandwagon actually began rolling, albeit slowly, in the late 1960s, though the term *Internet* had not yet been coined.[19] At that time, the Defense Advanced Research Projects Agency (DARPA) developed the switched data network ARPANET. DARPA had the vision of a nationwide (perhaps worldwide) network on which analysts working on defense issues would be interconnected via time sharing. Analysts on such a network would be able to share programs and data and communicate via e-mail with one another.

Unfortunately, the realization of this vision was problematic because long-distance charges would have been prohibitive. Costs would have been especially high if analysts attempted to use their computers in an interactive fashion. To do so, they would have needed to remain on-line and to incur continual long-distance charges.

DARPA hoped to solve this problem through the use of new technology, namely, packet switching and transmission. Packet technology was developed for data communications and is very economical in its use of transmission facilities. It held the promise of reducing long-distance charges sufficiently to make DARPA's vision a practical reality.

In the late 1960s, packet technology had not yet advanced sufficiently to support an effective nationwide data network. DARPA therefore decided to fund the development of packet technology. The result was one of the most successful research efforts of modern times. DARPA also developed and made operational the modern concept of a large switched data network. Today's basic Internet functions of Telnet and FTP were developed for ARPANET during its early period. The early ARPANET also supported e-mail, but e-mail predated ARPANET.

The development of software for ARPANET was especially important. This software included TCP/IP, which has become the standard Internet protocol. The software was designed to be used by disparate networks that used different hardware and operating systems.

The "IP" part of TCP/IP stands for "Internet Protocol." IP defines the structure of the packets. "TCP" is "Transmission Control Protocol." It is the protocol for communication between the originating and terminating packet switches. TCP serves the important function of ensuring that packets that are lost in transmission are retransmitted.[20]

Much of the software written for ARPANET entered the public domain and could be readily obtained and easily used. From the start, the availability of that software facilitated the use of ARPANET. In recent years, it has also facilitated the use of the Internet and has been a key contributor to its success.

ARPANET, like its successor the Internet, embodied strong bandwagon effects. As ARPANET expanded, users benefited from being able to communicate via e-mail with more persons (network externalities). Likewise, more information was shared, for example, on electronic bulletin boards (complementary bandwagon effects). By 1975, the DoD apparently regarded the network, given its size at that time, as worth the cost. The DoD therefore undertook to provide permanent funding for it, and DARPA relinquished control to the Defense Communications Agency.

Because the DoD was the proprietor of ARPANET and provided the funding, it had full power to determine the rules. A dramatic illustration of the DoD's exercising this power was the shift to TCP/IP in 1983. The DoD had previously determined that the value of ARPANET to the defense community as a whole would be maximized if TCP/IP completely supplanted the older standard NCP. But the DoD was not certain that its announced decision to discontinue supporting NCP was credible. To enhance credibility, it announced that it was going to reject, and actually did reject, all NCP packets on one day in mid-1982. The DoD was still not certain that it had achieved credibility and rejected NCP packets for two days in the fall of 1982. Finally, NCP was turned off for good on January 1, 1983.

While this implementation plan had a distinctly military flavor, the action can be explained in terms of bandwagon theory. The inconvenience that users of NCP suffered was, in the opinion of the DoD, more than outweighed by the bandwagon benefits to others of a single transmission protocol.

The DoD's incentives to develop ARPANET were enhanced by the regulatory policy of promoting high long-distance rates that did not reflect costs. Those prices created artificial incentives to use packet switching and thereby to limit usage of high-priced long-distance services. Nevertheless, DARPA's ultimate vision of a nationwide network of interconnected time-sharing computer users would probably have been prohibitively expensive even with cost-based long-distance rates. For example, suppose that rates were 10 cents per minute or $6.00 per hour in the late 1960s. This is less than half of the actual prices in 1973 and close to Rohlfs's (1978) estimates of costs. A computer user who was on-line one thousand hours per year would still have generated long-distance costs of $6,000 per year. This corresponds to approximately $23,000 per year in current dollars. Long-distance expenditures of this magnitude for a single user were probably not cost-effective, compared to the alternative of using local computers.

Thus, ARPANET really did constitute a way to use telecommunications facilities more efficiently for data applications. Although it was stimulated by non-cost-based regulatory pricing, it was not simply the exploitation of an arbitrage opportunity.

13.6 Other Packet-Switched Networks

Prior to the Internet, ARPANET was the largest packet-switched network. It was not, however, the only one. A variety of other networks began operations in the 1970s and 1980s. These included both commercial and noncommercial networks.[21]

13.6.1 Distant Commercial Time-Sharing

Commercial packet-switched networks began to operate in the 1970s. The earliest, Telenet (not to be confused with the Internet application Telnet), began operations in 1974. In addition, the time-sharing service Tymshare launched a public packet-switched network (Tymnet) in 1977.

Commercial packet-switched networks originally connected users to computers for time-sharing applications. For example, they provided a cost-effective way for a commercial time-sharing service to serve users who were not in the same local calling area.

Distant time-sharing applications involve internal supply-side scale economies. Transmission facilities with more channels have lower unit costs.[22] Also, as usage grows, each channel can carry more traffic, while maintaining quality of service, according to the laws of (telecommunications) traffic engineering.[23] In addition, suppliers of time-sharing services enjoy internal scale economies. They can satisfy greater demand at lower unit cost by using larger computers. For these reasons, the supply price of distant time-sharing services, including the cost of transmission via a packet-switched network, is inversely related to the amount of usage.

Distant time-sharing services do not, however, involve significant (external) bandwagon effects. The economies are internal from the perspective of suppliers and can be adequately modeled without using bandwagon models.

There is no particular reason to suspect that demand for distant commercial time-sharing was limited by any failure to solve a start-up problem. Sales were, of course, limited by the extent of demand. The need for distant commercial time-sharing services was always limited. Furthermore, it has declined steadily over time, as the power of smaller and less-expensive computers has increased.

13.6.2   Commercial Gateways

Commercial gateways (e.g., CompuServe, Dow Jones, and The Source) developed later. Their growth was facilitated by the proliferation of PCs. They were the forerunners of today's ISPs. They connected end users to a choice of many commercial information service providers. Commercial information service providers had schedules of fees for the information they supplied. Two of the largest were affiliated with gateways, namely, Dow Jones and H&R Block (the parent of CompuServe). In addition, many independent commercial information service providers existed. Furthermore, several governmental agencies (e.g., the IRS and the State Department) provided information on-line for no charge.

A gateway uses commercial packet-switched networks, as described in the preceding subsection, for transmission. The gateway bills its subscribers for the commercial information services that they use. It then passes the proceeds, less a cut, on to the information service providers. In addition to taking this cut, the gateway charges monthly subscription fees to its subscribers.

Gateways are subject to complementary bandwagon effects. As more users subscribe to gateways, the complementary supply of information services becomes more profitable and can be expected to increase. As a greater variety of information services is supplied, more users will get modems on their computers.[24] The process then leads to positive feedback, as more users subscribe to gateways, and so forth.

Like many bandwagon services, gateways encountered a start-up problem. In the United States, the problem was relatively easily overcome for the following reasons:

• PCs were rapidly proliferating, apart from this particular application.

• Nationwide commercial packet-switched networks were already in place.

• Information service providers could aim to serve a national clientele and thereby enjoy internal scale economies.

• Many information service providers could be reached via multiple gateways. Thus, the gateways were at least partially interlinked. A user of one gateway derived bandwagon benefits associated with users of other gateways.

It seems likely that the start-up problem for gateways in the United States was largely solved by the mid-1980s. At that time, there were several nationwide gateways. By 1986, the three largest—CompuServe, Dow Jones, and The Source—together had 620,000 subscribers.[25] There were literally hundreds of information service providers, including many that were highly successful. For example, Lexis had already been launched, notwithstanding initial skepticism that lawyers would use computers. In addition, services that catered to very specialized needs (e.g., those of traveling rock bands) had been launched.

The start-up problem was more difficult in other countries, because PCs were not as prevalent as in the United States. An especially innovative approach was used to solve the start-up problem in France. France Telecom launched the Teletel network. It distributed low-cost terminals ("Minitels") free to its telephone subscribers as an alternative to printed directories. Minitels could be used to access directory information throughout France. In addition, they could be used, for a fee, to access commercial information service providers. The service was highly successful for several years, but the Internet has now largely displaced it.

Many of the commercial information service providers on Teletel supplied sexually related ("X-rated") material. More generally, the supply of such material has been a widespread and profitable use of several new telecommunications technologies. The new technologies provide a way to distribute such material where the use of traditional media has been barred. Many public policymakers have not been pleased with the use of new technology to meet this "market need." With respect to the Internet, in particular, there has been concern that the material may be viewed by children. In the high-tech world, many things change very rapidly, but some things stay the same.

Although the start-up problem for gateways was solved, at least in the United States and France, the growth of gateways was limited by the demand for commercial information services. Most computer users have little need to purchase information from service vendors. Gateways thus served a relatively small niche.

13.6.3   Commercial E-Mail Services

Commercial e-mail began to be offered in the late 1970s and grew throughout the 1980s. Many different types of firms offered e-mail:

• Some manufacturers of mainframe computers and minicomputers offered e-mail systems for time-sharing users of their systems.

• Some suppliers of LANs offered e-mail for users connected to the LAN.

• Some of the gateways described in section 13.6.2 offered e-mail as an on-line service to their subscribers.

• Western Union offered e-mail as an adjunct to its international telex service.

• The two largest LDCs (AT&T and MCI) had e-mail services that were not adjuncts to other products or services.

The first two of types of e-mail listed above are private systems. They are used for internal communications within an organization. In themselves, they are not bandwagon services.

The latter three types of e-mail are public systems. Public systems are quintessential bandwagon services. Their value derives entirely from communicating with other subscribers. The value of the service to each subscriber increases as the user set expands.

E-mail grew relatively rapidly throughout the 1980s. By 1983, there were already approximately 76,000 users of private systems and an equal number of users of public systems.[26] By 1988, these numbers had increased to 4,250,000 users of private systems and 1,750,000 users of public systems.[27] Most of the users of public systems were customers of gateways. The other public e-mail systems had many fewer subscribers. In 1989,

- EasyLink (Western Union's product) had 200,000 subscribers,
- MCI Mail had 100,000 subscribers, and
- AT&T Mail had 50,000 subscribers.[28]

The rapid growth of e-mail is easy to explain. Private systems had significant value and cost very little to supply. Gateways could also provide e-mail capability at very low incremental cost. They found it worthwhile to offer e-mail, even though subscribers made relatively little use of it. Western Union's EasyLink could also be provided at low incremental cost to the subscribers of its international telex service. All these services were offered to specific sets of customers who had purchased other services. In contrast, the services of AT&T and MCI were offered to the general population, but those services were more costly to supply.

The growth of commercial e-mail subscribers during the 1980s substantially increased the bandwagon benefits of commercial e-mail; that is, users benefited from being able to communicate with more persons via e-mail. Conceivably, as the bandwagon benefits grew, commercial e-mail could have evolved into a large general communications medium.

Unfortunately, there was a serious impediment to such evolution, namely, lack of interlinking. Private systems did not generally interlink to public systems, and the public systems did not, for most of the 1980s, interlink with one another. Consequently, each subscriber enjoyed bandwagon benefits only with respect to the subscribers of his or her particular e-mail system. These benefits did not suffice for commercial e-mail to reach a critical mass and evolve into a large general communications medium.

It is easy to understand why private systems did not interlink with the public systems. Doing so would have involved large costs to achieve technical compatibility and substantial transactions costs. The benefits would usually not have been commensurately large. Furthermore, to achieve the full bandwagon benefits, a private system would have had to incur the costs of negotiating many agreements to interlink with each of the public systems.

With regard to public systems, the incentives to interlink were discussed on a theoretical level in section 4.4. In the case of commercial e-mail, CompuServe was by far the largest gateway.[29] It therefore had a competitive advantage over other commercial e-mail suppliers, since its users could enjoy bandwagon benefits from a larger user set. It was reluctant to give up this competitive advantage. Even so, interlinking with a supplier that offered a very different service mix to its clientele (e.g., MCI Mail) may well have been mutually advantageous.

In any event, the unwillingness of the various suppliers to interlink made the start-up problem much more difficult. Each individual supplier could offer its customers only the limited bandwagon benefits from a relatively small user set. Consequently, demand was also limited, and a critical mass was never achieved. The e-mail networks remained a collection of disparate communities of interest until they were overtaken by the Internet.

Commercial e-mail services began to interlink around 1989. In that year, Telemail (Telenet's product), MCI Mail, and AT&T Mail announced an agreement to interlink. Also that year, several major commercial e-mail providers began to interlink with the Internet. By that time, however, the Internet already had unstoppable momentum. Since the Internet offered ubiquitous e-mail at low cost, commercial e-mail could not compete and was nearing the end of its product life cycle.

13.6.4   Noncommercial Packet-Switched Networks

Some noncommercial packet-switched networks were developed quite early. For example, the Merit network connected state universities in Michigan in 1969. ALOHAnet connected universities in Hawaii in 1970.

Nevertheless, noncommercial packet-switched networks (other than ARPANET) were not widely used until some time later. In the mid-1970s government agencies established some networks, for example, MFENet and HEPNet by the Department of Energy and SPAN by NASA. A number of universities were included in ARPANET, which was used primarily by computer science departments. The users at those universities had packet-switched connections to one another, as well as to other members of ARPANET. This development largely took place in the early 1970s.

Not surprisingly, universities that were not included in ARPANET perceived that they were disadvantaged. To help correct this imbalance, BITNET was launched in 1981 to connect academic mainframe computers. CSNET, which was funded by the NSF, was launched that same year to connect computer science departments at universities that did not participate in ARPANET.

Around this time, the use of packet-switched networks by universities started to spread beyond the traditional enclave, which consisted primarily of computer science departments. Many departments of mathematics and natural sciences got connected. Later on, humanities and social science departments began to get connected.

All these noncommercial networks were designed to serve the needs of specific community-of-interest groups. Several of the networks had self-sufficient user sets, in that the funders thought they were getting their money's worth, given the user set. But the networks were generally not interlinked. Bandwagon benefits were based on the number of users in each separate network—not the total number of network users.

There were obvious benefits to interlinking these various noncommercial networks. The most significant interlinking agreement actually reached was that between ARPANET and CSNET in 1981. Under that agreement, costs were shared on the basis of statistical data, but there were no usage charges. This arrangement demonstrated the feasibility of interlinking networks and provided a model of how to implement interlinking in practice.

Nevertheless, relatively little further interlinking of noncommercial networks occurred. The communities of interest of the various networks were largely separate, and interlinking would have required that cost-sharing agreements be negotiated. A separate agreement would have been required for each pair of networks that were to be interlinked. Apparently, the proprietors of the networks believed that the benefits of interlinking were not worth the cost and bother of these negotiations.

13.7   NSFNET

Widespread interlinking of noncommercial networks in the United States occurred only after NSFNET was funded in 1985.[30] NSFNET provided, at no cost to users, the backbone for interlinking networks. The NSF imposed two requirements on use of the backbone:

• The IP protocol had to be used. This requirement ensured that all users enjoyed the bandwagon benefits of a single technical standard.

• Only uses in support of research and education were permitted (the "Acceptable Use Policy").

For (noncommercial) networks that met these two requirements, interlinking had substantial benefits and no significant costs. As would be expected under these circumstances, interlinking occurred very rapidly. As a result, bandwagon benefits increased enormously.

• Users could communicate with many more persons via e-mail.

• Information suppliers, being able to reach a larger audience, had incentives to supply more information. Internet users benefited from the availability of that information.

This rapid growth was further spurred a few years later when the Acceptable Use Policy was relaxed. NSFNET collaborated with Merit, IBM, and MCI to create a new nonprofit entity: Advanced Network Systems (ANS). ANS worked out a way by which for-profit firms could use the Internet without being subsidized.[31]

Figure 13.1, discussed earlier, shows the growth of data usage over time. As the figure shows, data traffic grew rapidly, even before NSFNET was funded. The initial rapid growth occurred as users rushed to take advantage of the new technology of packet switching. What NSFNET did was to allow this rapid rate of growth to be sustained. It did so by facilitating interlinking and thereby allowing the Internet to reach a critical mass. Once a critical mass had been achieved, growth of the Internet became subject to positive feedback. Each increment of growth provided additional bandwagon benefits that fueled further growth. This positive feedback has been sustained for over fifteen years and still shows no signs of slowing down.

13.8   The Internet after NSFNET

In April 1995, the NSF discontinued its funding of the Internet. Readers who (to their credit) are not familiar with practical politics may not appreciate what a great accomplishment that was. The general rule of thumb for governments at any level is that appropriations to special-interest groups become permanent. After the appropriations are made, the benefiting special-interest groups feel that they have a "right" to continuation of the status quo. They then exert strong political pressure to keep their "right" from being abridged.[32] Internet users were certainly no exception to this rule. They rallied to preserve their "right" to subsidized Internet usage. Nevertheless, NSF had the fortitude to pull the plug.

NSF's subsidy of the Internet succeeded beyond virtually everyone's expectations. Nevertheless, NSF wanted to get out of operational responsibility for the Internet, and there were important advantages to terminating the subsidies:

• A critical mass had been reached, so continuing subsidies were not necessary to sustain future growth.

• Continuing subsidies might have led to (additional) unwanted government intervention in Internet operations.

13.9   Externalities and Transactions Costs

The success of NSFNET derived from the external economies of bandwagon effects. As a result of interlinking, bandwagon benefits to virtually all users increased enormously. In this sense, NSF internalized the externalities for the greater public good.

As Coase showed, however, any story about internalizing externalities can equally well be told in terms of transactions costs. In this case, the benefits of an interlinking arrangement between two networks were internal to the two networks, considered together. Consequently, NSFNET was not necessary per se to internalize these externalities. Rather, NSFNET obviated the transactions costs of negotiating inter-linking arrangements. Users simply had to get their packets to the back-bone, and NSF took it from there. It appears that the transactions costs prior to NSFNET were sufficiently high to prevent large-scale interlink-ing. Thus, the role of NSFNET was determinative in getting interlinking started.

When NSFNET withdrew funding in 1995, there was again a need to negotiate interlinking arrangements. But the conditions at that time dif-fered substantially from those in 1986. In 1986, the Internet was a small collection of disparate networks; by 1995, it was generating enormous economic value. The negotiators in 1995 simply had to decide on some way to share this value or else lose it. As would be expected under these circumstances, the negotiations were successful.

Interlinking arrangements on the Internet are not, of course, 100 percent economically efficient (or even close).[33] They have resulted largely from bargaining rather than competition (which affords strong incentives for firms to improve efficiency).[34] The players do, however, have the incentive to negotiate more efficient arrangements over time—always assuming that they can work out some way to divide the gains rather than lose them.

13.10   Current Internet Usage

Many commercial transactions (e-commerce) now take place on the Internet. In addition, the Internet now provides the primary gateway to commercial information service providers. Nevertheless, the main uses of the Internet are still e-mail and other exchanges of free information.

The Internet is enormously larger than the commercial packet-switched networks that preceded it. To some extent, this growth reflects the proliferation of computers. A more important reason, however, is that demand for free information far exceeds that for information at a positive price (from commercial information service providers). Greater demand at a zero price is, of course, hardly surprising. What is much more surprising is the huge supply of free information that has been forthcoming. Much of the freely supplied information is advertising, but a great deal of noncommercial information is also supplied. Both the suppliers and the users of noncommercial information benefit from the free exchange of that information.

The Internet evolved through interlinking from the noncommercial packet-switched networks that preceded it. It still performs the same function as those networks—the free exchange of information—but for a much larger user set. Indeed, notwithstanding increased use of the Internet for commercial transactions in recent years, its essence is still the free exchange of information on an incomparably large scale.

13.11   A Final Reflection

Managers of the old Bell System enjoyed smugly recounting Alexander Graham Bell's attempt to sell his telephone patents to Western Union, the dominant communications firm at the time. Western Union had no interest. The alleged reason (which may be apocryphal) was, "Why would anyone want [to pay a high price for] a telephone when they could easily go to their local telegraph office and send telegrams?"

The modern variant of this story is an early attempt to commercialize ARPANET. Two of the early developers, Larry Roberts and Bob Kahn, visited AT&T in the early 1970s to try to get AT&T to take over ARPANET. AT&T refused.[35] Its reasoning may have been, "Why would anyone want to use a packet-switched network, when they could just as easily use the basic telephone network?"[36]

We may now be approaching the time when the Internet overtakes traditional telecommunications, in the same way that telephone overtook telegraph a century earlier. Perhaps in a few decades, the giants of the emerging telecommunications industry of the twenty-first century will smugly recount Roberts and Kahn's visit to AT&T and have a good laugh.

13.12   Lessons from Case Study

There is really only one lesson from the history of Internet, but it is perhaps the most important lesson of bandwagon economics: namely the great potential value of interlinking. Before interlinking, there was a small set of disparate networks. With interlinking, the Internet has become an astoundingly valuable global information resource. In addition to its huge commercial value, it provides enormous benefits to users from the free exchange of information. It is also an incomparable medium for free expression and free speech.

The U.S. government's role (through DoD and NSF) in making this happen is one of the great successes of government intervention in the economy. With expenditures that were temporary and modest by federal government standards, the Internet was launched. It is hard to find any sizable investment in either the public or private sector that yielded so large a rate of return.

IV
Conclusions

Our bandwagon tour has now ended. It is time to sum up what we learned on the way.

14

Summary of Results

Bandwagon effects[1] increase the benefits that consumers derive from a product or service as the user set expands. In the formal terms of economic theory, bandwagon effects are **external demand-side scale economies**. Where they apply to networks, they are often called **network externalities**. **Complementary bandwagon effects** apply where the benefit of a product (e.g., hardware) depends at least partially on the supply of complementary products (e.g., software) produced by independent vendors.

A property sometimes ascribed to network services is **Metcalfe's Law**, which states that the value of a network increases proportionately to the square of the number of users. The fundamental insight underlying the law—that bandwagon effects increase the value of a network to each user—is certainly correct. Nevertheless, the quantitative statement of Metcalfe's Law is incorrect as a matter of economic theory and likely to substantially overstate the value of large networks—except possibly for internal networks within organizations.

Bandwagon markets usually have multiple equilibria. In general, the largest sustainable **equilibrium user set** is best for both consumers and suppliers, but markets often have a tendency to end up at far smaller and less satisfactory equilibria. In such cases, concerted efforts by suppliers and/or government intervention may be required to solve the start-up problem and get to a larger, better equilibrium. Solving the start-up problem is often a question of reaching a **critical mass**. After a critical mass is achieved, demand for the product is subject to **positive feedback** and may grow extremely rapidly.

A key concept in bandwagon markets is **interlinking**. With interlinking, each consumer enjoys bandwagon benefits with respect to *all* consumers—not just those of his or her own supplier. Interlinking is sometimes achieved if the physical networks of various suppliers are interconnected. It is sometimes achieved through **compatibility** of the products of various suppliers, for example, if the hardware produced by different suppliers can use the same software.

Interlinking almost always has substantial benefits. It increases the value of the product or service to each user. It therefore increases demand. It eases the start-up problem, because this expansion of demand makes it easier to reach a critical mass.

Interlinking does, however, involve costs, which vary depending on the particular circumstances. The costs of interlinking are lowest before a new product is manufactured. Manufacturers can at relatively little cost adopt to a single **technical standard** which achieves compatibility for their products. Once incompatible hardware is produced, interlinking may not be economically feasible. Interlinking (**interconnection**) of physical networks is an intermediate case. The costs are significant but not especially large with modern technology.

Bandwagon services usually involve customer equipment that resides on the customer's premises. Proprietor services are low-cost alternatives that often predate bandwagon services and perform similar functions. Service suppliers provide such services on their own premises. Proprietor services are subject to internal supply-side scale economies, but they are not subject to external bandwagon effects.

In bandwagon markets, low prices do necessarily constitute **predatory pricing**, even if the prices are below the relevant measure of cost. Low prices increase bandwagon benefits and can increase the supplier's long-run profits, apart from any competitive consequences. Of course, the pricing may reflect predatory intent, but other evidence, in addition to below-cost pricing, would be required to demonstrate that intent.

The eight markets in our case studies are quite varied. The bandwagon effects work/worked in different ways in the different markets. Nevertheless, a number of general principles emerge from our analysis:

14.1 Start-Up Problem

Suppliers must have extraordinarily good products or services to reach a critical mass. All the successful products and services that we examined constituted major technological advances and met important customer needs. At the other extreme, Picturephone was a hard product to sell—even apart from the Bell System's failure to solve the start-up problem. In between are several products that constituted important technological advances but could not reach a critical mass. These include analog fax machines, digital compact cassette players, minidisc players, digital videodisc players, and commercial e-mail (before the rapid growth of the Internet).

A valuable stand-alone application is extremely helpful in solving the start-up problem. Such an application can generate a large initial user set before suppliers have to do anything to solve the start-up problem. If the stand-alone application is sufficiently valuable, the start-up problem solves itself. That is precisely what happened to VCRs, because the stand-alone application of time-shifting of television programs was so valuable. The start-up problem is much more difficult for pure bandwagon products, which have no such stand-alone application.

14.2 Vertical Integration

Vertical integration can help solve the start-up problem where there are complementary bandwagon effects. It can help coordinate start-up efforts and afford strong incentives for suppliers to make such efforts. For example, RCA's ownership of NBC was a critical factor in starting up original (black-and-white) television and color television. Philips' partial ownership of Polygram Records helped solve the start-up problem for CD players. On the other hand, the rapid proliferation of independent videocassette rental stores and of manufacturers of television sets show how effective competitive markets can be in meeting consumer needs—*after the user set has become sizable.*

14.3   Bandwagon Markets without Interlinking

These markets tend to gravitate toward a single supplier. Customers of the largest supplier usually enjoy the greatest bandwagon benefits. Consequently, new consumers tend to choose the largest supplier, and continuing customers often switch to the largest supplier to enjoy greater bandwagon benefits. As a result, the largest supplier tends to increase its market share until it has captured the entire market. This tendency is analogous to that of markets with internal supply-side scale economies. It is exemplified by the all-encompassing role of the Internet in data communications, the enduring dominance of Intel and Microsoft in the PC market, and the complete victory of VHS over Beta for home VCRs in the United States.

Notwithstanding the above, smaller suppliers often survive by serving market niches. In bandwagon markets, a niche is based on a community of interest among users. For example, early independent telephone companies overcame the disadvantage of their small size by serving geographic areas that Bell did not serve. They offered substantial bandwagon benefits to customers within those geographic areas. Apple Computer has largely served users with special interests—especially users in educational institutions. For such users, the applications software written for Apple is adequate (in some cases, superior), and they often enjoy better user support than do users of computers that run Microsoft Windows.

Suppliers in a bandwagon market without interlinking should not be too greedy for short-run profits. During the start-up phase, the goal of suppliers should be to maximize their customer base, subject to reasonable financial constraints. By pursuing this goal, they increase the value of the product or service to their customers, and they benefit as demand increases. They also gain competitive advantage, relative to other suppliers. Consumers benefit from this policy through lower prices in the short run and increased bandwagon benefits in the long run. Microsoft's pricing best exemplifies the success of this strategy. Similarly, JVC and Matsushita both offered low prices for VHS VCRs during the critical start-up phase. At the other extreme, the early Bell System made itself unnecessarily vulnerable to competition by pricing too high during the start-up period for telephone.

A supplier may need to vertically integrate in order to appropriate the gains from bandwagon effects; but vertical integration can be carried too far. The history of IBM illustrates the adverse consequences of too little vertical integration (though IBM may actually have had no choice, because it was so late in entering the PC market). Because the IBM PC had very little proprietary hardware and software, it became interlinked with its clones. The clones ultimately overwhelmed IBM, because they offered customers a low-cost way to enjoy the full bandwagon benefits of IBM-compatible PCs. At the other extreme, Apple internally produced almost all the components of its computer systems. This excessive vertical integration contributed substantially to Apple's loss of market leadership. Apple could have saved money and offered customers greater flexibility by relying more (though not wholly) on independent producers of components, including keyboards, disk drives, and modems.

Misjudgments by suppliers have enduring consequences in this market structure. Bandwagon markets without interlinking are very unforgiving. A supplier who makes a misjudgment during the critical start-up period is often seriously harmed (e.g., by falling behind in the bandwagon race) and gets no second chance. The structure of a mature industry therefore reflects the past misjudgments of suppliers, as well as the fundamentals of the industry. This point is important, because misjudgments inhere in high-technology industries. Market participants must plan their actions on the basis of guesses about markets and technology in the future, and those guesses often turn out to be wrong. The entire structure of the current PC industry is largely the result of early misjudgments by IBM and Apple. The competitive market structure for telephone service in the early part of the twentieth century is largely attributable to the failure of the Bell companies to develop the market more aggressively during the period of the Bell patents.

14.4   Agreeing to a Technical Standard

Where different suppliers use incompatible technical standards, their customers are not interlinked. The suppliers then each compete to become the dominant supplier, as described above. The market becomes a high-stakes, winner-take-all game. One firm may win big, while the others all leave the table with empty pockets.

In contrast, interlinking leads to traditional competition. No firm can reasonably hope to achieve market dominance. Many firms may, however, be able to participate in the market without losing their shirts.

Interlinking has the advantage of increasing consumer benefits and demand over time. The transitory profits that can be earned as the market grows in this way may outweigh the value to suppliers of a seat in the winner-take-all bandwagon game. Furthermore, without the consumer benefits of interlinking, the start-up problem may be impossible to solve.

Regardless of whether interlinking benefits suppliers, it often substantially benefits consumers. Consumers benefit from both increased bandwagon benefits and increased competition in the long run. These benefits are likely to outweigh the transitory gains from price cuts during a standards war.

Agreeing to a technical standard is likely to be profitable for all suppliers if no supplier has a strong technological edge. Interlinking yields substantial benefits to consumers. Suppliers can then profit from the resulting increase in demand—especially during the transitory period of rapid growth. A supplier has no reason to give up those gains for a seat in the winner-take-all game, unless it has a substantial edge in that game. The digital fax of the early 1980s exemplifies the benefits to suppliers of interlinking under these circumstances. The analog fax (in the 1970s) and commercial e-mail (before the rapid growth of the Internet) exemplify the adverse consequences to suppliers of *not* interlinking.

A supplier with a strong technological edge may benefit from interlinking by licensing competitors. Such a supplier might have a good chance to become the dominant supplier in a bandwagon market without interlinking. Nevertheless, it may be better off giving up that prospect and licensing its technology to other suppliers. Doing so has the disadvantage of allowing competitors to compete effectively, even though they would otherwise have inferior technology. On the upside, interlinking eases the start-up problem, which may otherwise be very difficult to solve. The licensing supplier also profits from licensing revenues. Philips very successfully pursued this strategy to develop the market for CD players.

14.5   Government Intervention

Government intervention to internalize bandwagon externalities has the potential to be very constructive. There is, of course, no guarantee that this potential will be realized. On the contrary, government intervention may turn out to be counterproductive. Nevertheless, government intervention in bandwagon markets has had some notable successes. The intervention by the U.S. government in developing the Internet was hugely successful. By subsidizing the Internet backbone, the NSF greatly facilitated interlinking among existing networks. This interlinking allowed the Internet to reach a critical mass. The subsequent growth of the Internet has been a tremendous boon. It has generated enormous economic value and has facilitated the free flow of information across the globe. The FCC's spectrum policies with regard to original black-and-white television have been justly criticized. They did, however, facilitate the solution of what would otherwise have been a difficult start-up problem for television. Similarly, the FCC's spectrum policies with regard to digital television have provided a solution to another difficult start-up problem. In this case, however, the policies appear to involve unnecessary risk and may lead to premature deployment of digital technology.

Government standard setting should emulate the successful practices of private standard setting. These practices include coordination of the activities of hardware and software suppliers and having multiple suppliers make technological contributions to the technical standards. These private practices are best exemplified by Philips and Sony's development of the technical standard for CDs. Both Japanese and U.S. governmental organizations (NHK and the FCC, respectively) appear to have done well in this regard with respect to developing technical standards for HDTV. Earlier, the FCC had success with this method in setting the original technical standards for (black-and-white) television. The FCC did not follow this path in originally setting technical standards for color television, and the outcome was much less successful.

15
Final Remarks

The case studies discussed in this book describe some of the most important technological developments of recent times. The proponents of these technologies have had a fundamental impact on modern life. They combined brilliant product innovations with the practical business acumen to succeed in the market.

These accomplishments are all the more impressive when one considers the difficulties of succeeding in a bandwagon market. The product must be extraordinary, a difficult start-up problem must be solved, and the market is very unforgiving of mistakes. The major product innovations in the bandwagon markets described in our case studies were truly remarkable achievements.

Mathematical Appendix

A.1 Equilibrium Adjustment Process

We assume that each consumer makes a simple yes-no decision about whether to subscribe to a particular service that embodies bandwagon effects. This assumption is not really restrictive, because the same individual could make yes-no decisions about whether to purchase successive units of the service. We further assume that the consumer chooses "yes," only if consuming the service increases his or her utility, compared to alternative purchases. He or she chooses "no" if alternative purchases would generate at least as much utility. (The bandwagon service loses ties.)

The adjustment process takes demand from the initial user set I to an equilibrium user set. Adjustment occurs as individuals sequentially (in some order) begin to subscribe or unsubscribe to the service. As the adjustment process progresses, no subscriber will ever want to unsubscribe, because the service becomes more valuable to existing users as the user set expands. Eventually an equilibrium is reached at which no one else wants to subscribe. This is the demand-based equilibrium user set, or D for short.

Theorem 1   The same equilibrium is arrived at, regardless of the order in which individuals subscribe.

Proof   Consider two sequences of individuals who subscribe, starting from an initial user set I:

$a_1, a_2, \ldots, a_m$ and

$b_1, b_2, \ldots, b_n$.

The end result of both sequences is an equilibrium user set. Let A equal the set $\{a_1, \ldots, a_m\}$ and B equal the set $\{b_1, \ldots, b_n\}$.

We know that $a_1 \in B$. If a_1 was willing to subscribe when the user set was I, he or she would certainly want to subscribe at the larger user set $I + B$.

It then follows that $a_2 \in B$. If a_2 was willing to subscribe when the user set was $I + a_1$, he or she would certainly want to subscribe at the larger user set $I + B$, which includes a_1.

Similarly, the remaining elements of A are all in B. Thus, $A \subseteq B$. We can then apply this process in reverse to prove that $B \subseteq A$. It follows that $A = B$.

End of Proof

Theorem 1 implies that D is well-defined. It depends only on I and not on the equilibrium adjustment process.

A.2 The Maximum Equilibrium User Set

The maximum equilibrium user set, or M for short, is the union of all possible equilibrium user sets.

Theorem 2 The union of all equilibrium user sets is an equilibrium user set.

Proof We need to prove that at the union of all equilibrium user sets: (a) no nonsubscriber would want to subscribe, and (b) no subscriber would want to unsubscribe.

(a) Suppose that a nonsubscriber wanted to subscribe: We could then apply the equilibrium adjustment process until an equilibrium was reached. The resulting equilibrium user set would contain the initial added subscriber. Thus, the original set would not be the union of all equilibrium user sets, contrary to assumption.

(b) No subscriber would want to drop out, since each is the member of some equilibrium user set that is contained in the union of all equilibrium user sets. If the subscriber did not want to drop out at the smaller equilibrium user set, he or she would also not want to drop out at the larger equilibrium user set.

End of Proof

Theorem 3 All users are better off at M than at any other equilibrium user set.

Proof Since M is the union of all equilibrium user sets, any other equilibrium user set is a proper subset of M. The additional users in M that are not in the other user set joined because doing so increased their utility. Some other subscribers may benefit from the addition of those new users through bandwagon effects, but no other subscriber is worse off.

End of Proof

A.3 Comparison of Equilibrium User Sets

Figure A.1 illustrates the user sets I, D, and M. In the figure, the user sets are nested. That is, I is a subset of D, which is a subset of M, which is a subset of the entire population. In all cases, the smaller set may be the same as the next larger set. In formal mathematical terms, it need not be a "proper" subset of the next larger set.

Figure A.2 illustrates user sets for the case in which I (and hence D) equals the null set. M may nevertheless be quite large, but the equilibrium adjustment process that we described above provides no way to get there. Of course, it is also possible that the product is a complete dud, and M (as well as I and D) is the null set.

A.4 Mathematical Description of Bandwagon Inverse Demand Curve

Figure A.3 illustrates the inverse demand curve for a bandwagon product. It is an elaboration of figure 3.1.

The figure can result from the following specification of the inverse demand function: Let individual i's reservation price for consuming the service be

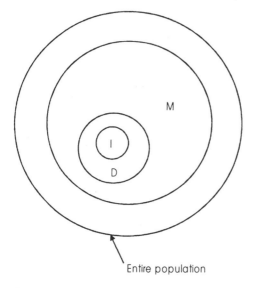

Entire population

Figure A.1
Equilibrium user sets.

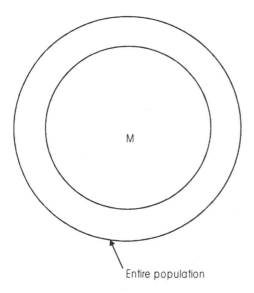

Entire population

Figure A.2
Equilibrium user sets where 1 equals the null set.

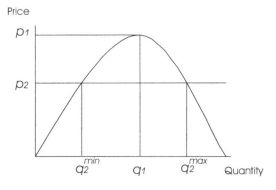

Price

Figure A.3
Equilibrium demand versus price: Simplest shape.

$$w(i) = v(i)f(n) \quad i = 1, \ldots, N, \tag{1}$$

where

w = reservation price (of consumer i),

n = the number of users,

N = the size of the population, and

f = a monotomically increasing function of n.

Let us assume that the reservation price is 0 if there are no other users; that is,

$$f(0) = f(1) = 0. \tag{2}$$

Let us also assume that consumers are ordered inversely according to v. Thus, v is a monotomically decreasing function of i. Finally, let us assume that the reservation price is 0 for the consumer who is least attracted to the service; that is,

$$v(N) = 0. \tag{3}$$

For an equilibrium user set with n users,

$$w(n) = v(n)f(n). \tag{4}$$

It follows from our previous assumptions that

$$w(0) = 0 \quad \text{and} \tag{5}$$

$$w(N) = 0. \tag{6}$$

However, w has positive values for $0 < n < N$.

It follows that the inverse demand curve is necessarily hump-shaped (under these assumptions). It may have multiple humps, as discussed in section A.6.

A.5   Stability of Demand Equilibria

The maximum sustainable price in figure A.3 is p_1. If price exceeds p_1, demand equals 0. For price equal to p_1, there is a unique equilibrium quantity q_1. For each positive price that is lower than p_1, (e.g., p_2), there are two possible equilibrium quantities ($q_2^{\min}$ and $q_2^{\max}$).

The equilibria on the downward-sloping part of the inverse demand curve are stable. For example, suppose that at price p_2, some marginal nonsubscribers join; so q is slightly greater than $q_2^{\max}$. The reservation prices of the new subscribers will then be slightly lower than the actual price. Hence, the equilibrium adjustment process will cause q to decline back to $q_2^{\max}$. Similarly, suppose that some marginal subscribers drop out; so q is slightly less than $q_2^{\max}$. The reservation prices of the new non-subscribers will then be slightly greater than the actual price. Hence, the equilibrium adjustment process will cause q to increase to $q_2^{\max}$.

In sharp contrast, the equilibria on the upward-sloping part of the inverse demand curve are unstable. Suppose that at price p_2, some marginal nonsubscribers join; so q expands to become slightly greater than $q_2^{\min}$, the reservation prices of the new subscribers will be slightly greater than the actual price. So will the reservation prices of nonsubscribers who value the service only slightly less than the new subscribers. Hence, the equilibrium adjustment process will cause q to increase. The process continues, until q reaches the stable equilibrium $q_2^{\max}$. Only then will there be no nonsubscribers whose reservation prices exceed the actual price.

Alternatively, suppose that at price p_2, some marginal subscribers drop out; so q contracts to become less than $q_2^{\min}$, the reservation prices of the new nonsubscribers will be less than the actual price. So will the reservation prices of subscribers who value the service only slightly more than the new nonsubscribers. Hence, the equilibrium adjustment process will cause q to decrease. The process continues, until q reaches 0. Only then will there be no subscribers whose reservation prices are less than the actual price.

A.6   More Complex Inverse Demand Curves

Figure A.3 shows only the simplest shape of the relation between equilibrium demand and price. Figure A.4 shows a somewhat more complex shape. In figure A.4, there are four equilibria at some prices, including p_2. As before $q_2^{\min}$ is a critical mass. Nevertheless, if that critical mass is achieved, demand does not increase to the maximum equilibrium user set. It increases only to q_2^x. The maximum equilibrium user set can be reached only if a secondary critical mass, q_2^y, is achieved.

A.7   Metcalfe's Law

Metcalfe's Law is couched in terms of the total "value" of a service. Value is, of course, not defined in the one-sentence law. We presume that it means the sum of consumers' reservation prices. In economics jargon, this equals revenue paid plus consumer surplus.

For a nonbandwagon service, the reservation price of any given consumer does not depend on the user set. If all consumers have equal

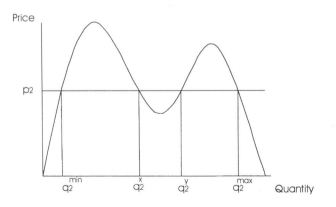

Figure A.4
Equilibrium demand versus price: More complex shape.

reservation prices, the total value of such a service increases proportionately with number of users.

This case is illustrated in the top part of figure A.5. In the figure, the value of the service to each person is 3 if that person is a user and zero otherwise. The total value of the service is obtained by summing the values of the persons who are users. For user sets of 1, 2, and 3 persons, the total values of the service are 3, 6, and 9, respectively. The total value is thus proportional to (and equals three times) the number of users.

In reality, any service has different values to different users. If we assume that the user set expands by bringing in users who place progressively less value on the service, we have the general result that the value of a nonbandwagon service increases *less than* proportionately with the number of users.

This point is illustrated in the bottom part of figure A.5. The value of the service is 5 to the first person, 3 to the second person, and 1 to the third person. For user sets of 1, 2, and 3 persons, the total values of the service are 5, 8, and 9, respectively. The total value of the service increases less than proportionately with the number of users. As the user set doubles by increasing from 1 to 2, the total value increases by only 60 percent. As the user set increases by another 50 percent (from 2 to 3), the total value increases by only 12.5 percent.

Let us now consider a bandwagon service. Suppose that the values of links to other network users are additive.[1] That is, the value of the service to any user is the sum of the values of the links with all the other members of the user set. If the value of all links were equal, we would get Metcalfe's Law; namely, the value of the network would, indeed, go up as the square of the number of users.

This point is illustrated in the top part of figure A.6. Each row of the table shows the value of the service to a particular person. Each column shows the values to other users of having that particular person in the user set. Each diagonal element shows the non-bandwagon value of the service—that is, the value to a person of being a user, apart from who else is in the user set. The value to each user of having any given user (including himself or herself) in the user set is assumed to be 3. The total value of the service to a user is obtained by summing across the user set in his or her row. The figure shows the calculations of total value of the

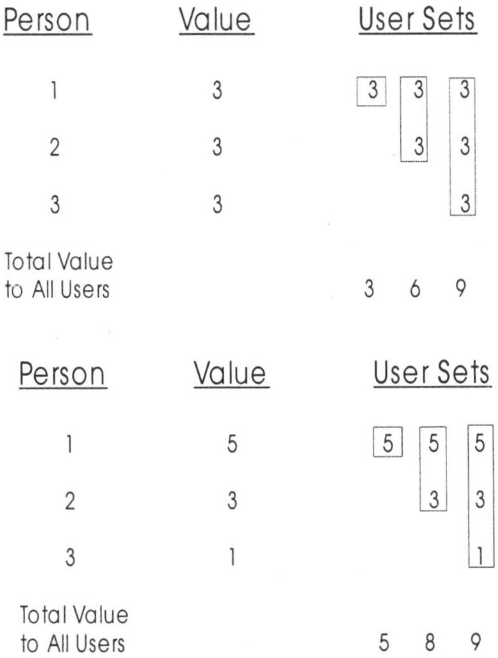

Person	Value	User Sets		
1	3	3	3	3
2	3		3	3
3	3			3
Total Value to All Users		3	6	9

Person	Value	User Sets		
1	5	5	5	5
2	3		3	3
3	1			1
Total Value to All Users		5	8	9

Figure A.5
(Top) Total value of nonbandwagon service: Equal values.
(Bottom) Total value of nonbandwagon service: Unequal values.

service. For user sets of 1, 2, and 3 persons, the total value of the service is 3, 12, and 27, respectively. The total value of the service is proportional to the *square* of the number of users. As the user set increases from 1 to 2 to 3, the total value increases by ratios of 1 to 4 to 9.

In reality, however, the values of network links can vary enormously. If we assume, not unreasonably, that the user set expands by bringing in users who place less and less value on the service,[2] the value of the network goes up *less than* proportionately to the square of the number of users. This point is illustrated in the bottom part of figure A.6. It is the same as the top part of the figure except that the values in the table at the bottom vary across users. In particular, the values associated with person 1's being a user are the greatest. The values associated with person 3's being a user are the least.

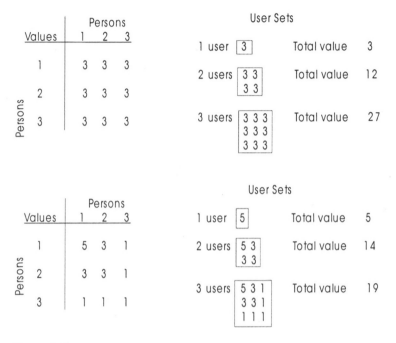

Figure A.6
(Top) Total value of bandwagon service: Equal values.
(Bottom) Total value of bandwagon service: Unequal values.

It is quite possible that the total value of a bandwagon service may increase more than proportionately with the number of users. In the bottom part of figure A.6B, the total value of the service increases more than proportionately as the user set expands from 1 to 2. The user set doubles, and the total value increases by a factor of 2.8 (but does not quadruple, as would be indicated by Metcalfe's Law). Such an outcome is not possible with nonbandwagon services.

The actual outcome may, however, be quite different. In the bottom part of figure A.6, the total value of the service increases less than proportionately as the user set expands 50 percent (from 2 to 3). The total value increases by only 35.7 percent (from 14 to 19). This is *far* short of the increase of 125 percent (the increase from a factor of 4 to a factor of 9) that would be indicated by Metcalfe's Law.

A.8 Continuous Formulation of Metcalfe's Law

The model underlying Metcalfe's Law can be formulated in continuous form as follows:

Let us assume that in equation (1),

$$f(n) = kn \qquad \text{for all } n \tag{7}$$

where k is a positive constant.

This assumption implies the complete absence of communities of interest. It implies that a marginal telephone subscriber is, indeed, someone I would want to talk to—as much as anyone else.

Let us further assume that

$$v(i) = ci^{\alpha}, \tag{8}$$

where

c is a positive constant, and

α is a nonpositive constant.

In equation (8), α indicates how rapidly the reservation prices of new subscribers (*with respect to any given user set*) decline as new subscribers who value the service progressively less are added.

If all persons value the service equally, $\alpha = 0$, and we get Metcalfe's Law. That is, in equilibrium,

$$
\begin{aligned}
w &= \int_0^n w(n)dn \\
&= \int_0^n v(n)f(n)dn \\
&= \int_0^n ckndn = \left(\frac{ck}{2}\right)n^2,
\end{aligned}
\tag{9}
$$

where w is the total value of the service. It is proportional to the square of the number of users.

If the user set expands by adding persons who value the service less and less, $\alpha < 0$. In the special case where $\alpha = -1$,

$$w = \int_0^n ckdn = ckn. \tag{10}$$

That is, the total value of the service increases proportionately with the number of users. More generally,

$$w = \int_0^n ckn^{\alpha+1}dn$$
$$= \left(\frac{ck}{\alpha+2}\right)n^{\alpha+2}. \tag{11}$$

Total value increases more or less than proportionately depending on whether α is greater than or less than -1. Metcalfe's Law is the (unrealistic) limiting case in which $\alpha = 0$.

A.9   Benefits of Interlinking

The benefits of interlinking are illustrated in figure A.7. The figure is based on the equal-value model that underlies Metcalfe's Law. The upper part of the figure is identical to the upper part of figure A.6, except that the user set consists of four persons. The upper part of figure A.7 shows that the value of the service is 48 if consumers are all interlinked (an implicit assumption underlying Metcalfe's Law).

The lower part of the figure shows what happens if users 1 and 2 are not interlinked with users 3 and 4. A possible reason for their not being interlinked is that the network that serves users 1 and 2 is not interconnected to the network that serves users 3 and 4. Alternatively, the products consumed by users 1 and 2 may be incompatible with those consumed by users 3 and 4. Regardless of the reason, users 1 and 2 derive no bandwagon benefits with respect to users 3 and 4, and vice versa. The total value of the service under these circumstances is 24—one half the value with interlinking, as shown in the upper part of the figure. More generally, in the equal-value model underlying Metcalfe's Law: The total value of a bandwagon service is fully n times as large if all consumers are interlinked, compared to their being served by n equal suppliers that are not interlinked.

As previously discussed, Metcalfe's Law is generally unrealistic, because different consumers are likely to value a bandwagon service very differently. Moreover, the user set served by each supplier is likely to have a community of interest within itself, because users will tend to choose

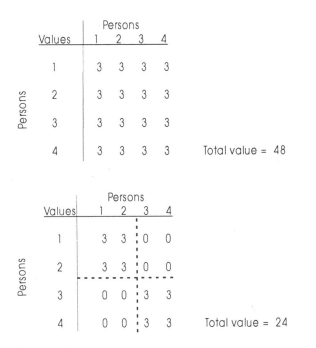

Figure A.7
(Top) Total value of bandwagon service with interlinking, equal values.
(Bottom) Total value of bandwagon service without interlinking, equal values.

the supplier from which they can enjoy the greatest bandwagon benefits. Figure A.8 illustrates the benefits of interlinking with diverse values and substantial communities of interest. These conditions reduce the value of interlinking. Even so, interlinking increases the total value of the band-wagon service from 34 to 48—an increase of 41 percent.

A.10   Start-Up Strategies

Some start-up strategies are illustrated in figure A.9 (which is an elabo-ration of figure A.4). The simple strategy is still to set price equal to p_2. If I is somewhere between $q_2^{\min}$ and q_2^x, D equals q_2^x.

An alternative strategy in this case is to lower price from p_2 to p_3. Demand would then increase all the way to $q_3^{\max}$, as a result of band-wagon effects. Price reductions from p_2 to p_4 may be unprofitable, but at

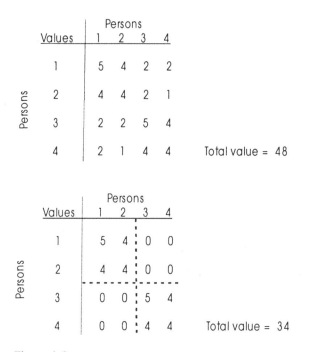

Total value = 48

Total value = 34

Figure A.8
(Top) Total value of bandwagon service with interlinking, unequal values.
(Bottom) Total value of bandwagon service without interlinking, unequal values.

p_4, demand becomes discontinuous. An infinitesimal further reduction leads to a large increase in demand. Such discontinuities are anomalous in standard demand models, but they are commonplace where bandwagon effects are present.

Another alternative strategy may be even more profitable. Suppose that the long-run profit-maximizing equilibrium is really p_2 and q_2^{max}. That equilibrium can be attained by raising price back to p_2 after demand has increased to q_3^{max}. Note, however, that the direct path from q_2^x to q_2^{max}, holding price equal to p_2, is blocked. The lesser quantity q_2^x is an equilibrium, and there is no tendency for q to increase further. One can get from q_2^x to q_2^{max} only via the indirect path of lowering price to some p_3 and then raising it again after demand has expanded beyond q_2^y.

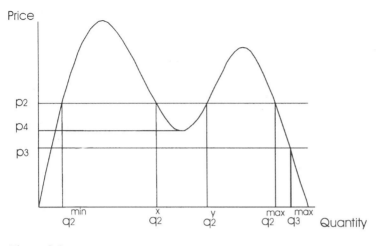

Figure A.9
Start-up strategy.

A.11 Principal Contacts in the User Set

Figure A.10 illustrates the construction of a user set by marketing the service to principal contacts of existing users. The numbers in the figures denote users in the order in which the new users are added. The solid lines connect individuals who are principal contacts of each other. These lines are the basis on which individuals are selected. After the user set becomes sufficiently large, it will be possible to add persons who have more than one principal contact within the user set. The additional contacts (above one) are indicated as dashed lines in the figure.

Each time the user set expands, an additional solid line is added. As a result, an existing user has one additional contact in the user set. Also, each new user has a principal contact in the user set. Thus, each time an additional person is added, two persons have an additional contact within the user set. If the user set consists of n persons, $n - 1$ of them were added through this process. Thus, the total number of principal contacts within the user set is

$$2(n - 1) = 2n - 2.$$

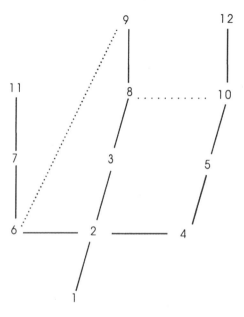

Figure A.10
Construction of a self-sufficient user set.

The average number of principal contacts per user is $2 - 2/n$. This average is close to 2 for any sizable n. Furthermore, there are likely to be some additional contacts via the dashed lines in the figure. Thus, the average number of principal contacts per user for any sizable user set is likely to exceed 2.

A.12   Microsoft's Pricing in the Static Essential-Component Model

Suppose that a computer system consists of base components plus the operating system, which we assume to be an essential component.[3] We assume that the base components and computer systems are both produced by competitive industries. The price of the base components is then equal to their marginal cost, which we assume to be fixed, from the perspective of the supplier of the essential component. The price of the computer system equals the price of the base components plus the price of the essential component. Thus,

$$p_s = mc_b + p_e, \tag{12}$$

where

p_s = the price of the system,

mc_b = the marginal cost of the base components, and

p_e = the price of the essential component.

The demand function for computer systems is

$$q_s = q_s(p_s),$$ (13)

where

q_s = the quantity of computer systems.

Profits of the supplier of the essential component are

$$\Pi_e = p_e q_s - c_e(q_s),$$ (14)

where c_e is the cost of producing the essential component, expressed as a function of output.

For static profit maximization

$$0 = q_s + p_e \frac{\partial q_s}{\partial p_e} - \frac{\partial c_e}{\partial p_e}.$$ (15)

But

$$\frac{\partial q_s}{\partial p_e} = \frac{\partial q_s}{\partial p_s} \frac{\partial p_s}{\partial p_e}.$$ (16)

Since mc_b in equation (11) is fixed from the perspective of the supplier of the essential components,

$$\frac{\partial q_s}{\partial p_e} = 1.$$ (17)

Thus,

$$\frac{\partial q_s}{\partial p_e} = \frac{\partial q_s}{\partial p_s}.$$ (18)

Also,

$$\frac{\partial c_e}{\partial p_e} = \frac{\partial c_e}{\partial q_s} \frac{\partial q_s}{\partial p_e}$$
$$= mc_e \frac{\partial q_s}{\partial p_s},$$ (19)

where

mc_e = the marginal cost of producing the essential component.

Substituting equations (18) and (19) in equation (15),

$$O = q_s + p_e\left(\frac{\partial q_s}{\partial p_s}\right) - mc_e\left(\frac{\partial q_s}{\partial p_s}\right). \tag{20}$$

Solving for p_e,

$$p_e = mc_e - \frac{q_s}{\left(\dfrac{\partial q_s}{\partial p_s}\right)}. \tag{21}$$

In terms of the elasticity of demand,

$$p_e = mc_e - \frac{p_s}{\eta_s}, \tag{22}$$

where

η_s = the demand elasticity of computer systems.

The price of computer systems is about \$2,000. The marginal cost of producing operating systems is approximately zero. Thus, in order for Microsoft's price of \$45 to \$65 to be the monopoly profit maximum, the demand elasticity for computer systems would have to be approximately −44 to −31.

In reality, the demand for computer systems is approximately −1.0. This value is not even remotely close to the value implied by the static essential-component model. We conclude that the static essential-component model is untenable.[4]

Notes

I Introduction

1. See Shiller. Our citation convention for books, academic articles, and Web sites is to cite only the author's name (or authors' names) in the text. Dates are given where we cite multiple works by the same author(s). Full references are given in the bibliography. Our citation convention for newspaper and magazine articles is to give the full citation in the text, but not to include the reference in the bibliography.

2. This and a number of other key economics concepts are defined in the glossary of economics concepts at the end of the book. These concepts are bold-faced in the text where they are first introduced and defined. They are again bold-faced where they first appear in the summary chapters 5 and 14.

Chapter 1. The High-Technology Bandwagon

1. Abbreviations and acronyms are defined where they are first introduced. They are additionally defined in the dictionary of abbreviations and acronyms that follows.

Chapter 2. A Bandwagon Tour

1. Several other papers from the mid-1970s discussed the issue of economically efficient pricing for a mature bandwagon service. See section 4.8.

II Bandwagons: How They Work

1. To avoid repetition in our theoretical discussions, we refer to "services" or "products" interchangeably, rather than to "services and products." The same theoretical results apply to both.

2. In formal economics terms, the gain to the consumer is the increase in his or her "consumer's surplus."

Chapter 3. Bandwagon Demand

1. This analytical approach follows Rohlfs (1974).

2. For further discussion of the demand-based equilibrium and the equilibrium adjustment process, see the mathematical appendix.

3. The mathematical appendix describes the properties of the maximum equilibrium user set. It also provides a mathematical comparison of the various user sets we have been discussing.

4. See the mathematical appendix for a mathematical description of demand in figure 3.2.

5. Further discussion of the stability properties of the inverse demand curve is given in the mathematical appendix.

6. For further discussion of more complex bandwagon demand models, see the mathematical appendix.

7. Shapiro and Varian quote Metcalfe as saying that the law was ascribed to him by George Gilder, but he is willing to take credit for it.

8. One needs to include the link between the user and himself/herself in order for the law to work out exactly. In reality, the self link may have little or no value, but the treatment of the self link makes relatively little difference for large n.

9. The role of expectations and their self-fulfilling property has been analyzed in previous economic analyses. See, for example, Katz and Shapiro.

Chapter 4. Bandwagon Supply

1. Two pioneering studies applying bandwagon models to compatibility issues are Farrell and Saloner (1985) and Katz and Shapiro.

2. These strategies are discussed in the mathematical appendix in the context of a specific model.

3. See, for example, Oi for an early discussion of two-part tariffs. Brown and Sibley treat the issue from the more general perspective of non-uniform pricing.

4. The economics of interlinking as a costly activity are explored in Farrell and Saloner (1992). That analysis applies to the use of "converters," but many of the results also apply to other costly ways of making incompatible products compatible. It can also be applied to interconnection of competing networks.

5. The start-up costs should be considered as investments, even though they may be treated as expenses in the firm's accounting records. The large accounting profits that the firm earns in later years are actually returns to those investments.

6. Related strategic issues arise when consumers must incur switching costs to change suppliers or are locked-in to their current supplier. Klemperer developed a theoretical model of switching costs and showed that

- new entrants will initially offer lower prices than they would in the absence of switching costs; and
- after a new entrant is established, it will offer higher prices than it would in the absence of switching costs.

See also Farrell and Shapiro (1988) and Beggs and Klempcrer.

7. See Schumpeter, pp. 81–106.

8. See Schumpeter, pp. 81–106.

9. Arthur demonstrates an analogous point in a lock-in model.

10. Of course, A's victory in the competitive battle is not inevitable. B may be able to win, notwithstanding bandwagon effects. Firm B is especially likely to win if the user set is not very large when it enters. B may also be able to initiate and have the financial resources to win a price war.

11. Expectations can also have the effect of turning a close victory into a landslide. Suppose, for example, that 55 percent of the people think that firm A's product is superior and 45 percent of the people think that firm B's product is superior. As a result, everyone may believe that A will win the bandwagon race and choose A's product.

12. Consumers may or may not be better off with interlinking. They will enjoy greater bandwagon benefits, but suppliers may raise their prices.

13. Grindley, p. 137.

14. Schmalensee at ¶¶ 103–106.

15. For further discussion of the advantages and disadvantages of vertical integration, see Panzar, Holmstrom and Tirole, Williamson, and Perry.

16. Making the distinction between proprietor services and customer equipment is, we believe, an innovation. The distinction is useful in several of our case studies in part III.

17. See Artle and Averous, Squire, and Littlechild for further discussion of this issue.

18. For example, Areeda and Turner propose the use of short-run variable costs for antitrust purposes. Regulatory commissions usually insist that the incumbent firm's prices in competitive markets exceed some variant of long-run incremental cost.

Chapter 5. Summary of the Results of Bandwagon Theory

1. Bold-faced words are defined in the glossary of economics concepts that follows.

III   Case Studies

Chapter 6.   Fax

1. The history of the fax in this section is taken from Coopersmith and Farrell and Shapiro (1992).

2. Data provided by Economides and Himmelberg (and used in their study).

3. Data provided by Economides and Himmelberg.

4. Economides and Himmelberg estimate a quantitative model of the growth of the fax as a bandwagon product during this period.

Chapter 7.   Early Telephone

1. Bell's sales agents were often construction companies that could do the required construction for an additional charge (Bornholz and Evans, p. 8).

2. Mueller, p. 35.

3. Bell also agreed to a costly settlement of a patent dispute with Western Union. See Brock, pp. 89–99, for further discussion of Bell's interactions with Western Union.

4. The actual policies of the Bell companies with respect to interlinking are discussed in section 7.2.

5. Bornholz and Evans, p. 25.

6. See WOW-COM.

7. Stehman, pp. 23–25.

8. Stehman, p. 26.

9. Stehman, pp. 27–28.

10. See also Bennett, pp. 2–3.

11. Bennett, p. 5. See also Brock, pp. 132–147. It should be noted that the European public monopolies generally did worse than Bell in developing telephone service outside the major cities.

12. For examples of the technical problems associated with early telephone service, see Brooks, pp. 85–87, and Fischer, pp. 37–38.

13. Mueller observes that for this reason, telephone service did not satisfy the usual conditions for natural monopoly. Rather, telephone service was a natural monopoly because of network externalities, not scale economies. According to Mueller, this point was well understood early in the century but had been largely forgotten by the time of the AT&T antitrust case.

14. A conceivable explanation of the lower rates in Europe is that exchanges were smaller and unit costs were therefore lower. Stehman (p. 47) adduces evidence that this was not the case. In particular, the London exchange was com-

parable in size to the New York exchange. The Stockholm exchange was comparable in size to the Washington exchange.

15. Brooks, pp. 82–85.

16. See Bornholz and Evans, pp. 22–25.

17. See Mueller, pp. 136–145.

18. In the Kingsbury Commitment of 1913, Bell agreed to interconnection with respect to toll services. Mueller (pp. 130–133) minimizes the importance of this agreement, because the conditions for interconnection were very favorable to AT&T. He notes that interconnection with non-Bell companies predated the commitment and did not accelerate thereafter.

Chapter 8. Picturephone

1. The analysis in this chapter draws on Rohlfs and Wish, and on Wish and Rohlfs.

Chapter 9. Compact-Disc Players

1. The analysis in this section is based largely on the history of CDs in Hill and in McGahan.

2. Smith, p. 128.

3. Steve McClure, "The SONY perspective," *Billboard* (September 26, 1992), p. CD 10.

4. "Compact discs spin industry into digital age," *Chicago Sun Times* (July 25, 1985).

5. Ibid.

6. "Compact discs spin industry into digital age," *Chicago Sun Times* (July 25, 1985), p. 91.

7. Laura Landro, "Merger of Warner Unit, Polygram angers troubled record industry," *The Wall Street Journal* (April 12, 1984).

8. William K. Knoedeleder Jr., "Record industry is suddenly a smash hit, fueled by boom in compact discs, firms' fortunes have soared," *Los Angeles Times* (October 15, 1987), p. 1.

9. "Polygram 32,000 shares priced at $16, 31.50 guilders," *Dow Jones News Service—Ticker* (December 14, 1989).

10. Susan Nunziata, "Music biz upset over Philips' plan for recordable CD," *Billboard* (October 10, 1992).

11. VCRs got off to this same bad start. As discussed in the next chapter, however, consumers could derive substantial utility from VCRs by recording and later replaying television programming. That stand-alone activity is not subject

to significant bandwagon effects. For this reason, the dual standard was less damaging to VCRs than to DCCs and MDs.

12. Hill.

Chapter 10. VCRs

1. Cusumano, Mylonadis, and Rosenbloom, p. 60.

2. Lardner, p. 143.

3. See Lardner's chapter on "Divorce, Japanese Style," pp. 136–155.

4. Some of the longer playing times shown in table 10.1 were achieved at the expense of somewhat lower picture quality.

5. Grindley, p. 4.

6. See Cusumano, Mylonadis, and Rosenbloom, pp. 83–84.

7. M. Schrage, "Experts differ on future of home video," *The Washington Post* (October 30, 1986), p. E3.

8. The history in this section is taken from Lardner, pp. 168–180.

9. Klopfenstein, p. 29.

10. Cusumano, Mylonadis, and Rosenbloom, p. 84.

11. Roehl and Varian draw a number of interesting parallels between the video-cassette business and commercial circulating libraries of the eighteenth century. For the latter, the complementary bandwagon effects related to the ability to read. The growth of libraries stimulated literacy, which then led to positive feedback.

12. Grindley, p. 123.

13. See Klopfenstein, pp. 26–27.

Chapter 11. Personal Computers

1. K. Polsson.

2. Grindley, p. 133.

3. See, for example, Andrew Pollack, *The New York Times* (May 11, 1983), p. 1.

4. Evans, Nichols, and Reddy, p. 4.

5. Grindley, p. 5.

6. Grindley, p. 142.

7. An important exception in recent times was the Bell System before the AT&T divestiture. Bell went to great lengths to control all phases of the production of telephone service. For example, it produced many of its own semiconductors. It owned a smelter to process precious metals. It produced its own screwdrivers

and its own notebooks, with a unique four-hole design that Bell regarded as superior to the standard three-hole design.

8. Nevertheless, the informal internal incentives within a firm work better for many activities. These include activities for which the output or its quality cannot be precisely defined, and contracts are therefore difficult to negotiate and enforce. See Panzar, Holmstrom and Tirole, Williamson, and Perry for further discussions of the advantages and disadvantages of vertical integration.

9. Deborah C. Wise, "Can John Scully clean up the mess at Apple: With Steve Jobs on the sidelines, the company will no longer go it alone," *Business Week* (July 29, 1985), p. 70.

10. Telecommunications terminal equipment (e.g., PBXs, modems, and answering machines) offers a striking parallel. Consumers had limited choice when such equipment was produced by the end-to-end Bell System monopoly. When terminal equipment was opened to competition, consumer choice increased, in many cases by a hundredfold or more. See Shooshan & Jackson Inc.

11. Grindley, pp. 25, 134.

12. Arguably, it is precisely through such passive play by Digital Research (namely, the delay in upgrading CP/M to 16 bits) that allowed Microsoft to get its start.

13. Fisher, p. 25.

14. This result is rigorously proved in the mathematical appendix, following Evans, Nichols, and Reddy. Schmalensee, in his testimony for Microsoft (fn. 131), states that Evans, Nichols, and Reddy, prepared their study under his (Schmalensee's) direction.

15. In this scenario, Microsoft's upgrade price would have to be comparable to the price that it charged computer manufacturers. Otherwise, users could buy computers without operating systems, install an older copy of Windows, and then buy the upgrade.

16. Om Malik, "Microsoft Office unlikely to budge from top spot," http://forbes.com/1999/08/30/mu7.html.

17. Stephanie Miles and Joe Wilcox, "Windows 95 remains most popular operating system," CNET News.com (July 20, 1999).

18. For a detailed history of the development of JAVA, see ⟨http://ils.unc.edu/blaze/java/javahist.html⟩.

Chapter 12. Television

1. This section is based on the historical account of Besen and Johnson, pp. 87–89.

2. The FCC did develop interconnection rules to ensure that wireless and wireline networks were interlinked.

3. In the past, no U.S. cellular supplier had near-nationwide coverage, and the uniform AMPS technical standard did indeed facilitate roaming and generate some external bandwagon benefits (though for most users, these benefits were/are secondary to the benefits from local calling). The uniform GSM (and 3G) standards also facilitate roaming across European countries.

4. See Cole and Oettinger, p. 24.

5. See Quinlan for discussion of the latter. Quinlan refers to the early postwar period at the FCC as "The Whorehouse Era."

6. As we shall see shortly, this same vertical integration contributed to color television's achieving a critical mass.

7. Upward compatibility was not an issue. Color television sets could easily be (and were) designed to show black-and-white programs in black and white. For black-and-white programming, however, the picture quality of color television sets was somewhat inferior to that of black-and-white television sets.

8. Besen and Johnson, p. 92.

9. Farrell and Shapiro (1992), p. 28.

10. Farrell and Shapiro (1992), p. 56.

11. Farrell and Shapiro (1992), p. 58.

12. Farrell and Shapiro (1992), p. 5.

13. Cabletelevision Advertising Bureau, *Cable TV Facts* (New York: 1997), p. 5.

14. In this report, we use the term "HDTV" generically to refer to all the analog and digital technologies for providing improved quality of picture and sound.

15. See Farrell and Shapiro (1992), pp. 13–18.

16. See Grindley, p. 212.

17. Grindley, p. 204.

18. This section and the next (on Japan) draw on Grindley, pp. 202–207.

19. PAL is used in the United Kingdom, Germany, Italy, and Spain. SECAM is used in France, Russia, and Eastern Europe.

20. This section draws on Farrell and Shapiro (1992).

21. These sorts of arrangements are actually being made under the FCC's actual (digital) HDTV policies. Manufacturers are underwriting the production of some digital programming. For example, Panasonic subsidized ABC's production of *Monday Night Football* in HDTV. Mitsubishi subsidized some of CBS's prime-time programming in HDTV (S. Donahue, "ABC will broadcast 'Monday Nigh Football' in high definition. MSGN already produces in high definition," *Electronic Media* (May 31, 1999), p. 32).

22. Farrell and Shapiro (1992), p. 25.

23. This technology substantially differs from the digital technology deployed by many cable television systems. The latter is used primarily to increase the

channel capacity of the cable. It does not require viewers to have digital television sets and does not produce the high picture quality of the FCC standard.

24. Farrell and Shapiro (1992), p. 25.

25. Noll, Peck, and McGowan, p. 81.

26. See Brinkley for a detailed discussion of the large influence of the broadcasters on the FCC's decision process.

27. Nevertheless, it was opposed by the cable and computer industries. The cable industry would, as previously discussed, be better off if broadcast HDTV never developed. The computer industry wanted the FCC to adopt a less flexible standard to ensure that broadcast television would be compatible with computer technology. Such a standard would further the interests of the computer industry, but the FCC decided that it would not further the broader public interest.

Chapter 13. The Internet

1. A user who downloaded all the information from one hundreds sites every day (an ambitious goal) would get through only 36,500 sites at the end of a year.

2. For example, see Cerf and see Leiner et al.

3. FCC (1998).

4. It is calculated as the book value of 1994 physical plant of AT&T Communications (the long-distance division of AT&T), adjusted upward to take account of four years' growth and to include an estimate of the plant of other LDCs. Since AT&T provided little of the Internet backbone in 1994, this estimate can reasonably be interpreted as the part of the long-distance network used for voice traffic.

5. The size estimates presented above do not include wireless carriers or carriers that compete with telcos to provide local telephone services—even where such carriers are vertically integrated with telcos or LDCs. The size estimates also do not include satellite carriers or equipment suppliers.

6. It is calculated as the property, plant, and equipment of the largest ISP, America On Line ("AOL"), adjusted upward to include other ISPs.

7. It is based on the transmission plant of AT&T Communications in 1994 with the following adjustments:

• upward adjustments to take account of four years' growth and the plant of LDCs other than AT&T;
• downward adjustments to reflect the smaller capacity of the Internet relative to the capacity used by LDCs for voice traffic.

AT&T data reflect voice capacity, since AT&T carried primarily voice traffic and supplied little of the Internet backbone.

8. See Coffman and Odlyzko in addition to Odlyzko for a more detailed analysis of Internet growth.

9. Odlyzko.

10. FCC (1994–1995) and (1998), table 2.5—Access Lines by Type of Customer for Reporting Local Exchange Carriers. The number represents the annualized growth in the total number of switched access lines.

11. In this regard, we need carefully to distinguish voice over Internet ("VoI") from voice over Internet protocols ("VoIP"). The former is actually carried on the Internet; the latter uses packet switching and transmission with the same technological protocols as the Internet, but may be carried partly or wholly on private networks instead of the Internet. Many carriers now offer voice services using VoIP. By largely using their own networks instead of the Internet, these carriers can ensure that the QoS is acceptable. With VoI, voice users must simply accept the low QoS of the Internet.

12. Sometimes U and V are served by the same telco switch. In that case, the call can be completed with a single switching occurrence and no inter-office transmission.

13. In addition, signaling costs, which are also small, are related to call attempts. The signaling system sets up the call and reserves capacity end to end before switching ports and transmission links are deployed.

14. Figure 13.3 is a common configuration, but the number of additional switching occurrences by the LDC varies. There may be only one or there may be more than two.

15. These terminals could handle interactions with a host computer, but they had far less computing capability than did personal computers, which were introduced later.

16. FCC (1999) at 14–8.

17. The relevant cost measure in this case is long-run marginal cost.

18. For further discussion of this point, see Rohlfs (1978).

19. This section and the following one rely largely on the Internet histories of Cerf and of Leiner et al.

20. An alternative Internet protocol is UDP/IP, which is used for VoIP. With UDP/IP, packets have the same structure (dictated by IP), but lost packets are not retransmitted.

21. For more detail on the timing of various packet-switched networks, see Zakon.

22. For example, the cost of installing a fiber-optic cable increases far less than proportionately if the cable contains additional fiber strands. Thus, the cost per strand declines with the number of strands. Also, by using sophisticated electronic and optical equipment, an enormous number of transmission channels can be put on a single fiber-optic strand. Through efficient use of such equipment, the cost per channel can be reduced as the number of channels increases.

23. An important dimension of QoS is the percentage of calls that get through. Calls sometimes fail to get through because random surges in demand exceed

capacity limitations. Such occurrences are less likely for a transmission facility that has more channels (operating at the same rate of capacity utilization). The same type of scale economies applies to queuing for a teller. You are less likely to have a long wait if there is a single line with two tellers and two persons ahead of you than if there is one teller and one person ahead of you. In particular, if one of the persons ahead of you in line takes a long time for some unexpected reason, you can go to the other teller.

24. Modems are standard equipment on modern PCs. However, when gateways were first launched, relatively few PCs had modems.

25. "Personal computers: With modem you can join the club," *The San Diego Union-Tribune* (July 26, 1986), p. D3.

26. "Electronic mail is a key ingredient in the mix of today's telecom services," *Communication News* (November 1, 1983).

27. David DeJean, "Electronic mail comes of age: But it still has a lot of growing up to do," *PC-Computing* (August 1, 1988), p. 159.

28. Brock N. Meeks, "Expert Advice E-MAIL ECONOMICS—Subtle differences in e-mail services will affect your choice of the perfect service," *BYTE* (April 1, 1989), p. 151; and Beth Schultz, "AT&T, MCI, Telenet offer e-mail links, *Communications Week* (May 8, 1989), p. 9.

29. CompuServe survived well into the Internet Age, but in 1997 it was swallowed up. MCI.WorldCom (the largest provider of the Internet backbone) acquired its network assets; AOL (the largest ISP) acquired its retail operations.

30. An analogous program, JANET, was funded in the United Kingdom, beginning in 1984.

31. See Varian for a more detailed discussion of this effort.

32. Property rights to the status quo play a fundamental role in Owen and Braeutigam's model of regulatory processes. See also Zajac, pp. 111–112, 120–121.

33. For discussion of some of these inefficiencies, see MacKie-Mason and Varian. Several articles in McKnight and Bailey also address this issue.

34. In formal economic terms, the negotiated agreements deviate from the contract curve.

35. See Roberts, p. 1310.

36. For further discussion of AT&T's contempt for packet switching, see Hafner and Lyon, pp. 62–64, 182.

Chapter 14. Summary of Results

1. Bold-faced words are defined in the glossary of economics concepts that follows.

Mathematical Appendix

1. This model is not completely general, but it may be a reasonable approximation in many cases. It is described mathematically in Rohlfs (1974), pp. 25–26.

2. This assumption is certainly reasonable with respect to the model in figure A.3. In more complex models, however, individuals cannot be uniquely ordered in terms of the value they place on the network service. Those values depend on the identities of the users in the user set. Nevertheless, one would expect there to be a general tendency for users who valued network links highly (in terms of willingness to pay) to join before those who valued them less highly or not at all.

3. This section is based on Evans, Nichols, and Reddy.

4. The model would be all the more untenable if we assumed that the marginal cost of producing operating systems were positive.

Glossary of Economics Concepts

Bandwagon effect (or benefit): A benefit that a person enjoys as others do the same thing that he or she does. In particular, a consumer may enjoy bandwagon benefits as others consume the same product or service that he or she does.

Chicken-and-egg problem (with respect to products that are subject to complementary bandwagon effects): The base product (the "chicken") may have no value apart from the supply of complementary products (the "egg"). The complementary products, in turn, may have no value without the base product. The problem is that the suppliers of the base product may not supply it unless the complementary products are already available. Suppliers of the complementary products may not supply them unless the base product is already available. Without coordination of the suppliers of base products and complementary products, there may be no way for *either* the chicken or the egg to come first.

Community of interest (with respect to the user set of a bandwagon product): A group whose members enjoy greater bandwagon benefits with respect to other members of the group than with respect to persons outside the group.

Compatibility (of products that are subject to complementary bandwagon effects): The ability of the base products (e.g., hardware) of all suppliers to work in conjunction with the same complementary products (e.g., software). Compatibility causes the base products to be interlinked.

Complementary bandwagon effects: Bandwagon effects that derive from the increased supply of complementary products as the user set of the base product expands.

Critical mass (for a bandwagon product): A user set that, if surpassed, sustains further growth (positive feedback).

Demand-based equilibrium user set: The equilibrium user set that results from demand adjustments, starting from the initial user set.

Demand curve: The graphical depiction of the relation between equilibrium demand and price. Equilibrium demand is modeled to depend on price.

Demand-side scale economies: See "External demand-side scale economies" and "Internal demand-side scale economies."

Disequilibrium: An economic state that tends to change, usually in the direction of a stable equilibrium.

Equilibrium: An economic state that has no tendency to change.

Equilibrium user set: A user set for which demand of each user and nonuser has no tendency to change.

External demand-side scale economies: Benefits that accrue to consumers as the user set expands. They are external to a single user, because the benefits to him or her derive from actions of others.

First-mover advantage: The competitive advantage enjoyed by a firm as a result of entering a market first (before its competitors).

Initial user set: Those who consume a bandwagon product when it is new— that is, before the user set grows and generates bandwagon benefits.

Interconnection: The ability of users of one network to communicate with users of another network. Interconnection always requires cooperation between the proprietors of the interconnecting networks. It may additionally require physical connection of telecommunications facilities. Interconnection is a form of interlinking.

Interlinking (of the products of multiple suppliers in a bandwagon market):   The ability of the products to generate bandwagon benefits based on the user set of customers of all suppliers—not just the customers of a single supplier.

Internal demand-side scale economies: Benefits to a user organization that increase more than proportionately as its total consumption of a product increases. The benefits are internal, because they accrue to the user organization that increases its consumption.

Internal supply-side scale diseconomies: The opposite of internal supply-side scale economies—that is, *increases* in unit cost of a firm as its output of a product increases.

Internal supply-side scale economies: Decreases in unit cost of a firm as its output of a product increases. The benefits are internal, because they accrue to the firm that expands output.

Internalize the externality: The process by which a group acts jointly to optimize decisions in the presence of externalities. Externalities are external to individuals in the group but are internal to the group, considered as a whole. On their own, individuals make decisions without fully taking into account the external benefits that might accrue to other members of the group. The group internalizes the externality by taking these external benefits into account in its group decision.

Inverse demand curve: The graphical depiction of the relation between price and equlibrium demand. For any level of demand, the inverse demand curve shows the price for which that level of demand is an equilibrium.

Marginal user: A user who would no longer consume the product if the price were slightly higher.

Market power: The ability of a firm to earn monopoly profits. Market power can derive from an oligopoly or monopoly industry structure.

Maximum equilibrium user set: The largest user set that is an equilibrium.

Metcalfe's Law: The hypothesis that the value of a network grows proportionally with the square of the number of users.

Monopoly profits: Profits in excess of what a competitive firm could expect to earn, given the same amount of invested capital. Monopoly profits can derive from market power in an oligopoly or monopoly industry structure.

Multipart tariffs: A price structure that has multiple elements. With a multipart tariff, the total amount that a consumer pays is not proportional to the amount that he or she purchases.

Network externalities: Bandwagon effects that apply to the user set of a communications network.

Oligopoly: An industry structure in which a few firms produce the same or very similar products.

Positive feedback: A process in which increases in an activity lead to further increases in that activity, which lead to still further increases, and so forth.

Predatory pricing: Offering low prices (often below cost) with the intent of driving competitors out of business.

Pure bandwagon model: The bandwagon model that posits that some users benefit from an expansion of the user set and no user is ever made worse off.

Pure competition: An industry structure in which many firms produce the same or very similar products.

Reservation price: The maximum price that an individual would be willing to pay for a product. If price is less than the reservation price, the individual consumes the product; if price exceeds the reservation price, he or she does not.

Scale economies: See "External demand-side scale economies," "Internal demand-side scale economies," and "Internal supply-side scale economies."

Stable equilibrium (with respect to demand): An equilibrium that demand (in disequilibrium) tends to move toward.

Supply-side scale economies: See "Internal supply-side scale economies."

Technical standards (of products that are subject to complementary bandwagon effects): The protocols that define how the base product works in conjunction with the complementary products. A single technical standard has the effect of interlinking the base products of multiple suppliers.

Transactions costs: In general, the costs of making an economic transactions; for example, negotiating a contract. The term was used by Coase to include all the impediments to internalizing externalities.

Unstable equilibrium (with respect to demand):   An equilibrium that demand (in disequilibrium) does *not* tend to move toward. A critical mass in a bandwagon market is an unstable equilibrium.

Vertical integration: The production by a single firm or affiliated firms of products in the multiple (vertical) stages of production. In particular, a vertically integrated firm produces upstream products that are used as inputs in its own production of downstream products.

Dictionary of Abbreviations and Acronyms

ACTV	Advanced Compatible Television
ADTV	Advanced Digital Television
ANS	Advanced Network Systems
ATTC	Advanced Television Testing Committee (a private committee of broadcasters, manufacturers, and programmers that tested technologies for advanced television)
BSB	British Satellite Broadcasting (BSB merged with Sky in November 1990, and the combined enterprise became BSkyB)
CBO	Congressional Budget Office
CD	compact disc
DARPA	Defense Advanced Research Projects Agency
DAT	digital audiotape
DBS	direct broadcast satellite
DCC	digital compact cassette
DoD	Department of Defense
DOJ	Department of Justice
EDTV	Enhanced Definition Television
fax	facsimile
FCC	Federal Communications Commission
FTP	file-transfer protocol
HDTV	high-definition television
ISP	Internet service provider

ISV	independent software vendor
LAN	local area network
LDC	long-distance carrier
MAC	Multiplexed Analog Components (European HDTV standard)
MD	minidisc
MUSE	Multiple Subnyquist Sampling Encoding (Japanese system for compressing HDTV for broadcasting)
NCTA	National Cable Television Association
NHK	Nippon Hoso Kyokai (Japanese state broadcaster)
NSF	National Science Foundation
NTSC	National Television Standards Committee
PAL	Phased Alternate Line (color television standard used in most of Western Europe)
PC	personal computer
PCS	Personal Communications System
QoS	quality of service
RMA	Radio Manufacturers' Association
SC-HDTV	Spectrum Compatible HDTV
SCMS	Serial Copy Management System (technical system that allows single copies but prevents chain copying of recordings)
SECAM	Systeme Electronique Couleur Avec Memoire (color television standard used in France, Russia, and Eastern Europe)
TCP/IP	Transmission Control Protocol/Internet Protocol (standard Internet protocol for data transmission)
telco	local telephone company
VCR	videocassette recorder
VDP	videodisc player
VoI	Voice over Internet
VoIP	Voice over Internet protocols

Bibliography

American Telephone and Telegraph Company. Comptroller's-Accounting Division, *Bell System Statistical Manual, 1950–1981*, June 1982.

Areeda, P., and D. F. Turner. "Predatory Pricing and Related Practices under Section 2 of the Sherman Act," *Harvard Law Review* 88 (1975), pp. 637–833.

Arthur, W. B. "Competing Technologies, Increasing Returns, and Lock-In by Historical Events," *Economic Journal*, 99, no. 394 (March 1989), pp. 116–131.

Artle, R., and C. Averous. "The Telephone Systems as a Public Good: Static and Dynamic Aspects," *Bell Journal of Economics and Management Science* 4, no. 1 (Spring 1973), pp. 89–100.

Baumol, W. J., and D. E. Bradford. "Optimal Departures from Marginal Cost Pricing," *American Economic Review* 60 (June 1970), pp. 265–283.

Beggs, A., and P. Klemperer. "MultiPeriod Competition with Switching Costs," *Econometrica* 60, no. 3 (May, 1992), pp. 651–666.

Bennett, A. R. *The Telephone Systems of the Continent of Europe.* New York: Arno Press, 1974.

Besen, S. M., and L. L. Johnson. *Compatibility Standards, Competition, and Innovation in the Broadcasting Industry*, R-3453-NSF. Santa Monica, CA: The RAND Corporation, November 1986.

Boiteux, M. "On the Management of Public Monopolies Subject to Budgetary Constraints," *Journal of Economic Theory* 3 (September 1971), pp. 219–240.

Bornholz, R., and D. S. Evans, "The Early History of Competition in the Telephone Industry," in D. S. Evans, *Breaking Up Bell: Essays in Industrial Organization and Regulation.* North-Holland, 1983.

Brinkley, J. *Defining Vision.* New York: Harcourt Brace & Company, 1997.

Brock, G. W. *The Telecommunications Industry: The Dynamics of Market Structure.* Cambridge: Harvard University Press, 1981.

Brooks, J. *Telephone: The First Hundred Years.* New York: Harper & Row, 1975.

Brown, S. J., and D. S. Sibley. *The Theory of Public Utility Pricing*. Cambridge University Press, 1986.

Cerf, V. "How the Internet Came to Be," Bell Laboratories, Lucent Technologies, 1993. Available at ⟨http://www.bell-labs.com/user/zhwang/vcerf.html⟩.

Church, J., and N. Gandal. "Network Effects, Software Provision, and Standardization," *Journal of Industrial Economics* 40, no. 1 (March 1992), pp. 85–103.

Coase, R. "The Problem of Social Cost," *Journal of Law and Economics* (October 1960), pp. 1–44.

Coffman, K. G., and A. M. Odlyzko. "The size and growth rate of the Internet," *First Monday*, October 1998. Available at ⟨http://firstmonday.org/⟩ and also available at ⟨http://www.research.att.com/~amo⟩.

Cole, B., and M. Oettinger. *Reluctant Regulators: The FCC and the Broadcast Audience*. Reading, MA: Addison-Wesley Publishing Company, 1978.

Coopersmith, J. *The Joys of Fax*, n.d. Available at ⟨http://people.tamu.edu/~jcfax1/spectrum.htm⟩.

Cusumano, M. A., Y. Mylonadis, and R. S. Rosenbloom. "Strategic Maneuvering and Mass-Market Dynamics: The Triumph of VHS over Beta," *Business History Review* 66 (Spring 1992): 51–94.

Day, K. "Newcomers to Computers Try to Polish Apple, *Los Angeles Times* (September 29, 1985), p. 1.

Ducey, R. V., and M. R. Fratrik. "Broadcasting Industry Response to New Technologies," *Journal of Media Economics* 2, no. 2 (Fall 1989), pp. 67–81.

Economides, N., and C. Himmelberg. *Critical Mass and Network Size with Application to the US FAX Market*, EC-95–11, New York University, Leonard N. Stern School of Business, August 1995.

Economides, N., and S. C. Salop. "Competition and Integration Among Complements, and Network Market Structure," *Journal of Industrial Economics* 40, no. 1 (March 1992), pp. 105–123.

Evans, D. S., A. Nichols, and B. Reddy. "The Rise and Fall of Leaders in Personal Computer Software," National Economic Research Associates, January 7, 1999.

Farrell, J., and G. Saloner. "Standardization, Compatibility, and Innovation," *Rand Journal of Economics* 16, no. 1 (Spring 1985), pp. 70–83.

Farrell, J., and G. Saloner. "Converters, Compatibility, and the Control of Interfaces," *Journal of Industrial Economics* 40, no. 1 (March 1992), pp. 9–35.

Farrell, J., and C. Shapiro. "Dynamic Competition with Switching Costs," *Rand Journal of Economics* 19 (1988), pp. 123–137.

Farrell, J., and C. Shapiro. "Standard Setting in High-Definition Television," *Brookings Papers: Microeconomics (1992)*, pp. 1–77.

Federal Communications Commission (FCC). In the Matter of Access Charge Reform, Price Cap Performance Review for Local Exchange Carriers, Transport Rate Structure and Pricing, and End User Common Line Charges, CC Docket Nos. 96–262, 94–1, 91–213, and 95–82, *First Report and Order* (released May 15, 1997).

Federal Communications Commission (FCC). *Statistics of Common Carriers, 1994–1995*, 1998.

Federal Communications Commission (FCC). Industry Analysis Division, Common Carrier Bureau. Table 14.6, "Average Revenue per Minute," in *Trends in Telephone Service*, September 1999.

Federal Communications Commission (FCC). In the Matter of Implementation of the Local Competition Provisions in the Telecommunications Act of 1996, CC Docket No. 96–98, *Third Report and Order and Fourth Notice of Proposed Rulemaking* (November 5, 1999).

Fischer, C. S. *America Calling: A Social History of the Telephone to 1940*. Berkeley: University of California Press, 1992.

Fisher, F. M. Direct testimony, *United States of America v. Microsoft*, 1999.

Gabel, D. "Competition in a Network Industry: The Telephone Industry, 1894–1910, *Journal of Economic History* 54, no. 3 (September 1994), pp. 543–572.

Grindley, P. *Standards Strategy and Policy: Cases and Stories*. Oxford: Oxford University Press, 1995.

Hafner, K., and M. Lyon. *Where Wizards Stay Up Late: The Origins of the Internet*. New York: Touchstone, 1996.

Hill, C. W. L. *Establishing a Standard: Competitive Strategy and Technological Standards in Winner-Take-All Industries*, Academy of Management, May 1, 1997. Copyright UMI Company.

Holmstrom, B. R., and J. Tirole. "The Theory of the Firm," in *Handbook of Industrial Organization*, vol. 1, ed. Richard Schmalensee and Robert D. Willig. Amsterdam: Elsevier Science Publishers B.V., 1989, pp. 61–133.

Internet Valley. "History of the Internet and Worldwide Web," n.d. Available at ⟨http://www.internetvalley.com/intvalstat.html⟩.

Jackson, C. L., and J. Haring. *Pitfalls in the Economic Valuation of the Electromagnetic Spectrum*. July 19, 1995.

Katz, M. L., and C. Shapiro. "Network Externalities, Competition, and Compatibility," *American Economic Review* 75, no. 3 (June 1985), pp. 424–440.

Klemperer, P. D. "Markets with Consumer Switching Costs," *Quarterly Journal of Economics* 102 (1987), pp. 375–394.

Klopfenstein, Bruce C. "The Diffusion of the VCR in the United States," *The VCR Age: Home Video and Mass Communication*, ed. Mark R. Levy. Newbury Park: Sage Publications, 1989.

Lardner, James. *Fast Forward: Hollywood, The Japanese, and the Onslaught of the VCR*. New York: W. W. Norton & Company, n.d.

Leibenstein, H. "Bandwagon, Snob, and Beblen Effects in the Theory of Consumers' Demand," *Quarterly Journal of Economics* 64, no. 2 (May 1950), pp. 183–207.

Leiner, B. M., et al. "A Brief History of the Internet," February 20, 1998. Available at ⟨http://www.isoc.org/internet-history/brief.html⟩.

Liebowitz, S. J., and S. E. Margolis. *Winners, Losers & Microsoft: Competition and Antitrust in High Technology*. Oakland, CA: The Independent Institute, 1999.

Littlechild, S. C. "Two-Part Tariffs and Consumption Externalities," *Bell Journal of Economics*, vol. 6, no. 2 (Autumn 1975), pp. 661–670.

MacKie-Mason, J. K., and H. R. Varian, "Pricing the Internet," University of Michigan, April 1993. Revised: February 10, 1994.

Matutes, C., and P. Regibeau. "Compatibility and Bundling of Complementary Goods in a Duopoly," *Journal of Industrial Economics* 40, no. 1 (March 1992), pp. 37–54.

McGahan, A. M. *Philips' Compact Disc Introduction (C)*, 9-892-037, Harvard Business School, October 23, 1991.

McKnight, L. W., and J. P. Bailey, ed. *Internet Economics*. Cambridge, MA: The MIT Press, 1998.

Mueller, M. L., Jr. *Universal Service, Competition, Interconnecting, and Monopoly in the Making of the American Telephone System*. Cambridge, MA: The MIT Press, and Washington, DC: AEI Press (1997), pp. 107–110.

Noll, R. G., M. J. Peck, and J. J. McGowan. *Economic Aspects of Television Regulation*. Washington, DC: The Brookings Institution, n.d.

Odlyzko, A. "The Current State and Likely Evolution of the Internet," n.d. Available ⟨http://www.research.att.com/~amo⟩.

Oi, W. Y. "A Disneyland Dilemma: Two Part Tariffs for a Mickey Mouse Monopoly," *Quarterly Journal of Economics* 85 (1971), 77–90.

Oren, S. S., and S. A. Smith. (1981). "Critical Mass and Tariff Structure in Electronic Communications Markets," vol. 12, no. 2, *Bell Journal of Economics*, pp. 467–487.

Owen, B. M., and R. Braeutigam. *The Regulatory Game: Strategic Use of the Administrative Process*. Cambridge, MA: Ballinger, 1978.

Panzar, J. C. "Technological Determinants of Firm and Industry Structure," in *Handbook of Industrial Organization*, Vol. I, ed. Richard Schmalensee and Robert D. Willig. Amsterdam: Elsevier Science Publishers B.V., 1989.

Perry, M. K. "Vertical Integration: Determinants and Effects," in *Handbook of Industrial Organization*, Vol. I, ed. Richard Schmalensee and Robert D. Willig. Amsterdam: Elsevier Science Publishers B.V., 1989.

Pigou, A. C. *Wealth and Welfare*. London: Macmillan, 1912.

Pigou, A. C. *The Economics of Welfare*. London: Macmillan, 1920.

Polsson, K. "Chronology of Events in the History of Microcomputers," October 3, 1999. Available at ⟨http://www.islandnet.com/~kpolsson/comphist.htm⟩.

Quinlan, S. *The Hundred Million Dollar Lunch*. Chicago: J. P. O'Hara, 1974.

Ramsey, F. P. "A Contribution to the Theory of Taxation," *Economic Journal* 37 (March 1927), pp. 47–61.

Reddy, B. J., D. S. Evans, and A. L. Nichols. "Why Does Microsoft Charge So Little for Windows?," National Economic Research Associates, January 7, 1999.

Roberts, L. G. "The Evolution of Packet Switching," *Proceedings of the IEEE* 66, no. 11 (November 1978).

Roehl, R., and H. R. Varian. *Circulating Libraries and Video Rental Stores*, June 14, 2000. Available at ⟨http://www.sims.Berkeley.edu/~hal/Papers/history/⟩.

Rohlfs, J. "A Theory of Interdependent Demand for a Communications Service," *Bell Journal of Economics and Management Science* 5, no. 1 (Spring 1974), pp. 16–37.

Rohlfs, J. "Economic-Efficient Bell System Pricing," Bell Laboratories, Murray Hill, New Jersey, 1978.

Rohlfs, J. H., and M. Wish. "Economic Analysis of Picturephone Demand" (January 22, 1974).

Schmalensee, R. L. Direct testimony, *United States of America v. Microsoft*, 1999.

Schumpeter, J. A. *Capitalism, Socialism and Democracy*. New York: Harper & Row, 1942; 3d ed. 1950.

Shapiro, C., and H. R. Varian. *Information Rules, A Strategic Guide to the Network Economy*. Boston: Harvard Business School Press, 1999.

Shiller, R. J. *Irrational Exuberance*. Princeton, NJ: Princeton University Press, 1999.

Shooshan & Jackson Inc. *Competition in the Provision of Customer Premises Equipment and Enhanced Services in the United States*, October 1983.

Smith, A. *The Wealth of Nations*. New York: Random House, 1937.

Squire, L. "Some Aspects of Optimal Pricing for Telecommunications," *Bell Journal of Economics and Management Science* 4, no. 2 (Autumn 1973), pp. 515–525.

Stehman, J. W. *The Financial History of the American Telephone and Telegraph Company*. New York: Augustus M. Kelley, 1967.

Varian, H. R. "Economic Issues Facing the Internet," June 10, 1996 (rev. September 15, 1996).

Williamson, O. E. "Transaction Cost Economics," *Handbook of Industrial Organization*, Vol. I, ed. Richard Schmalensee and Robert D. Willig. Amsterdam: Elsevier Science Publishers B.V., 1989.

Wish, M., and J. H. Rohlfs. "Preconceptions, Perceptions, and Opinions about PICTUREPHONE Service" (April 15, 1974).

WOW-COM, Statistics & Surveys, "The Cellular Telecommunications Industry Association's Annualized Wireless Industry Data Survey Results, June 1985 to June 1999," March 1, 2000. Available at ⟨http://www.wow-com.com/statsurv/survey/199906b.cfm⟩.

Zajac, E. E. *Political Economy of Fairness*. Cambridge, MA: The MIT Press, 1995.

Zakon, R. H. *Hobbes' Internet Timeline v4.2*, September 21, 1999. Available at ⟨http://www.isoc.org/guest/zakon/Internet/History/HIT.html⟩.

Index